Learning Core
Audio

Learning Core Audio

A Hands-On Guide to Audio Programming for Mac and iOS

Chris Adamson
Kevin Avila

✦✦ Addison-Wesley

Upper Saddle River, NJ • Boston • Indianapolis • San Francisco
New York • Toronto • Montreal • London • Munich • Paris • Madrid
Cape Town • Sydney • Tokyo • Singapore • Mexico City

The publisher offers excellent discounts on this book when ordered in quantity for bulk purchases or special sales, which may include electronic versions and/or custom covers and content particular to your business, training goals, marketing focus, and branding interests. For more information, please contact:

U.S. Corporate and Government Sales
(800) 382-3419
corpsales@pearsontechgroup.com

For sales outside the United States, please contact:

International Sales
international@pearsoned.com

Visit us on the Web: informit.com/aw

Library of Congress Cataloging-in-Publication Data

Adamson, Chris, 1967-
Learning Core audio : a hands-on guide to audio programming for Mac and iOS / Chris Adamson, Kevin Avila.
    p. cm.
  ISBN 978-0-321-63684-3 (pbk. : alk. paper) — ISBN 0-321-63684-8 (pbk. : alk. paper)
  1. Computer sound processing—Computer programs. 2. Core audio. 3. Apple computer—Programming. I. Avila, Kevin, 1980- II. Title.
  TK7881.4.A244 2012
  006.4'5—dc23
                                            2012000862

ISBN-13: 978-0-32-163684-3
ISBN-10: 0-32-163684-8

Text printed in the United States on recycled paper at R.R. Donnelley in Crawfordsville, Indiana.

First printing, April 2012

Editor-in-Chief
Mark Taub

Senior Acquisitions Editor
Trina MacDonald

Development Editor
Chris Zahn

Managing Editor
Kristy Hart

Senior Project Editor
Lori Lyons

Copy Editor
Krista Hansing Editorial Services, Inc.

Senior Indexer
Cheryl Lenser

Proofreader
Kathy Ruiz

Technical Reviewers
Mark Dalrymple
Mark Granoff
Michael James
Chris Liscio
Robert Strogan
Alex Wiltschko

Publishing Coordinator
Olivia Basegio

Multimedia Developer
Dan Scherf

Cover Designer
Chuti Prasertsith

Compositor
Nonie Ratcliff

Contents

Acknowledgments

From Chris Adamson

This book wouldn't exist without Kevin Avila and Mike Lee, who found a publisher who not only wasn't scared off by the thought of a difficult niche Mac and iOS title, but actually relished the challenge of bringing this beast to market. They knew there was a crowd out there that has been aching for years to get Core Audio presented in a practical form that lets normal programmers draw out its ferocious power. Behind the scenes, Chuck Toporek championed this book, pulled me in when it got stuck, and saw it through to the finish. More than anyone else, he's the one to thank for finally getting a Core Audio book published.

We wouldn't have been able to get it all done without the generous support of the Core Audio developer community, particularly the membership of the `coreaudio-api` mailing list. Core Audio founder William Stewart and Apple's Doug Wyatt have long been generous with their time and attention to questions posted to the list and got us unstuck on a number of occasions.

We're also grateful to our many tech reviewers and readers of the "Rough Cuts" edition who reported errors and provided feedback as this book worked through its long road to completion.

At home, thanks to my wife, Kelly, and our kids, Keagan and Quinn, for cutting me enough slack to get this thing done and not completely freaking out when the example code went wrong and horrible buzzes blasted forth from Dad's office in the basement.

Obligatory end-of-book tune check: This time it was We Are The City, … And You Will Know Us by the Trail of Dead, Daft Punk, Dr. Dog, Fun, and (fittingly) Hatsune Miku.[1]

From Kevin Avila

I would like to acknowledge the Big Bang, gravity, and the eventual copulation between my parents for making this possible.

Chuck Toporek (@chuckdude), Chris Adamson (@invalidname), Mike Lee (@bmf): There truly are no words that express my gratitude for all the blood, sweat, and grammar you've contributed, not only to this book, but to the entire developer community. Thank you.

---

[1] Find up-to-date listening stats at www.last.fm/user/invalidname.

Bill Stewart, Jeff Moore, Doug Wyatt, Michael Hopkins, Bob Aron, James McCartney, Mehul Trivedi, Cynthia Maxwell, Torrey Walker, Nick Thompson, Matthew Mora, Brad Ford, Murray Jason, and Edward Agabeg: Thanks for sharing with me your passion and knowledge of audio.

Special thanks to David Avila, Daniel Kaufman, Andre LaBranche, Quentin Carnicelli, Ed Wynne, and Steve Jobs.

What's on my iPod: AC/DC, Rush, Beach Boys, Sublime, Primus, KRS-One, Beastie Boys, Mac Dre, Vokab Kompany, and the insanely great George Carlin.

About the Authors

Chris Adamson is an independent writer, editor, and developer who lives in Grand Rapids, Michigan. Now focusing on iOS and Mac development, he is the coauthor of *iOS SDK Development* (Pragmatic Programmers, 2012). He is also the author of *QuickTime for Java: A Developer's Notebook* (O'Reilly Media, 2005) and coauthor of *Swing Hacks* (O'Reilly Media, 2005). He was formerly the editor of *java.net* and *ONJava.com*. He consults and publishes through his corporate identity, Subsequently and Furthermore, Inc., with a focus on user-facing and digital media development for Mac and iOS. He blogs on digital media software development at www.subfurther.com/blog. In a previous career, he was a writer/associate producer at *CNN Headline News,* and over the years, he has managed to own 11 1/2 Macs.

Kevin Avila (a.k.a. dogbert) is a smooth blend of carbon compounds, oxygen, hydrogen, and nitrogen, with some impurities for added flavor. Additionally, he has more than 15 years' experience developing for the Mac and, since its release, the iPhone. Kevin has been involved in every corner of the audio market, from being an engineer at Apple to configuring professional recording studios. He currently is a code mercenary for various clients while he sits in his underwear at home, sipping coffee.

We'd Like to Hear from You

You can visit our website and register this book at:

www.informit.com/title/9780321636843

Be sure to visit the book's website for convenient access to any updates, to download the book's sample code, or for errata that might be available for this book.

As the reader of this book, you are our most important critic and commentator. We value your opinion and want to know what we're doing right, what we could do better, what areas you'd like to see us publish in, and any other words of wisdom you're willing to pass our way.

When you write, please be sure to include this book's title and the name of the author, as well as your name, phone, and/or e-mail address. I will carefully review your comments and share them with the author and others who have worked on this book.

E-mail: trina.macdonald@pearson.com
Mail: Trina MacDonald
            Senior Acquisitions Editor, Addison-Wesley
            Pearson Education, Inc.
            1249 8th Street
            Berkeley, CA 94710 USA

For more information about our books or conferences, see our website at:

www.informit.com

Foreword

Reflect for a minute on your craft. Think of those in ages past who shared the same experiences. Think of the painters who drove themselves mad trying to gather the forces within to produce something of meaning. Think of the industrialists, who believed they were standing at the dawn of a new age, one that they themselves were capable of building.

Think of the ancient acolytes of magic, seeking to unlock the power in arcane knowledge. Then think of that moment when, having learned street magic tricks such as flow control and data structures, you finally gained access to the API libraries. Think of that sorcerer's apprentice staring glassy-eyed at the universe of possibilities in a room of musty books.

It's one of those key moments in any programmer's career, cresting that foothill only to see the mountain beyond. It is the daunting realization that programming is a lifelong journey of learning. Many would-be magicians simply turn around and head back out the door, leaving that world behind to pursue a more normal life of sane pursuits.

That you have found your way here suggests you are part of the other group, a select few blessed with some genetic predisposition to solving hard problems. They are the ones who cross that threshold and enter that world, losing themselves to learning new spells and exploring new kinds of magic.

For what is programming but magic? Wielding secret words to command powerful forces you just barely understand, calling forth the spirits of bygone spell casters to ease your burdens, simplify your workflows, and grant you the ability to surprise and delight the masses.

As you pore over each tome, practicing new forms of magic, you start combining them with the things you learned before creating new spells, thus unlocking new possibilities. Everything you learn leads to new tricks to learn, new roads forking into other new roads, until one day you run into a dead end.

Many of the ancient texts refer to such dark arts as audio programming but do not deal with them directly. As vital as Core Audio is, there seem to be no books on the subject, no scrolls of spells or sample code to practice. There are plenty of use cases for audio programming, but as black magic, the only materials you can find to read about it are terse and confusing.

Chris Adamson tracked down a practitioner of the audio arts named Kevin Avila, a graying wizard well versed in C. Through a combination of bribery and honest inquiry, he established himself as a protégé. The rabbit hole he entered goes on forever, and as his ears led him through its many dark twists and turns, he learned a new language to describe sound—and, with it, a new way of looking at the universe.

An eternity later, he himself a graying wizard, he thought back on that library to the missing volumes and realized it was his destiny to shed light on the dark art of Core Audio. It is the definition of mastery that we must teach what we have learned. This is the truth that fuels the cycle of master and protégé. This is the engine that drives generations forward, each propelling the next further ahead as we move toward that grand ineffable vanishing point we call the future.

As with all rites of passage, it was a herculean task, requiring a whole new sets of skills and a different type of discipline. We must tear apart our knowledge, and ourselves, to find not just truth, but the beauty that underlies the truth and allows it to resonate across the ages and to be understood.

All such that at some unknowable time in the future, where once there was a dead end and a blank space between Core Animation and Core Data, some young acolyte might find wisdom and guidance. They might combine this new knowledge with what they already know so that, when they find their own dead end and their own dark arts, they, too, will be ready.

That moment, dear reader, is now. That acolyte is you, and the grimoire that you hold in your hand has all the wisdom and more than enough spells to take your magic to the next level. This book is your key to wielding unspeakable power, the power of sound and nature, the power of Core Audio.

Does all that seem a bit much for a book about audio programming? Rest assured that, if anything, I have undersold it. Sound is an incredibly powerful force that affects the human brain in ways we only barely understand. Consider the impact of music on your life. Now consider that all of music is maybe 10% of the story of sound.

The power of audio programming goes so far beyond anything you can experience with your ears. Swiping a credit card used to require an expensive machine. Now you can do the same trick with a cheap plastic dongle plugged into the headphone jack of your iPhone. You don't have to make music to make magic with sound.

With this book, you dig into your first Core Audio code in Chapter 1, "Overview of Core Audio," even as you are learning what exactly Core Audio is and when you should (and should not) attempt to use its power.

Core Audio, like all black arts, has roots in the inherent properties of nature. Chapter 2, "The Story of Sound," takes to heart the story of sound, not as ineffable natural phenomena, but as simple science. You'll learn the language and techniques of converting vibrating air molecules into the mathematical language of computers, and vice versa.

You'll also learn the human language of audio and the real meanings of technical terms you've heard, and perhaps even used, for years: sample rate, frame rate, buffer, and compression. You'll see these ideas carried through Chapter 3, "Audio Processing with Core Audio," as you peel back the wrapper on audio formats and learn about the canonical formats Core Audio uses internally.

When you know the basics of Core Audio, you'll want to apply your skills by learning the parlor tricks of recording and playback with Chapters 4, "Recording," and 5, "Playback," using the high-level Audio Queue architecture.

Of course, "high-level" can be a misnomer, especially if you're coming from an object-oriented background such as Cocoa. Setting aside the comforting warmth of Objective-C to take the reins of C can certainly be scary, but with a little understanding, you'll come to see how much like Cocoa a C framework can be, as familiar friends, like key-value pairs, emerge in unfamiliar clothes.

When you understand Audio Queues, you'll be a master of audio formats—almost. First you must complete your quest by learning to convert between formats and come to understand the relevance of canonical formats.

Then it's time to say goodbye to high-level shores as you strap on your diving suit and descend into the depths of Core Audio, the modular Audio Units that implement the magic. Chapters 7, "Audio Units: Generators, Effects, and Rendering," and 8, "Audio Units: Input and Mixing," will make or break you as an audio programmer, for here you can craft end-to-end sonic solutions that are not possible "the easy way."

Once time is your plaything, it's time to tackle space. In Chapter 9, "Positional Sound," you enter another dimension as you learn to change sounds by positioning audio in space using OpenAL, the 3D audio framework.

Core Audio has its roots in the Mac but has evolved with Apple's fortunes. In Chapter 10, "Core Audio on iOS," you focus on iOS and the challenges and changes brought by the post-PC world of ultraportable hardware running ultra-efficient software.

Mobile hardware is not the only way to take audio beyond the computer. In Chapter 11, "Core MIDI," you gain the means to connect the computer to musical instruments and other hardware using Core Audio's implementation of the industry-standard Musical Instrument Digital Interface, Core MIDI.

With that, you'll be at the end of your quest, but your journey will have just begun. In Chapter 12, "Coda," you look to the future, to the once inexplicable advanced concepts you are now equipped to tackle, such as digital signal processing and sampling.

If you want to be a master of the arcane arts, you have a long road ahead of you. There's no sense sugarcoating it: This is going to be hard. But don't worry—you're in good hands. Your authors have used plain language and plenty of sample code to banish the demons and show you the way to the underlying logic that will make these concepts yours.

Core Audio is the most powerful system for audio programming man has yet to create, but its power has largely remained out of the hands of most app makers and locked in the brains of audio nerds like Kevin. Chris has done what nobody else has managed to do and may never manage to do again: Explain Core Audio in a way other people can understand.

This book has been years in the making, and it took an incredible amount of work and the best tech editor in the industry, the legendary Chuck Toporek, and his talented colleagues at Pearson to finally bring it into existence. The people into whose waiting hands this enchanted volume has been given will be the people who deliver the coming wave of incredible audio apps.

Imagine the possibilities of connecting to people in new ways with the magic of sound. That incredible future is yours to invent. It is the dawning of the age of magic in computing, and you are a magician. Mastering the Core Audio frameworks will change the way you think about the world.

Mike Lee, Amsterdam

Introduction

Macs are great media computers, and the iPhone is the best iPod ever made—but how did they get that way? How did some of the first iOS applications turn the iPhone into a virtual instrument, yet developers on other mobile platforms remain happy enough to just to reskin another simple MP3 player? Why is the Mac the choice of so many digital media professionals, and what secret makes applications such as Bias Peak, Logic, and Soundtrack Pro possible?

Core Audio, that's what.

Core Audio is the low-level API that Apple provides for working with digital audio on Mac OS X and iOS. It provides APIs for simultaneously processing many streams of multichannel digital audio and interfaces to the audio hardware for capture (microphones) and output (speakers and headphones). Core Audio lets you write applications that work directly with the uncompressed audio data captured from a microphone, perform effects on it, mix it with other audio, and either play the result out to the speakers or convert it into a compressed format that you can then write to the file system or send over the network. If you're not developing full applications, Core Audio lets you write just the custom effect and wrap it in a plug-in called an *audio unit*, which lets users add your effect to their Core Audio-based applications.

Apple debuted Core Audio in Mac OS X 10.0, where it eventually displaced the SoundManager that was part of the Classic Mac OS. Because Core Audio is a C-based API, it can be used with Cocoa applications written in Objective-C and Carbon applications written in C++. You can even skip these application frameworks and call into Core Audio from a plain-C POSIX command-line executable (in fact, most of this book's examples are written this way). Since it is written in and called with C, Core Audio is extremely high-performance, which is crucially important when you're dealing with processing hundreds of thousands of audio samples every second.

Core Audio is based on the idea of "streams" of audio, meaning a continuous series of data that represents an audio signal. Because the sound changes over time, so does the data. Throughout Core Audio, your primary means of interacting with the audio is by working with these streams: getting them from files or input devices, mixing them, converting them to different formats, sending them to output devices, and so on. In doing this, your code makes calls to Core Audio or gets callbacks from Core Audio every time a stream has more data to process. This is a different metaphor than you might have seen in other media APIs. Simple media players such as the HTML5 `<audio>` tag or the iOS `AVAudioPlayer` treat an audio source (such as a file or URL) as an opaque box of audio: You can usually play, pause, and stop it, and maybe skip ahead or back to different parts of the audio, but you can't really inspect the contents of the box or do anything with the data. What makes Core Audio cool is that it's all about *doing stuff* with the data.

If only it were that easy.

Core Audio has a well-earned reputation as one of the hardest frameworks to deal with on Mac OS X and iPhone. This is because choosing to operate at this level means dealing with a lot of challenges: working with streams of samples in their native form, working with Core Audio's highly asynchronous programming models, and keeping things running fast enough that you don't starve Core Audio when it needs data to send to the speakers or headphones. It didn't help that, in iPhone OS 2.0, the first to support third-party applications, Core Audio was the *only* media framework; developers who simply wanted to play a file had to go all the way down to the stream level to process samples by hand, in C. It's great if you want or need to work with that level, but developers who needed a simpler, higher-level abstraction did a *lot* of public complaining.

Core Audio is not arbitrarily cruel or obtuse. It's complex because the nature of the problem domain is. In our opinion, storing a web app purchase in a database is trivial compared to modeling sound waves in a stream of samples, performing effects on them through mathematical manipulations, and delivering the results to the hardware hundreds or thousands of times a second—and doing it fast enough that the user perceives the result as instantaneous. Doing something really hard, really fast is inherently challenging: By the time you get to the end of this book, we think you'll have an appreciation for just how much Core Audio does for you.

And by that point, we think you'll be ready to do some cool things of your own.

Audience for This Book

One book can't be everything to everyone, so it's best to set the terms right at the start: This book is going to kick your butt. But like Nietzche said, "That which does not kill you only makes you stronger." When you've mastered this material, you'll be ready to do some serious butt-kicking of your own.

Who Should Read this Book

The primary audience for this book is experienced programmers who are familiar with Mac or iOS but have not yet explored Core Audio. Familiarity with C is assumed, but no prerequisite knowledge of digital audio is required; we cover that in Chapter 2. We assume that, to be interested in an audio programming book at all, you've used enough media applications to have a sense of what's possible: audio capture, real-time effects, MP3 playback, virtual instruments, web radio, voice over IP, and so on. If the thought of this stuff doesn't get your programmer parts all tingly, there's probably a nice book on Ruby on Rails two racks over.

Who Shouldn't Read This Book

As self-declared "world's toughest programmer" Mike Lee once said, "Core Audio is some serious black arts shit." You'll find yourself digging around low-level APIs, and if you're not comfortable with getting your hands dirty, this book might not be where you should start (but keep it in mind as something to come back to when you're skilled enough).

You need to know Xcode, C, and Objective-C, and you need to be comfortable reading and interpreting header files. You never know when you'll need to dive deeper into something, and having those skills under your belt will definitely make reading this book a better experience for you.

What You Need to Know

This book assumes a working knowledge of C, including pointers, `malloc()`, and the usual hazards of low-level memory management. If you don't have experience with C or any Clike language (C++, Java, and C#), stop right now and read a good book on C before you attempt to tackle this book.

The book also assumes that you're familiar and comfortable with Xcode and programming in Objective-C. You won't find any primers on how to create a project in Xcode or how to debug; you can find plenty of entry-level books for newbies and converts from other platforms and programming environments. If you're messing around with Core Audio and low-level C APIs, we can assume that you've already got that grounding.

Because the book covers use of Core Audio on the Mac and iOS, we also assume that you have an Apple developer account; if not, you should (they're cheap these days!). Go to **developer.apple.com/mac** or **developer.apple.com/ios** to sign up today—$198 gets you access to all the relevant updates for both Mac OS X and iOS, as well as Xcode, Apple's developer documentation, sample code, and even the session videos from WWDC.

Looking Up Documentation

Every Core Audio developer is constantly flipping over to Core Audio's online documentation to look up function names, parameter lists, and semantic information (such as what you're allowed to pass in a parameter or what to expect a function to do). It's all available on Apple's website, but Apple's online documentation has a habit of moving around, which makes it hard for us to provide URLs that won't break six months after we publish.

Instead, we encourage you to get familiar with Xcode's documentation browser, if you aren't already. In Xcode 4.2, you access it with the **Help > Documentation and API Reference** menu item, which takes you to the Organizer window and opens the Documentation tab. When you first visit this documentation, you'll see a Quick Start screen that lists some introductory resources for using Xcode. The right pane of this view has buttons for browsing, searching, and managing bookmarks in the documentation. Via Browse, you can select the top-level docsets to work with. Figure I.1 shows the home page for the Mac OS X 10.7 Core Library.

Figure I.1   Xcode documentation viewer showing home page of
Mac OS X 10.7 Core Library documentation

The column on the left side of the content pane arranges documentation by type, topic, and then level of the Mac OS X or iOS architecture. If you scroll down to the Media Layer level, you'll find Core Audio, Core Audio Kit, and Audio Toolbox, which is where Core Audio exposes most of its functionality to applications. Click on one of these to see a list of reference guides, technical Q&A documents, and sample code. For example, you could click on Audio Toolbox Framework Reference and then use the Bookmarks toolbar button to find your way back here easily.

Actually, we rarely browse the documentation. The second toolbar button in the left pane exposes a search interface, which is what we use most of the time. Type in a term here to get a list of matching API references (methods, functions, types, structs, and so on), as well as occurrences of the term in other documentation, such as sample code or programming guides, all of which is readable within the documentation viewer. We mentioned the term *audio unit* earlier in the Introduction; Figure I.2 shows what happens when we search for "AudioUnit" with the documentation viewer. As you can see, the term shows up in function names, typedefs, #defines and more in the API section, as well as programming guides, Q&A documents, and sample code in the full-text section.

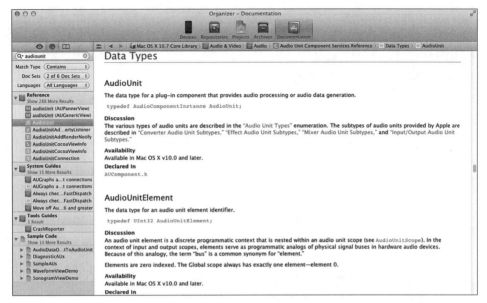

Figure I.2   Searching for "AudioUnit" in Xcode documentation viewer

You can also search for a term directly from your source; just option-double-click on a term in your source to pop up a brief overview of its documentation (see Figure I.3); full documentation is available if you click the book icon at the top of the pop-up window. There's also a button with a **.h** document icon that takes you to the term's definition. Both of these functions are available by Control-clicking (or right-clicking) the term in the text: Look for the menu items Find Text in Documentation *and* Jump to Definition.

Throughout the book, we count on the fact that you can look up information through this interface. For example, when we introduce a new function, we trust you can type its name into the search field and find its API documentation if you want the official word on how it works. When a function uses custom types, these are typically hyperlinked within the documentation so you can follow those links to find related documentation.

How This Book Is Organized

Before you start your journey, let's talk about what's at stake. The path will be treacherous, and you must always remind yourself of the great bounty that awaits you at the end of this book.

We start by giving a high-level overview of what Core Audio does. We briefly describe and provide use cases for the input and output of audio data, "transcoding" between formats, audio effects, playback and recording, and MIDI.

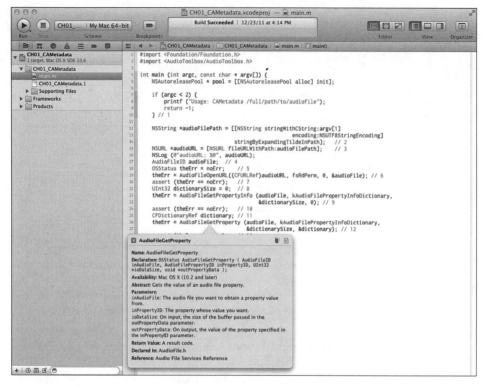

Figure I.3   Looking up documentation from the Xcode source editor

Then we give an overview of the API itself. We describe its procedural, property-driven nature and then give a quick tour of each of its architectural units, starting from high-level API, Audio Queue, OpenAL, Extended Audio File; moving through the mid- and low-level APIs (Audio Units, Audio File, Audio Converter); and finally heading into related topics such as Core MIDI, OpenAL, and how Core Audio works on iOS.

Part I: Understanding Core Audio

This section lays the foundation on which the rest of the book is built. That it seems like a lot of material to get through before writing any code is indicative of the subject. Understanding the problem of digital audio and the solutions Core Audio offers is an absolute must if subsequent sections and their sample code are to make any sense.

- **Chapter 1: Overview of Core Audio**

  We start our journey with a nuts-and-bolts investigation of Core Audio as a Mac or iOS framework: where the files are, how to integrate it into your projects, and where to go for help.

  We start with an overview of the API itself. We describe its procedural, property-driven nature. Then we take a quick tour of each of its architectural units, starting from high-level API (Audio Queue, OpenAL, Extended Audio File), moving through the midlevel API (Audio Units, Audio File, Audio Converter), and working into the low-level API (IOKit/IOAudio, HAL, and, on iOS, Remote I/O). We also work through a simple application to use Core Audio to fetch metadata from a sound file, to give you a taste of writing Core Audio code.

- **Chapter 2: The Story of Sound**
  The central problem of digital audio lies in representing the analog waveform of a sound on a digital computer. We talk about how sampling converts the sounds you hear into the 1s and 0s of a binary computer. We cover bit rates and the trade-offs of quality, performance, and file size. To get a hands-on understanding of sampling, you'll write your own sound waves directly to a file, sample by sample, and see (well, *hear,* actually) how different wave forms sound different to the human ear.

  When you have the raw stream of bits, you need to quantize them into frames and packets. We talk about the difference between constant and variable bit rates and frame rates.

- **Chapter 3: Audio Processing with Core Audio**
  When you understand the concepts of audio in English, it's time to express them in C. We talk about the implementation details here—how Core Audio represents audio streams and provides functionality to work with those streams. We talk about file formats and stream formats and highlight the difference between them. Then we'll write an example that inspects what kinds of audio format/file format combinations Core Audio supports.

  Following our description of formats, we switch to Core Audio's processing model and look at how Core Audio encapsulates its functionality as Audio Units, how these are combined in interesting ways, and why they use a pull model to move audio data through the system.

Part II: Basic Audio

This section begins the hands-on use of the API and concepts from the previous chapter. We start by discussing the flow of data between files and the audio systems, first by recording and then by playing file-based audio data. Then we discuss transcoding API for moving data between formats and explain the important behind-the-scenes function that serves.

- **Chapter 4: Recording**
  Why address recording before playback? Because it's easier and it generates sample files to play with later. This chapter introduces the high-level API for getting data in and out of files and explores the Audio Queue API for making use of that data. We'll develop a complete example that captures audio from the default input device and writes it to a file. In the process, we'll deal with some of the tricky parts of compressed formats, such as working with format-specific magic cookies and figuring out how big buffers need to be to write data for arbitrary formats.

- **Chapter 5: Playback**
  From a programming perspective, recording and playback are two sides of the same coin. Playback moves data from a file to a series of buffers; recording moves data from a series of buffers into a file.

  This chapter provides a full example of reading audio from a file and playing it to the default output. Again, we look at techniques for dealing with variable-bit-rate formats. We also take a look at some of the neat things you can do with an audio queue's properties and parameters and dig into the latency implications of working with so many buffers.

- **Chapter 6: Conversion**
  For people used to object-oriented programming, Core Audio's high-level API seems pretty low level. This chapter demonstrates the complexity behind the scenes, diving into the nitty-gritty details of modern audio codecs and the complexity necessary to convert them into canonical data. We work through an example that directly uses Audio Converter Services to convert a compressed file to an uncompressed version and then simplify this through the use of Extended Audio File Services, which combine I/O and data conversion into a single step.

Part III: Advanced Audio

Now that you understand how to move audio data back and forth, it's time to get fancy. We start by adding effects to audio data, move into 3D positional audio, and then talk about performance and low-level architecture.

- **Chapter 7: Audio Units: Generators, Effects, and Rendering**
  Core Audio provides an elegant architecture for digital signal processing plug-ins, called Audio Units. However, audio units are the lowest commonly used level of the Core Audio API and introduce new challenges for the programmer. This chapter introduces audio units to play sounds from files and the Mac OS X speech synthesizer and to perform effects on the sound, all coordinated via the AUGraph API. We also look at how to provide your own programmatically generated audio data as input to audio units.

- **Chapter 8: Audio Units: Input and Mixing**
  To help you further flex our muscles with the Audio Units API, we look at how to use the IO unit to perform audio capture and jump through some rather tricky threading hoops to get the captured data to run through an AUGraph of effects and other sources. To combine it all, we make use of the powerful multichannel mixer unit.

- **Chapter 9: Positional Sound**
  Up to now, the discussion has focused on sound itself, but the human experience of sound adds an entirely new dimension to the problem. This section discusses OpenAL, the 3D positional sound API, which enables you to associate sounds with

locations in a 3D space. We start with loops, but by the end of the chapter, you will be able to play arbitrarily long streams of sound from 3D sources.

Part IV: Additional Topics

By this point, we've covered most of Core Audio, but not all of it. This section explores some of the miscellany that doesn't fit into the rest of book. We start with a chapter dedicated to iOS, then talk about handling MIDI data, and end with a chapter on extending Core Audio.

- **Chapter 10: Core Audio on iOS**
  Conceptually, there's little difference between sound on an iPhone and sound on a Macintosh, but the devil is in the details. This chapter addresses the differences, with a particular concentration on the limitations and exceptions that come with limited hardware resources.

  We also discuss the Audio Session API, which is vital to making sure your application behaves properly in the preemptive, multisource, multidestination iPhone environment.

- **Chapter 11: Core MIDI**
  Musicians love the MIDI standard, which is a lynchpin of connecting musical instruments and processing digital music data. In this chapter, we look at how Core MIDI processes music events between the Mac or iOS device and instruments connected either physically or wirelessly. You'll also see how MIDI data can be delivered into an Audio Unit, enabling you to convert note and timing data into sound.

- **Chapter 12: Coda**
  In the final chapter, we look at what we've covered and what's left to discover. We also point out the newest and shiniest audio bits unveiled in Mac OS X 10.7 (Lion) and iOS 5.

This book doesn't use every function Core Audio defines or conceptually cover everything you can do with it, but it does dig deeply into the most used and most important topics. After you make it through the book, you'll have the hang of how Core Audio does things, and we think you'll be well equipped to explore any remaining functionality you need for your applications.

About the Sample Code

The source code for the projects in this book is available as a downloadable disk image (.dmg). To get it, click on the Resources tab on the book's catalog page:

www.informit.com/title/9780321636843

The disk image contains a README file and folders with the projects for each chapter.

This book contains a lot of sample code, and Core Audio can be pretty verbose to the modern eye. To keep the code size manageable, most of the examples in this book are written as OS X command-line executables, not full-fledged Cocoa (Mac OS X) GUI applications. You'll be able to run these directly in Xcode or from the command line (in Terminal or xterm). The iOS examples in Chapter 10 and thereafter are genuine iOS apps—the iPhone doesn't have a command line, after all—but we don't bother with a GUI unless absolutely necessary.

Core Audio is mostly the same between Mac OS X and iOS, so iOS developers can use the concepts from these examples in iPhone, iPod Touch, and iPad apps. In most cases, the code works exactly the same; we've pointed out any differences between Mac and iOS, either in the APIs themselves or in how they work on the different platforms. For the parts of Core Audio that are unique to iOS, see Chapter 10.

Our baseline SDK for this book is Xcode 4.2, which includes the SDKs for Mac OS X 10.7 (Lion) and iOS 5. For Core Audio development on a Mac, you don't need anything else: All the libraries, headers, and documentation are included with the Xcode tools.[1] Our sample code is written to support versions 10.6 and 10.7 on the Mac, and iOS 4 and 5. Because of changes and deprecations over the years, some of the Mac examples won't run as is on version 10.5 (Leopard) or earlier, although, in many cases, the difference is only a changed constant here or there (for example, the kAudioFileReadPermission constant introduced in version 10.6 replaces the fsRdPerm found in earlier versions of Mac OS X).

---

[1] Core Audio used to be a separate download, which has confused a few developers when they've seen it listed separately on Apple's Development Kits page. That download is needed only if you're developing on Tiger (Mac OS X 10.4.x).

Understanding Core Audio

1

Overview of Core Audio

Core Audio is the engine behind any sound played on a Mac or iPhone OS. Its procedural API is exposed in C, which makes it directly available in Objective-C and C++, and usable from any other language that can call C functions, such as Java with the Java Native Interface, or Ruby via RubyInline. From an audio standpoint, Core Audio is high level because it is highly agnostic. It abstracts away both the implementation details of the hardware and the details of individual audio formats.

To an application developer, Core Audio is suspiciously low level. If you're coding in C, you're doing something wrong, or so the saying goes. The problem is, very little sits above Core Audio. Audio turns out to be a difficult problem, and all but the most trivial use cases require more decision making than even the gnarliest Objective-C framework. The good news is, the times you don't need Core Audio are easy enough to spot, and the tasks you can do without Core Audio are pretty simple (see sidebar "When Not to Use Core Audio").

When you use Core Audio, you'll likely find it a far different experience from nearly anything else you've used in your Cocoa programming career. Even if you've called into other C-based Apple frameworks, such as Quartz or Core Foundation, you'll likely be surprised by Core Audio's style and conventions.

This chapter looks at what's in Core Audio and where to find it. Then it broadly surveys some of its most distinctive conventions, which you'll get a taste for by writing a simple application to exercise Core Audio's capability to work with audio metadata in files. This will give you your first taste of properties, which enable you to do a lot of the work throughout the book.

When Not to Use Core Audio

The primary scenario for not using Core Audio is when simply playing back from a file: On a Mac, you can use AppKit's NSSound, and on iOS, you can use the AVAudioPlayer from the AV Foundation framework. iOS also provides the AVAudioRecorder for recording to a file. The Mac has no equivalent Objective-C API for recording, although it does have QuickTime and QTKit; you could treat your audio as QTMovie objects and pick up some playback, recording, and mixing functionality. However, QuickTime's video orientation and its philosophy of being an editing API for multimedia documents makes it a poor fit for purely audio tasks. The same can be said of AV Foundation's `AVPlayer` and `AVCaptureSession` classes, which debuted in iOS 4 and became the heir apparent to QuickTime on Mac in 10.7 (Lion).

Beyond the simplest playback and recording cases—and, in particular, if you want to do anything with the audio, such as mixing, changing formats, applying effects, or working directly with the audio data—you'll want to adopt Core Audio.

The Core Audio Frameworks

Core Audio is a collection of frameworks for working with digital audio. Broadly speaking, you can split these frameworks into two groups: audio engines, which process streams of audio, and helper APIs, which facilitate getting audio data into or out of these engines or working with them in other ways.

Both the Mac and the iPhone have three audio engine APIs:

- **Audio Units.** Core Audio does most of its work in this low-level API. Each unit receives a buffer of audio data from somewhere (the input hardware, another audio unit, a callback to your code, and so on), performs some work on it (such as applying an effect), and passes it on to another unit. A unit can potentially have many inputs and outputs, which makes it possible to mix multiple audio streams into one output. Chapter 7, "Audio Units: Generators, Effects, and Rendering," talks more about Audio Units.

- **Audio Queues.** This is an abstraction atop audio units that make it easier to play or record audio without having to worry about some of the threading challenges that arise when working directly with the time-constrained I/O audio unit. With an audio queue, you record by setting up a callback function to repeatedly receive buffers of new data from the input device every time new data is available; you play back by filling buffers with audio data and handing them to the audio queue. You will do both of these in Chapter 4, "Recording."

- **OpenAL.** This API is an industry standard for creating positional, 3D audio (in other words, surround sound) and is designed to resemble the OpenGL graphics standard. As a result, it's ideally suited for game development. On the Mac and the iPhone, its actual implementation sits atop audio units, but working exclusively with the OpenAL API gets you surprisingly far. Chapter 9, "Positional Sound," covers this in more detail.

To get data into and out of these engines, Core Audio provides various helper APIs, which are used throughout the book:

- **Audio File Services.** This framework abstracts away the details of various container formats for audio files. As a result, you don't have to write code that specifically addresses the idiosyncrasies of AIFFs, WAVs, MP3s, or any other format. It enables your program to open an audio file, get or set the format of the audio data it contains, and start reading or writing.

- **Audio File Stream Services.** If your audio is coming from the network, this framework can help you figure out the format of the audio in the network stream. This enables you to provide it to one of the playback engines or process it in other interesting ways.

- **Audio Converter Services.** Audio can exist in many formats. By the time it reaches the audio engines, it needs to be in an uncompressed playable format (LPCM, discussed in Chapter 2, "The Story of Sound"). Audio Converter Services helps you convert between encoded formats such as AAC or MP3 and the uncompressed raw samples that actually go through the audio units.

- **Extended Audio File Services.** A combination of Audio Converter Services and Audio File Stream Services, the Extended Audio File APIs enables you to read from or write to audio files and do a conversion at the same time. For example, instead of reading AAC data from a file and then converting to uncompressed PCM in memory, you can do both in one call by using Extended Audio File Services.

- **Core MIDI.** Most of the Core Audio frameworks are involved with processing sampled audio that you've received from other sources or captured from an input device. With the Mac-only Core MIDI framework, you synthesize audio on the fly by describing musical notes and how they are to be played out—for example, whether they should sound like they're coming from a grand piano or a ukulele. You'll try out MIDI in Chapter 11, "Core MIDI."

A few Core Audio frameworks are platform specific:

- **Audio Session Services.** This iOS-only framework enables your app to coordinate its use of audio resources with the rest of the system. For example, you use this API to declare an audio "category," which determines whether iPod audio can continue to play while your app plays and whether the ring/silent switch should silence your app. You'll use this more in Chapter 10, "Core Audio on iOS."

As you develop your application, you'll combine these APIs in interesting ways. For example, you could use Audio File Stream Services to get the audio data from a net radio stream and then use OpenAL to put that audio in a specific location in a 3D environment.

Core Audio Conventions

The Core Audio frameworks are exposed as C function calls. This makes them broadly available to Cocoa, Cocoa Touch, and Carbon apps, but you have to be ready to deal with all the usual issues of procedural C, such as pointers, manual memory management, *structs*, and *enums*. Most modern developers have cut their teeth on object-oriented languages such as Objective-C, C++, and Python, so it's no longer a given that professional programmers are comfortable with procedural C.

In C, you don't have classes, object orientation, implementation hiding, or many of the other important language traits that most developers have depended on for years. But Core Audio, like Apple's other C-based frameworks, does provide a measure of these modern traits, even within the C idiom.

Apple's model C framework is Core Foundation, which underlies Foundation, the essential Objective-C framework that nearly all Mac and iPhone applications use. You'll recognize Foundation by classes such as NSString, NSURL, NSDate, and NSObject. In many cases, the Objective-C classes assemble their functionality by calling Core Foundation, which provides opaque types (pointers to data structures whose actual members are hidden) and functions that work on these objects. For example, an NSString is literally the same as a CFStringRef (you can freely cast between the two), and its length method is equivalent to the function CFStringGetLength(), which takes a CFStringRef as its object. By combining these opaque types with consistent naming conventions for functions, Core Foundation provides a highly manageable C API with a clarity similar to what you're used to in Cocoa.

Core Audio is highly similar in its design. Many of its most important objects (such as audio queues and audio files) are treated as opaque objects that you hand to predictably named functions, such as AudioQueueStart() or AudioFileOpenURL(). It's not explicitly built atop Core Foundation—an AudioQueueRef is not technically a CF opaque type; however, it does make use of CF's most important objects, such as CFStringRef and CFURLRef, which can be trivially cast to and from NSStrings and NSURLs in your Cocoa code.

Your First Core Audio Application

Now let's get a feel for Core Audio code by actually writing some. The audio engine APIs have a lot of moving parts and are, therefore, more complex, so we'll make trivial use of one of the helper APIs. In this first example, we'll get some metadata (information about the audio) from an audio file.

> **Note**
>
> In this book, most of the examples are command-line utilities instead of full-blown AppKit or UIKit applications. This helps keep the focus on the audio code, without bringing in GUI considerations.

Launch Xcode, go to File > New Project, select the Mac OS X Application templates, and choose the Command Line Tool template; select the Foundation type in the pop-up menu below the template icon. When prompted, call the project **CAMetadata**. The resulting project has one user-editable source file, *main.m*, and produces an executable called *CAMetadata*, which you can run from Xcode or in the Terminal.

Select the *CAMetadata.m* file. You'll see that it has a single main() function that sets up an NSAutoReleasePool, prints a "Hello, World!" log message, and drains the pool before terminating. Replace the comment and the `printf` so that `main()` looks like Listing 1.1. We've added numbered comments to the ends of some of the statements as callouts so that we can explain what this code does, line by line.

Listing 1.1 **Your First Core Audio Application**

```
int main (int argc, const char * argv[]) {
    NSAutoreleasePool * pool = [[NSAutoreleasePool alloc] init];
    if (argc < 2) {
        printf ("Usage: CAMetadata /full/path/to/audiofile\n");
        return -1;
    }                                                           // 1

NSString *audioFilePath = [[NSString stringWithUTF8String:argv[1]]
                           stringByExpandingTildeInPath];       // 2
    NSURL *audioURL = [NSURL fileURLWithPath:audioFilePath];     // 3
    AudioFileID audioFile;                                      // 4
    OSStatus theErr = noErr;                                    // 5
    theErr = AudioFileOpenURL((CFURLRef)audioURL,
                              kAudioFileReadPermission,
                              0,
                              &audioFile);                      // 6
    assert (theErr == noErr);                                  // 7
    UInt32 dictionarySize = 0;                                 // 8
    theErr = AudioFileGetPropertyInfo (audioFile,
                                kAudioFilePropertyInfoDictionary,
                                &dictionarySize,
                                0);                             // 9
    assert (theErr == noErr);                                  // 10
    CFDictionaryRef dictionary;                                // 11
    theErr = AudioFileGetProperty (audioFile,
                                kAudioFilePropertyInfoDictionary,
                                &dictionarySize,
                                &dictionary);                   // 12
    assert (theErr == noErr);                                  // 13
    NSLog (@"dictionary: %@", dictionary);                     // 14
    CFRelease (dictionary);                                    // 15
    theErr = AudioFileClose (audioFile);                       // 16
    assert (theErr == noErr);                                  // 17

    [pool drain];
    return 0;
}
```

Now let's walk through the code from Listing 1.1:

1. As in any C program, the `main()` method accepts a count of arguments (`argc`) and an array of plain C-string arguments. The first string is the executable name, so you must look to see if there's a second argument that provides the path to an audio file. If there isn't, you print a message and terminate.

2. If there's a path, you need to convert it from a plain C string to the `NSString`/`CFStringRef` representation that Apple's various frameworks use. Specifying the UTF-8 encoding for this conversion lets you pass in paths that use non-Western characters, in case (like us) you listen to music from all over the world. By using `stringByExpandingTildeInPath`, you accept the tilde character as a shortcut to the user's home directory, as in ~/*Music/*....

3. The Audio File APIs work with URL representations of file paths, so you must convert the file path to an `NSURL`.

4. Core Audio uses the `AudioFileID` type to refer to audio file objects, so you declare a reference as a local variable.

5. Most Core Audio functions signal success or failure through their return value, which is of type `OSStatus`. Any status other than `noErr` (which is 0) signals an error. You need to check this return value on *every* Core Audio call because an error early on usually makes subsequent calls meaningless. For example, if you can't create the `AudioFileID` object, trying to get properties from the file that object was supposed to represent will always fail. In this example, we've used an `assert()` to terminate the program instantly if we ever get an error, in callouts 7, 10, 13, and 17. Of course, your application will probably want to handle errors with somewhat less brutality.

6. Here's the first Core Audio function call: `AudioFileOpenURL`. It takes four parameters, a `CFURLRef`, a file permissions flag, a file type hint, and a pointer to receive the created `AudioFileID` object. You do a toll-free cast of the `NSURL` to a `CFURLRef` to match the first parameter's defined type. For the file permissions, you pass a constant to indicate read permission. You don't have a hint to provide, so you pass 0 to make Core Audio figure it out for itself. Finally, you use the `&` ("address of") operator to provide a pointer to receive the `AudioFileID` object that gets created.

7. If `AudioFileOpenURL` returned an error, die.

8. To get the file's metadata, you will be asking for a metadata property, `kAudioFilePropertyInfoDictionary`. But that call requires allocating memory for the returned metadata in advance. So here, we declare a local variable to receive the size we'll need to allocate.

9. To get the needed size, call `AudioFileGetPropertyInfo`, passing in the `AudioFileID`, the property you want information about, a pointer to receive the result, and a pointer to a flag variable that indicates whether the property is writeable (because we don't care, we pass in `0`).

10. If `AudioFileGetPropertyInfo` failed, terminate.

11. The call to get a property from an audio file populates different types, based on the property itself. Some properties are numeric; some are strings. The documentation and the Core Audio header files describe these values. Asking for `kAudioFilePropertyInfoDictionary` results in a dictionary, so we set up a local variable instance of type `CFDictionaryRef` (which can be cast to an `NSDictionary` if needed).

12. You're finally ready to request the property. Call `AudioFileGetProperty`, passing in the `AudioFileID`, the property constant, a pointer to the size you're prepared to accept (set up in callouts 8–10 with the `AudioFileGetPropertyInfo` call) and a pointer to receive the value (set up on the previous line).

13. Again, check the return value and fail if it's anything other than `noErr`.

14. Let's see what you got. As in any Core Foundation or Cocoa object, you can use `"%@"` in a format string to get a string representation of the dictionary.

15. Core Foundation doesn't offer autorelease, so the `CFDictionaryRef` received in callout 12 has a retain count of 1. `CFRelease()` releases your interest in the object.

16. The `AudioFileID` also needs to be cleaned up but isn't a Core Foundation object, per se; therefore, it doesn't get `CFRelease()`'d. Instead, it has its own end-of-life function: `AudioFileClose()`.

17. `AudioFileClose()` is another Core Audio call, so you should continue to check return codes, though it's arguably meaningless here because you're two lines away from terminating anyway.

So that's about 30 lines of code, but functionally, it's all about setting up three calls: opening a file, allocating a buffer for the metadata, and getting the metadata.

Running the Example

That was probably more code than you're used to writing for simple functionality, but it's done now. Let's try it out. Click build; you get compile errors. Upon inspection, you should see that all the Core Audio functions and constants aren't being found.

This is because Core Audio isn't included by default in Xcode's command-line executable project, which imports only the Foundation framework. Add a second #import line:

```
#import <AudioToolbox/AudioToolbox.h>
```

Audio Toolbox is an "umbrella" header file that includes most of the Core Audio functionality you'll use in your apps, which means you'll be importing it into pretty much all the examples. You also need to add the framework to your project. Click the project icon in Xcode's file navigator, select the CAMetadata target, and click the Build Phases tab. Expand the Link Binaries with Libraries section and click the + button to add a new library to be linked at build time. In the sheet that slides out, select the AudioToolbox.framework, as shown in Figure 1.1.

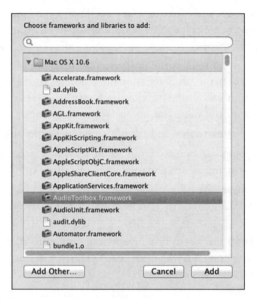

Figure 1.1   Adding the AudioToolbox.framework to an Xcode project

Now you should be able to build the application without any errors. To run it, you need to provide a path as a command-line argument. You can either open the Terminal and navigate to the project's build directory or supply an argument with Xcode. Let's do the latter:

- From the Scheme pop-up menu, select Edit Scheme.
- Select the Run CAMetadata item and click the Arguments tab.
- Press + to add an argument and supply the path to an audio file on your hard drive.

- If your path has spaces in it, use quotation marks. For example, we're using an MP3 bought online, located at ~/*Music*/*iTunes*/*iTunes Music*/*Amazon MP3*/*Metric*/*Fantasies*/*05 - Gold Guns Girls.mp3*. Click OK to dismiss the Scheme Editor sheet.
- Bring up Xcode's Console pane with Shift-⌘-C and click Run.

Assuming that your path is valid, your output will look something like this:

```
2010-02-18 09:43:17.623 CAMetadata[17104:a0f] dictionary: {
    album = Fantasies;
    "approximate duration in seconds" = "245.368";
    artist = Metric;
    comments = "Amazon.com Song ID: 210266948";
    copyright = "2009 Metric Productions";
    genre = "Alternative Rock";
    title = "Gold Guns Girls";
    "track number" = "5/10";
    year = 2009;
}
```

Well, that's pretty cool: You've got a nice dump of a lot of the same metadata that you'd see in an application such as iTunes. Now let's check it out with an AAC song from the iTunes Store. Changing the command-line argument to something like ~/*Music*/*iTunes*/*iTunes Music*/*Arcade Fire*/*Funeral*/*07 Wake Up.m4a* gets you the following:

```
2010-02-18 09:48:15.421 CAMetadata[17665:a0f] dictionary: {
    "approximate duration in seconds" = "335.333";
}
```

Whoa! What happened to the metadata call?

Nothing, really: Nothing in the documentation promises what you can expect in the info dictionary. As it turns out, Core Audio offers richer support for ID3 tags in *.mp3* files than the iTunes tagging found in *.m4a* files.

No Need for Promises

Speaking from experience, you'll want to prepare yourself for unpredictable results, such as different levels of metadata support for MP3 and AAC files. Mastering Core Audio isn't just about understanding the APIs; it's also about developing a sense of the implementation, how the library actually works, and what it does well and where it comes up short.

Core Audio isn't just about the syntax of your calls; it's about the semantics, too. In some cases, code that's syntactically correct will fail in practice because it violates implicit contracts, acts differently on different hardware, or even just it uses too much CPU time in a time-constrained callback. The successful Core Audio programmer doesn't march off in a huff when things don't work as expected or don't work well enough the first time. Instead, you must try to figure out what's really going on and come up with a better approach.

Core Audio Properties

The Core Audio calls in this example were all about getting properties from the audio file object. The routine of preparing for and executing property-setter and property-getter calls is essential in Core Audio.

That's because Core Audio is a *property-driven* API. Properties are key-value pairs, with the keys being enumerated integers. The values can be of whatever type the API defines. Each API in Core Audio communicates its capabilities and state via its list of properties. For example, if you look up the `AudioFileGetProperty()` function in this example, you'll find a link to a list of Audio File Properties in the documentation. The list, which you can also find by looking in Core Audio's *AudioFile.h* header, looks like this:

```
kAudioFilePropertyFileFormat          =    'ffmt',
kAudioFilePropertyDataFormat          =    'dfmt',
kAudioFilePropertyIsOptimized         =    'optm',
kAudioFilePropertyMagicCookieData     =    'mgic',
kAudioFilePropertyAudioDataByteCount  =    'bcnt',
...
```

These keys are 32-bit integer values that you can read in the documentation and header file as four character codes. As you can see from this list, the four-character codes take advantage of the fact that you can use single quotes to represent char literals in C and spell out clever mnemonics. Assume that `fmt` is short for "format," and you can figure out that `ffmt` is the code for "file format" and `dfmt` means "data format." Codes like these are used throughout Core Audio, as property keys and sometimes as error statuses. If you attempt to write to a file format Core Audio doesn't understand, you'll get the response `fmt?`, which is `kAudioFileUnsupportedDataFormatError`.

Because Core Audio makes so much use of properties, you'll see common patterns throughout its API for setting and getting properties. You've already seen `AudioFileGetPropertyInfo()` and `AudioFileGetProperty()`, so it probably won't surprise you later to encounter `AudioQueueGetProperty()`, `AudioUnitGet Property()`, `AudioConverterGetProperty()`, and so on. Some APIs provide property listeners that you can register to receive a callback when a property changes. Using callback functions to respond to asynchronous events is a common pattern in Core Audio.

The values that you get or set with these APIs depend on the property being set. You retrieved the `kAudioFilePropertyInfoDictionary` property, which returned a pointer to a `CFDictionaryRef`, but if you had asked for a `kAudioFileProperty EstimatedDuration`, you'd need to be prepared to accept a pointer to an `NSTimeInterval` (which is really just a `double`). This is tremendously powerful because a small number of functions can support a potentially infinite set of properties. However, setting up such calls does involve extra work because you typically have to use the "get property info" call to allocate some memory to receive the property value or to inspect whether the property is writable.

Another point to notice with the property functions is the Core Audio naming conventions for function parameters. Let's look at the definition of `AudioFileGetProperty()` from the docs (or the *AudioFile.h* header):

```
OSStatus AudioFileGetProperty (
    AudioFileID          inAudioFile,
    AudioFilePropertyID  inPropertyID,
    UInt32               *ioDataSize,
    void                 *outPropertyData
);
```

Notice the names of the parameters: The use of `in`, `out`, or `io` indicates whether a parameter is used only for input to the function (as with the first two, which indicate the file to use and the property you want), only for output from the function (as with the fourth, `outPropertyData`, which fills a pointer with the property value), or for input and output (as with the third, `ioDataSize`, which accepts the size of buffer you allocated for `outPropertyData` and then writes back the number of bytes actually written into that buffer). You'll see this naming pattern throughout Core Audio, particularly any time a parameter works with a pointer to populate a value.

Summary

This chapter provided an overview of the many different parts of Core Audio and gave you a taste of programming by using Audio File Services to get the metadata properties of audio files on the local drive. You saw how Core Audio uses properties as a crucial idiom for working with its various APIs. You also saw how Core Audio uses four character codes to specify property keys, and to signal errors.

Of course, you haven't really dealt with audio itself yet. To do that, you first need to understand how sound is represented and handled in a digital form. Then you'll be ready to dig into Core Audio's APIs for working with audio data.

2

The Story of Sound

In the previous chapter, you got your first taste of the Core Audio API: what it offers, how to add it to a project, and how to call its functions. Now it's time to take a step back and look at the bigger picture: the problems that Core Audio addresses in the first place.

This chapter introduces the basic science of sound, what it is and how it works. As it turns out, the digital nature of computers makes them not well suited to processing continuous analog signals. This leads to the idea of sampling a signal, or chopping the smooth sound waves into discrete values frequently enough that the human ear can't notice the difference. This chapter covers how these samples are represented and arranged in digital form.

It's one thing to talk about samples and another to actually handle them, so the example project writes sound waves to a file, one sample at a time.

Finally, you'll wrap up with some of the issues that always arise with digital audio: buffers (and their inherent latency concerns) and the various kinds of digital audio formats.

Making Waves

If you shove someone on the sidewalk, that person just moves. But if you shove someone in a crowded place, such as at a concert, he bounces off the person in front of him and returns to his original position. This triggers a chain reaction as the force of your shove travels through the crowd, eventually hitting your friend across the room. You've just shoved your friend via a couple dozen annoyed proxies.

In scientific terms, a bunch of objects close enough to bounce off each other is called a medium because of the way energy can travel through it. The movement of the person you shoved—first forward, then back—is called a cycle. The time it takes to complete a cycle is its period. If you pushed the person repeatedly, the pattern of people bouncing off each other would be a compression wave.

This wave has two attributes. The strength with which you push is the wave's amplitude. The speed with which you push is the wave's frequency. The more frequently you

push, the higher the frequency of the wave created as a result. If you varied the amplitude and frequency of your pushing, your friend would feel those changes. You would no
longer be just making waves; you'd be transmitting data over a medium.

When you talk to someone, your vocal cords move back and forth, or vibrate, pushing the molecules in the air. Those molecules bounce off each other like people at a
concert until they hit your friend's ear drums. Speakers and microphones are just
machines that do the same thing. Sound is nothing but energy shoving its way through a
medium.

To record a sound, all you have to do is describe the way the sound makes a membrane vibrate. To play back the sound, you vibrate a membrane as described. One way
to describe sound is to graph the position of the membrane over time, as shown in
Figure 2.1.

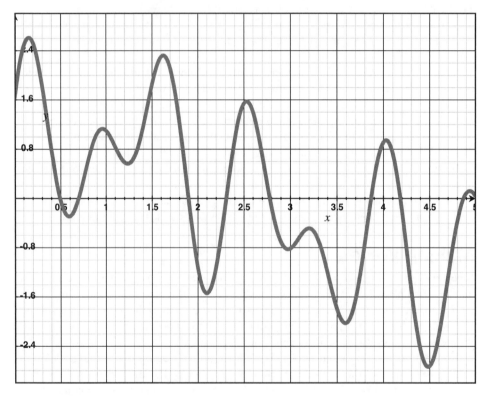

Figure 2.1   A sound wave as it relates to the position
of a vibrating membrane

The middle of the graph represents the resting state of the membrane. The top and bottom of the graph represent the maximum displacement of the membrane. As time moves

from left to right, the position of the membrane moves up and down. The y-axis, then, represents amplitude as a percentage of maximum, and the frequency with which the values move between positive and negative represents the sound's frequency.

One way to represent this wave is to carve a picture of it into some physical object. The advantage of this technique, called analog recording, is that it produces a very accurate reproduction. The disadvantage is that the recording is as nuanced and inexact as the sound wave it describes. This inexactness comes into play when making copies. It's also incompatible with computers, which require that things be described in exact numerical terms.

Digital Audio

For computers, you need to represent the wave numerically. You can approximate the wave by plotting a series of (x,y) points along its path. If you provide enough points, you'll have a good-enough representation. The standard for this is *pulse code modulation (PCM),* which works by recording y at regular intervals of time, meaning x is implicit. In its most common form, linear pulse code modulation, you assign a value that represents a proportion of the maximum value of y. For example, if a graph represents values between 0 and 1, and a given point has a y value that's half of the maximum, you assign it the value 0.5. This process of assigning values at regular intervals is called sampling. Each value is itself a sample.

CD-quality audio has a sample rate of 44.1 kHz, or 44,100 samples per second. One way of looking at that is to realize that every second of CD-quality audio has 44,100 gaps of just under 23 microseconds. For these gaps, no data exists. Anything that happened to the sound wave during that time is lost. Figure 2.2 illustrates the effect of sample rate on the data's capability to accurately approximate the curves of the sound wave. All three images in Figure 2.2 represent the same wave as in Figure 2.1, but at decreasing sample rates. As you can see, the representation of the wave gets less accurate as you use fewer samples. In particular, the peak at $t = 2.5$ and the valleys at $t = 2.1$ and $t = 4.4$ are completely lost in the rightmost image.

You could make better approximations by taking more samples, but it would be helpful to know if there's some granularity that's "good enough." The key to finding a good enough approximation is that you don't hear individual samples, but instead you hear the waves of sound pushing through the air. What you hear are frequencies, repeated patterns of vibration, whether from a guitar chord or a larynx. You need to figure out how often to sample in order to reproduce these frequencies.

You actually get this number from the *Nyquist-Shannon Sampling Theorem*, which says that if you have a function with no frequencies greater than B Hz (cycles per second), you can render it accurately by using points spaced $1/(2B)$ seconds apart. For audio purposes, this means that to reproduce any frequency, you need to sample the signal at double that frequency or more.

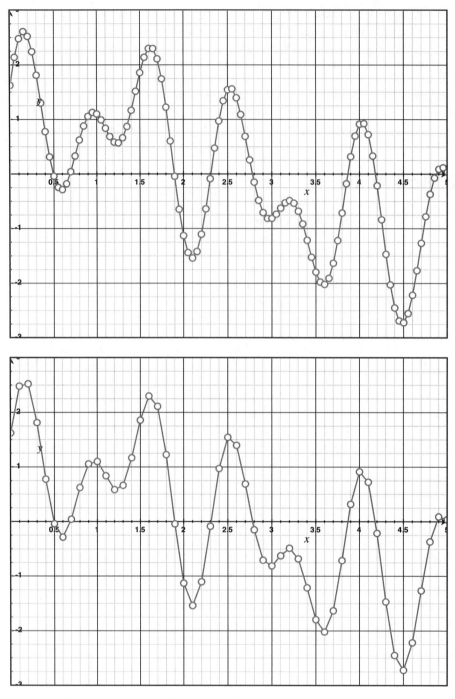

Figure 2.2(a, b)   A sound wave approximated by several sample rates

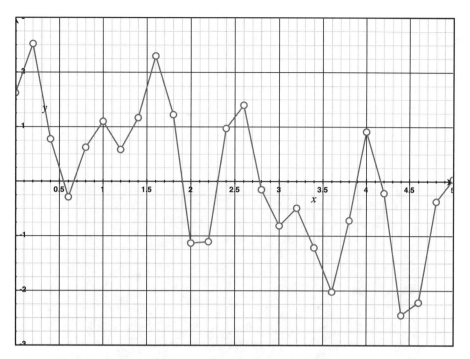

Figure 2.2(c)   A sound wave approximated by several sample rates

This explains the value of 44.1 kHz chosen for CD-quality audio. Half of that is 22.05 kHz, which is beyond the range of most human hearing. The ability to perceive high frequencies deteriorates with age. Young people can hear up to about 20 kHz, but a middle-age person might hear only up to around 14 or 15 kHz. So by sampling at 44.1 kHz, you might lose some information, but not enough to matter—what's important is the listener's ability to perceive the vibration frequencies in the audio signal.

Each sample represents the amplitude of the wave, or the displacement of the membrane, as a percentage of the maximum possible value. The advantage of using percentages is hardware independence. Half is half, regardless of what you're halving.

Unlike integers, in which larger numbers require more digits to express, fractions need more digits to express smaller numbers. Writing 100 takes more digits than writing 10, but writing [1/100] takes more digits than writing [1/10]. A sample's bit depth is the number of digits it has. If the difference between two sounds is smaller (as a percentage of the maximum possible displacement) than the sample has digits to express, that difference is lost.

The bit depth (measured in bits per sample) multiplied by the sample rate (measured in samples per second) results in the bit rate (measured in bits per second). That is the number of bits required to describe 1 second of audio. A higher bit rate gives a higher-quality recording but also means more bits for the hardware to store and process.

The fundamental problem of digital fidelity lies in making the best approximations, given the limits of the hardware. Every different format is a different solution set of compromises to solve this problem. This is true not only in digital audio, but generally. Digital photography, for example, has the same sorts of problems, with the same alphabet soup of formats, each offering its own solution.

In a digital image, the sample rate translates into the number of pixels, whereas the bit depth translates into the number of colors per pixel. Each additional bit yields an increase of a power of two. The difference between the two adjacent images in Figure 2.3 is a single bit.

Figure 2.3   Bit depth and sample rate in digital photography

One niggling implementation detail is that this metaphor works only with a grayscale image. Computers can't actually display color pixels the way humans see them. Each color pixel consists of red, green, and blue lights. Each requires its own set of data, called a channel. Most image formats combine one sample from each channel into a bundle representing a single pixel.

Digital audio shares these issues. A monaural sound wave is like a grayscale image, but many sound systems have multiple speakers. Just as a pixel requires channels for red, blue, and green, stereo sound requires channels for left and right. Surround sound adds extra channels. A typical 5.1 surround-sound signal has six channels: left and right channels for the front and rear, a center channel, and a nondirectional channel for low-frequency effects, known to aficionados simply as bass.

As with their graphical brethren, audio formats typically combine one sample per channel into a bundle, called a *frame*. Whereas a pixel represents all color channels in one area in space, a frame represents all audio channels at one moment in time. So for mono sound, a frame has one sample; for stereo, it has two. If you put multiple channels of sound in one stream, you call the channels *interleaved*. This is common for playback: Because you want to read all the channels at the same time, it makes sense to arrange the data to do this easily. However, when processing audio (such as when adding effects or doing some other signal processing), you might want noninterleaved audio that so you can focus on each channel in isolation.

Some audio formats combine multiple frames as *packets*. This concept is entirely a creation of a given audio format and represents an indivisible unit within that format. LPCM doesn't use packets, but compressed audio formats do because they use mathematical techniques with a group of samples to approximate their values. A given sample can often be predicted to some degree by those around it, so compressed formats can use groups of samples, arranged in frames, to produce a similar (if not identical) wave from much less data than the uncompressed LPCM original.

We mentioned the bit rate earlier, the amount of data over a given period of time to represent audio in some format. For PCM, the bit rate is constant: CD-quality audio has a bit rate of 1,411,200 bits per second, or 1,411 kbps, because it has 2 channels × 16 bits × 44,100 samples per second. PCM is said to have a *constant bit rate* because this data rate never changes for a given combination of channel count, bit depth, and sample rate. Compressed formats often use a *variable bit rate,* meaning that the amount of data needed to compress any particular part of the data changes. Core Audio supports *variable frame rate* formats: The amount of data for any given frame may vary, but the packets remain the same size. Core Audio also supports *variable packet rate,* in which even the packet rate may change. However, currently no variable packet rate formats are in widespread use.

One reason to care about this distinction is that constant bit rate (CBR) data sometimes employs simpler API calls than variable bit rate (VBR). For example, when you read audio data from a file or stream, VBR data supplies you with a block of data and an array of packet descriptions that help you figure out what samples go with what times. For CBR, this is unnecessary; the amount of data for every frame is constant, so you can find a given time's samples by multiplying the frame size by the time.

DIY Samples

We've talked a lot about samples and audio waves. It might help to take a look at audio samples by writing some yourself.

In Listing 2.1, we'll again use Audio File Services, this time to create a file and write raw samples to it. Create a command-line tool project and call it CAToneFileGenerator. As before, the template provides you with one source file, whose *main()* method sets up an autorelease pool and prints a "Hello, world!" message. Add *AudioToolbox.framework* to the project and rewrite *CAToneFileGenerator.m* as follows:

Listing 2.1   **Writing a Sound Wave to a File, Sample by Sample**

```
#import <Foundation/Foundation.h>
#import <AudioToolbox/AudioToolbox.h>

#define SAMPLE_RATE 44100                                        // 1
#define DURATION 5.0                                             // 2
#define FILENAME_FORMAT @"%0.3f-square.aif"                      // 3

int main (int argc, const char * argv[]) {
    NSAutoreleasePool * pool = [[NSAutoreleasePool alloc] init];

    if (argc < 2) {
        printf ("Usage: CAToneFileGenerator n\n(where n is tone in Hz)");
        return -1;
    }

    double hz = atof(argv[1]);                                   // 4
    assert (hz > 0);
    NSLog (@"generating %f hz tone", hz);

    NSString *fileName = [NSString stringWithFormat:
                          FILENAME_FORMAT, hz];                  // 5
    NSString *filePath = [[[NSFileManager defaultManager] currentDirectoryPath]
                          stringByAppendingPathComponent: fileName];
    NSURL *fileURL = [NSURL fileURLWithPath: filePath];

    // Prepare the format
    AudioStreamBasicDescription asbd;                            // 6
    memset(&asbd, 0, sizeof(asbd));                              // 7
    asbd.mSampleRate = SAMPLE_RATE;                              // 8
    asbd.mFormatID = kAudioFormatLinearPCM;
    asbd.mFormatFlags = kAudioFormatFlagIsBigEndian |
        kAudioFormatFlagIsSignedInteger | kAudioFormatFlagIsPacked;
    asbd.mBitsPerChannel = 16;
    asbd.mChannelsPerFrame = 1;
    asbd.mFramesPerPacket = 1;
```

```
    asbd.mBytesPerFrame = 2;
    asbd.mBytesPerPacket = 2;

    // Set up the file
    AudioFileID audioFile;
    OSStatus audioErr = noErr;
    audioErr = AudioFileCreateWithURL((CFURLRef)fileURL,        // 9
                                  kAudioFileAIFFType,
                                  &asbd,
                                  kAudioFileFlags_EraseFile,
                                  &audioFile);
    assert (audioErr == noErr);

    // Start writing samples
    long maxSampleCount = SAMPLE_RATE * DURATION;              // 10
    long sampleCount = 0;
    UInt32 bytesToWrite = 2;
    double wavelengthInSamples = SAMPLE_RATE / hz;            // 11

    while (sampleCount < maxSampleCount) {
        for (int i=0; i<wavelengthInSamples; i++) {
            // Square wave
            SInt16 sample;
            if (i < wavelengthInSamples/2) {                  // 12
                sample = CFSwapInt16HostToBig (SHRT_MAX);     // 13
            } else {
                sample = CFSwapInt16HostToBig (SHRT_MIN);
            }
            audioErr = AudioFileWriteBytes(audioFile,          // 14
                                  false,
                                  sampleCount*2,
                                  &bytesToWrite,
                                  &sample);
            assert (audioErr == noErr);
            sampleCount++;                                     // 15
        }
    }
    audioErr = AudioFileClose(audioFile);                      // 16
    assert (audioErr == noErr);
    NSLog (@"wrote %d samples", sampleCount);

    [pool drain];
    return 0;
}
```

There's more to this code than the previous example, but it's still only about 70 lines. Let's walk through the callouts of the key points.

1. #define a sample rate of 44,100 samples per second, or 44.1 kHz, the same as with CD audio.

2. Next, #define how many seconds of audio you want to create.

3. Put the filename in a #define'd format string so you can change the name later. The first example creates square waves, the simplest kind of wave form, so incorporate "square" in the filename.

4. As in the previous chapter's example, you take a command-line argument here. This time, it's a floating point number for the tone frequency you want to generate. If you want to run this from Xcode (instead of the command line), go to the Scheme editor, as before, and add an argument. You could use 261.626 for the note that's middle C on a piano, or 440 for the A above that (which is known as middle A or concert A).

5. These two lines create the path to a file, using the FILENAME_FORMAT and the frequency to create a name, such as *261.626-square.aif*. They then make an NSURL because the Audio File Services functions take URLs, not file paths.

6. To create an audio file, you must provide a description of the audio that the file contains. You do this with what might be the most important and commonly used data structure in Core Audio, AudioStreamBasicDescription. This struct defines the most universal traits of a stream of audio: how many channels it has, the format it's in, the bit rate, and so on.

7. In some cases, Core Audio fills in some of the fields for an AudioStreamBasic-Description that you don't (or can't) know when you're writing the code. To do this, the field must be initialized to 0. As a common practice, always blank out the fields of an ASBD with *memset()* before you set any of them.

8. The next eight lines use individual fields of the AudioStreamBasicDescription to describe the data you're going to write to the file. Here, they describe a stream that's one-channel (mono) PCM, at a data rate of 44,100. You use 16-bit samples (again, the same as a CD), so each frame will have 2 bytes (one channel × 2 bytes of sample data). LPCM doesn't use packets—they're useful only for variable bit rate formats—so the bytesPerFrame and bytesPerPacket are equal. The other field to note is mFormatFlags, whose contents vary based on the format you're using. For PCM, you must indicate whether your samples are big-endian (the high bits of a byte or word are numerically more significant than the lower ones) or vice versa. Here you'll write to an AIFF file, which can take only big-endian PCM, so you need to set that in your ASBD. You also need to indicate the numeric format of the samples (kAudioFormatFlagIsSignedInteger), and you pass in a third flag to indicate that your sample values use all the bits available in each byte (kAudioFormatFlagIsPacked). mFormatFlags is a bit field, so you combine these behavior flags with the arithmetic OR operator (|).

9. You can now ask Core Audio to create an `AudioFileID`, ready for writing at the URL you've set up. The *AudioFileCreateWithURL()* function takes a URL (notice that you again use toll-free bridging to cast from a Cocoa `NSURL` to a Core Foundation `CFURLRef`), a constant to describe the AIFF file format, a pointer to the `AudioStreamBasicDescription` describing the audio data, behavior flags (in this case, indicating your desire to overwrite an existing file of the same name), and a pointer to populate with the created `AudioFileID`.

10. You're nearly ready to start writing samples. Before going into a loop to do so, you calculate how many samples you'll need for `DURATION` seconds of sound at `SAMPLE_RATE` samples per second. Along with a counter variable, `sampleCount`, you set up `bytesToWrite` as a local variable only because the call to write the samples requires a pointer to this `UInt32`; you can't just put the value into the parameter directly.

11. You need to keep track of how many samples are in a wavelength so you can calculate the values for samples that make up a wave.

12. For this first example, you'll write one of the simplest waves, the *square wave*. The samples for this are trivial: For the first half of the wavelength, you provide a maximum value, and for the rest of the wavelength, you use a minimum value. So only two possible sample values ever are used: one high and one low. For the 16-bit signed integers, you'll use the C constants that represent the maximum and minimum values, `SHRT_MAX` and `SHRT_MIN`.

13. You declared the audio format as big-endian signed integers in the `AudioStreamBasicDescription`, so you have to be careful to keep the 2-byte samples in that format. Modern Macs run on little-endian Intel CPUs, and the iPhone's ARM processor is also little-endian, so you need to swap bytes from the CPU's representation to big-endian. The Core Foundation function `CFSwapInt16HostToBig()` does this for you. This call also works on a big-endian CPU, such as the PowerPC on older Macs, because it would just realize that the host's format is big-endian and would not do anything.

14. Having calculated your sample, you write it to the file with `AudioFileWrite-Bytes()`. This call takes five parameters: the `AudioFileID` to write to, a caching flag, the offset in the audio data that you're writing to, the number of bytes you're writing, and a pointer to the bytes to be written. You get to use this function because you have constant bit rate data; in more general cases, such as when writing compressed formats, you must use the more complex `AudioFileWritePackets()`.

15. Increment `sampleCount` so that you're writing your new data further and further into the file.

16. Finally, call `AudioFileClose()` to finish and close the file.

Build and run this program with Xcode 4. To find the file that was written, open the Organizer, go to the Projects tab, select the `CAToneFileGenerator` project, and click the round arrow next to the Derived Data path. This opens a Finder window with the project metadata and products, in which you'll find the path `Build/Products/Debug`. Inside this folder, you should see the CAToneFileGenerator executable and a sound file with a name representing the frequency you set as an argument to the executable, as in `880.000-square.aif`. You can play it with QuickTime Player, with iTunes, or even in the Finder by selecting it and pressing the spacebar—but before you do, turn the volume down! Square waves are pretty hard on the ear.

That brings up an important point. The frequency with which waves repeat is what you perceive as pitch: how "high" or "low" a sound is. But that's not the whole story. The shape of the waves gives the sound its character, its *timbre*.

Let's consider three kinds of basic waveforms that you can easily create programmatically:

- *Square waves,* as you've seen, just alternate between two values.

- *Sawtooth waves* have a linear increase from a minimum value to a maximum over the length of the wave, and then reset to the minimum for the next wave.

- *Sine waves* are curves that conform to the properties of trigonometric functions. They sound somewhat more natural because the sine function can represent simple harmonic motion, which resembles natural phenomena such as instrument strings vibrating.

Figure 2.4 shows these three wave types.

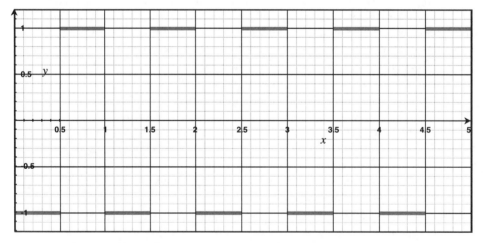

Figure 2.4(a)   Square, sawtooth, and sine waves
as mathematical functions

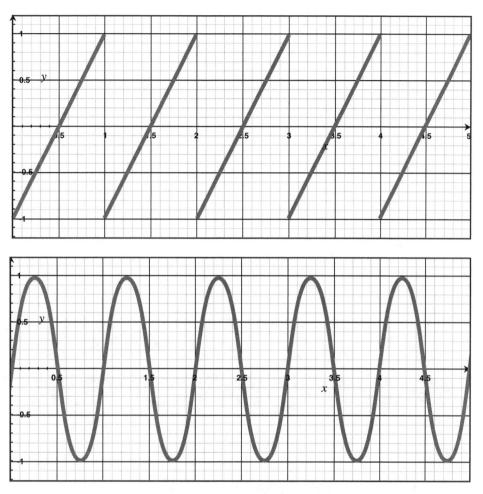

Figure 2.4(b, c) Square, sawtooth, and sine waves
as mathematical functions

Changing the program to generate these different wave types is a simple matter. Let's start with the sawtooth wave. First, change the #define for the filename format so you can distinguish among the various files:

```
#define FILENAME_FORMAT @"%0.3f-saw.aif"
```

Then rewrite the for loop as follows:

```
    for (int i=0; i<wavelengthInSamples; i++) {
        // saw wave
        SInt16 sample = CFSwapInt16HostToBig (((i / wavelengthInSamples) *
SHRT_MAX *2) -
                                 SHRT_MAX);
```

```
audioErr = AudioFileWriteBytes(audioFile,
                               false,
                               sampleCount*2,
                               &bytesToWrite,
                               &sample);
assert (audioErr == noErr);
sampleCount++;
}
```

The only difference is the calculation of the sample. This function divides i, the loop counter, by the length of the wave and then uses some scaling so that the values increase evenly from SHRT_MIN to SHRT_MAX.

After you build and run this version, you can compare the sound of square waves versus sawtooth waves. You can hear that they're both the same pitch, but the sound is slightly different.

If you have an audio editor that zooms down to the raw sample level, you can use it to inspect these files, too. Figure 2.5 shows Felt Tip Software's Sound Studio 3 application editing 880.000-saw.aif, an 880 Hz sawtooth wave generated by your program.

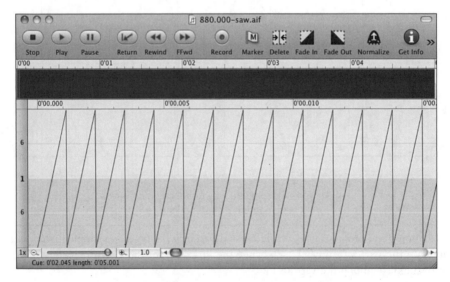

Figure 2.5   Inspecting a sawtooth wave file created
by the CAToneFileGenerator example

Let's tweak the code once more, this time to create a sine wave. This is the classic reference signal; in television, the "bars and tone" used to calibrate equipment uses a

1,000 Hz tone that engineers can validate against an oscilloscope. First, change the file-name format so you can keep track of your output files.

```
#define FILENAME_FORMAT @"%0.3f-sine.aif"
```

Then rewrite the `for` loop. You can even reuse the sawtooth wave's `for` loop and just change the line that calculates the sample:

```
SInt16 sample = CFSwapInt16HostToBig ((SInt16) SHRT_MAX *
                          sin (2 * M_PI *
                          (i / wavelengthInSamples)));
```

Yeah, welcome back to high school trigonometry. This converts the phase (i / `wavelengthInSamples`) to radians for the sine function (by multiplying it by 2π), multiplying the result by `SHRT_MAX` (because the sine function returns values between −1.0 and 1.0), and casts the whole thing to a 16-bit value that you can then endian-swap and write to the file.

> **Note**
>
> If you declared your `AudioStreamBasicDescription` as using floating-point samples, you wouldn't have to scale up like this. However, the iOS 4 version of Core Audio can only do integer samples in PCM, not floating point, and we wanted to keep the code portable to both platforms.

Try this—you'll hear that it's a much more pleasant tone than either the square or sawtooth wave, even though you'll also be able to clearly hear that, for a given frequency, they're all playing the same pitch.

You might also try to set the frequency increasingly higher and see if you can identify when you get to a point that you can't hear the tone anymore. You should be able to hear tones around 10,000 Hz easily enough, but you probably won't be able to hear those at 20,000 Hz or higher. In fact, your ability to hear high frequencies deteriorates with age, so if you can hear 15,000 Hz now, you might not be able to in ten years.

Consider one final point on this example. What happens when the frequency is 22,050 Hz? That's exactly half of the sample rate. In any of the versions of the example, the value of `wavelengthInSamples` will be 2. That means there are just two samples to represent the wave; for the square wave, you get one sample of `SHRT_MIN` and one of `SHRT_MAX`. But at least there's a pattern, something that repeats. At higher frequencies, you have less than two samples per wave—and, therefore, no repeating pattern. This is another way you can think about Nyquist and its seemingly arbitrary concept of sampling at double the highest frequency you want to reproduce.

Buffers

You might have noticed that writing all the samples to your file took a few seconds. A 5-second run time for generating 5 seconds of audio is not very performant!

Reading or writing one sample at a time is highly inefficient. If you think back to the `AudioFileWriteBytes`, you might remember that the last two parameters were the number of bytes to write to the file and a pointer to the sample. Instead of writing one sample at a time to the file, racking up the overhead of a function call more than 200,000 times for this simple example, you could have created a memory buffer to hold a bunch of samples and then written those samples en masse to the file.

This isn't just a problem with writing files. It's also a problem when you generate sound at runtime. In a nutshell, the different parts of the computer don't operate at the same speed. The time it takes for the audio hardware to produce or consume a packet of audio data is much less than the time it takes to move the packets in and out of memory. This slowdown is called the von Neumann bottleneck.

When the audio hardware runs out of things to do, it makes terrible noises and ruins the magic. To prevent this from happening, you can use buffers to shuttle audio packets back and forth. A lot of big buffers means that any hiccups in the slow parts of the computer can be fixed before the fast parts of the computer notice: By the time one buffer of audio data has been exhausted, another has (hopefully) arrived.

Aside from further increasing the complexity of the subject, buffering has the unpleasant side effect of making it harder to get the hardware's attention when you actually want it. Think of it as data-level bureaucracy—some of it's necessary, but too much of it makes everything take too long.

The technical term is *latency,* the delay between initiating an action and seeing the result of that action. For example, the hardware latency of the iPhone and iPod Touch is about 15 to 30 milliseconds, depending on model. When you push a buffer of samples out from your code to one of the audio engines mentioned in the previous chapter, a few milliseconds elapse before the first sample of that sound starts coming out of the speaker or headphones.

Buffers and latency are a delicate balancing act: Big buffers makes for higher latency, but if you push your luck in search of lower latency, you risk exhausting your buffers and hearing silence (dropouts) or noise.

Audio Formats

In the example, you used an `AudioStreamBasicDescription` to describe the format of the audio stream your code generated: 16-bit integer samples, one channel, sample rate of 44,100, and so on. But this isn't the whole story. You then put that audio into an AIFF file. And as you might know from managing your own iTunes collection, many different file formats exist: AIFF, WAV, MP3, M4A, and so on.

> **Note**
>
> Describing audio and storing audio data to the file system are entirely different problems. Data formats solve the first problem; file formats solve the latter.

Think of an audio file as a container that holds audio data. Some file formats are customized for specific data formats, such as MP3; an .mp3 file can't contain PCM or Windows Media data—only MP3 data. As noted, AIFF files handle PCM audio data, but only if it's big-endian. Conversely, PCM in WAV files has to be little-endian. Other file formats are more agnostic and deal with several data formats. For example, the MP4 file format can contain data in a number of data formats, including AAC, PCM, and AC3.

The most content-agnostic file format Core Audio supports is its own Core Audio Format, abbreviated as CAF and indicated by the file extension .caf. A CAF file contains *any* audio format supported by Core Audio: MP3, AAC, Apple Lossless, you name it. This makes CAF an excellent choice as a container format for audio that is internal to your application, such as background music or sound effects.

CAF also employs a number of tricks to improve performance. For example, consider MP3 audio: Because it has a variable bit rate, jumping ahead to any point in an .mp3 file requires decompressing all the data from the current playback position until it reaches the time you want to jump to. You have no other way to know what part of the file represents the target time. This requires significant I/O and CPU costs and often takes a noticeable amount of time to execute. CAF sets up internal lookup tables that map times to samples, so it can make the jump almost immediately.

> **Note**
>
> The internal structure of the various container formats is beyond the scope of this book. Formats are frequently proprietary and wildly variable. Core Audio handles this implementation detail by completely abstracting them away.
>
> In the example, you could replace the file format constant `kAudioFileAIFFType` with `kAudioFileM4AType` or `kAudioFileCAFType`, change the filename to use a suitable extension, and not have to change anything else in your code. Core Audio would take responsibility for figuring out how to put your PCM data into the specified format, as long as the audio format and file format are compatible.

Summary

You've come a long way in this chapter! You started in the real world, talking about how natural sources generate sound, how sound moves through the air as waves of pressure, and how your ears pick up that sound. Then you saw how to model this in a digital representation with numeric representations of sound waves, which are more amenable to being processed by computers, stored on digital media, and sent across networks. To concretize these concepts, you wrote your own sound waves, sample by sample, to files on the hard drive, again using Core Audio's Audio File Services. You briefly considered the difference between audio stream formats and audio file formats. Finally, you saw how Core Audio abstracts away the differences in the various file formats, meaning that you read and write `.aif`, `.caf`, and `.m4a` files more or less the same way.

With this grounding in the concepts of digital audio, it's time to really take on Core Audio—how it represents and processes audio.

3

Audio Processing with Core Audio

The last chapter introduced some essential concepts of digital audio. So how does Core Audio handle them? Chapter 1, "Overview of Core Audio," gave you an overview of the major areas of interest in Core Audio. This chapter digs down to a more detailed level to see how Core Audio models and processes digital audio data.

We'll start with the issue of representing sample data and formats in Core Audio's various data structures, and then turn our attention to the APIs that can do interesting stuff with those structures.

Audio Data Formats

Core Audio views audio data as streams of packets. The contents of a stream's packets are described by its `AudioStreamBasicDescription`, which we introduced briefly in the last chapter. The ASBD is critically important to just about any Core Audio program, so let's take a deeper look at it.

As shown in Listing 3.1, this C structure contains metadata describing the packet's data layout: the sample rate, the number of bits in a channel, the number of channels in a frame, and so on. It doesn't contain the data; it simply describes the data.

Listing 3.1   **The AudioStreamBasicDescription Structure**

```
struct AudioStreamBasicDescription {
    Float64 mSampleRate;
    UInt32  mFormatID;
    UInt32  mFormatFlags;
    UInt32  mBytesPerPacket;
    UInt32  mFramesPerPacket;
    UInt32  mBytesPerFrame;
    UInt32  mChannelsPerFrame;
```

Listing 3.1   **Continued**

```
    UInt32  mBitsPerChannel;
    UInt32  mReserved;
};

typedef struct AudioStreamBasicDescription  AudioStreamBasicDescription;
```

> **Note**
>
> Moving audio data is called streaming, so a bunch of audio data in memory is called an audio stream. Don't confuse this with streaming audio over a network, which is a different use of the same metaphor.

The important point about a stream's ABSD is that its meaning is an implementation detail of its format: You don't want to compare the mFramesPerPacket value of an ASBD representing AAC data against an ASBD for MP3 because the packets of those formats are totally different.

When you're reading data from some source, such as a file or a network stream, various parts of Core Audio populate the ASBD's values. For example, Audio File Services fills in the ABSD for audio loaded from disk. In some cases, Core Audio even fills in values when you're writing data: When you want to write compressed data, you often don't know or can't know the value of some of the fields, so you set them to 0 and let Core Audio figure it out.

The names of the ASBD's struct members begin with m. Want to know the sample rate? Check mSampleRate. Let's look at the members one by one:

- mSampleRate is defined to be the number of samples per channel per second of uncompressed data. This makes it equal to the number of frames per second, which means you can multiply it by mFramesPerPacket to determine packet length in seconds.

- mFormatID is a four-character code that serves as the name of the format. Without naming a format, the struct is meaningless, so this value must be defined. The default types Core Audio supports are defined in CoreAudioTypes.h. There you'll see the four character codes for the default formats and constants you can use in your code. For example, the kAudioFormatLinearPCM format constant used in the last chapter is the four-character code lpcm.

- mFormatFlags is the format's subtype, or preference panel. This field is a UInt32 bit field in which you set or check various 1-bit flags. Setting flags answers questions left open by formats that support noninterleaved data, multiple sample types, or variable data structures. Unfortunately, the only way to know how to interpret this value is to look up the documentation—search for "AudioStreamBasic-Description Flags" to find the defined flags. Formats that do not have flags can set this value to 0.

- `mBytesPerPacket` answers the first of several questions about the structure of this format's data: How much data are we talking about? Variable bit rate formats, by definition, cannot answer this question. These formats set this value to 0 and use an `AudioStreamPacketDescription`, described later.

- `mFramesPerPacket` subdivides the raw bytes of the packet into some number of frames. This is an issue only for compressed formats; uncompressed formats always set this to 1. Core Audio can also support formats with a variable frame rate. These formats set this value to 0 and use `AudioStreamPacketDescriptions`, described later.

- `mBytesPerFrame` establishes the size of a single frame—that is, the total number of digits used to represent each moment in time. When a frame does not contain a sample per channel, as with compression, this value is set to 0.

- `mChannelsPerFrame` subdivides the frame into channels, regardless of compression. This value cannot be 0 because an audio stream with no channels is, by definition, empty.

- `mBitsPerChannel` is the sample's bit depth. As with bytes per frame, it represents the actual structure of the data. Compressed formats whose frames do not contain a sample per channel set this value to 0.

- The `mReserved` member is for data alignment purposes, padding the structure to an even multiple of 8. It must always be 0.

For compressed data, whose packet structure cannot be adequately derived from its measurements, each packet must be accompanied by another structure, `AudioStream-PacketDescription` (see Listing 3.2). Unlike `AudioStreamBasicDescription`, which describes every packet, `AudioStreamPacketDescription` describes an individual packet. Thus, when you get a buffer of compressed audio data, you work with an array of `AudioStreamPacketDescriptions`, each describing one packet in the buffer.

Listing 3.2   **The AudioStreamPacketDescription Structure**

```
struct  AudioStreamPacketDescription {
        SInt64  mStartOffset;
        UInt32  mVariableFramesInPacket;
        UInt32  mDataByteSize;
    };
typedef struct AudioStreamPacketDescription AudioStreamPacketDescription;
```

- `mStartOffset` represents the packet's location, relative to other packets in the buffer, in bytes. This is important because packets of different sizes cannot use an implied *x*-axis value as in a linear PCM format. (In layman's terms, you can't find a sample by doing Offset = Time × Sample rate × Frame size + Channel number.)

- `mVariableFramesInPacket` represents the number of frames in the packet, but only if the packets use a variable frame rate. If the `AudioStreamBasicDescription` has a value for `mFramesPerPacket`, `mVariableFramesInPacket` should be 0, and vice versa.
- `mDataByteSize` contains the packet's actual size, in bytes.

With these two structures, you're largely ready to handle just about any audio format thrown at you. For any data specific to a format that is not handled by the stream's `AudioStreamBasicDescription` or an individual packet's `AudioStreamPacket-Description`, several of the Core Audio helper APIs—notably, Audio File Services, Audio File Stream Services, Audio Conversion Services, and Audio Queue Services—support the idea of a *magic cookie*. The cookie (unrelated to the browser terminology of the same name) is an opaque block of data whose contents are specific to the format being encoded or decoded. In practice, this means that when you open a file or network stream of compressed data, you check for a magic cookie property. If present, you read it in as a block of untyped data and pass it along to Core Audio without worrying about what might be inside it.

Example: Figuring Out Formats

As you've seen, the way Core Audio represents audio data isn't as simple as saying "an MP3" or "an Audible book." There's a big difference between a file format and the audio data inside that file, or between the data that describes that audio data, which could involve three separate descriptors: the `AudioStreamBasicDescription` needed for all audio streams, the magic cookie of certain compressed formats, and the `AudioStreamPacketDescription` needed for every packet of compressed format.

A lot of what we've said about the various formats might seem arbitrary, so you can use code to tell you what can and can't go into a given file. Audio File Services provides an interesting function called `AudioFileGetGlobalInfo` that gives information not about an individual file, but about Core Audio's handling of audio files in general. Look up this function in the documentation and follow the link to "Audio File Global Info Properties"; you'll see a number of interesting-looking properties to inspect. In this example, you use a property called `kAudioFileGlobalInfo_AvailableStream-DescriptionsForFormat` to get Core Audio to spill the beans about what can and can't go into your audio files.

Specifically, here's what the documentation for `kAudioFileGlobalInfo_AvailableStreamDescriptionsForFormat` promises to give you:

An array of audio stream basic description structures, which contain all the formats for a particular file type and format ID.

The audio stream basic description structures have the following fields filled in: `mFormatID`, `mFormatFlags`, and `mBitsPerChannel` for writing new files. When accessing this property, provide a pointer, in the `inSpecifier` parameter, to an audio file type and format ID structure.

So this property tells you how to set up an ASBD for writing to a file, for any supported audio format and file type. That sounds useful—you can try it out next.

Create another Xcode command-line tool project, called `CAStreamFormatTester`. As always, you need to add `#import <AudioToolbox/AudioToolbox.h>` in the .m file and add the `AudioToolbox.framework` to the project.

As before, you can write this example just by editing the default `main()` function and removing the "Hello, World!" log statement. Listing 3.3 shows the example code.

Listing 3.3   Inspecting Core Audio's File Format Support

```
int main (int argc, const char * argv[]) {
        NSAutoreleasePool * pool = [[NSAutoreleasePool alloc] init];

    AudioFileTypeAndFormatID fileTypeAndFormat;                    // 1
    fileTypeAndFormat.mFileType = kAudioFileAIFFType;
    fileTypeAndFormat.mFormatID = kAudioFormatLinearPCM;

    OSStatus audioErr = noErr;                                     // 2
    UInt32 infoSize = 0;

    audioErr = AudioFileGetGlobalInfoSize                          // 3
        (kAudioFileGlobalInfo_AvailableStreamDescriptionsForFormat,
         sizeof (fileTypeAndFormat),
         &fileTypeAndFormat,
         &infoSize);
    assert (audioErr == noErr);

    AudioStreamBasicDescription *asbds = malloc (infoSize);        // 4
    audioErr = AudioFileGetGlobalInfo                              // 5
        (kAudioFileGlobalInfo_AvailableStreamDescriptionsForFormat,
         sizeof (fileTypeAndFormat),
         &fileTypeAndFormat,
         &infoSize,
         asbds);
    assert (audioErr == noErr);

    int asbdCount = infoSize / sizeof (AudioStreamBasicDescription);
                                                                  // 6
    for (int i=0; i<asbdCount; i++) {
        UInt32 format4cc = CFSwapInt32HostToBig(asbds[i].mFormatID);
                                                                  // 7
        NSLog (@"%d: mFormatId: %4.4s, mFormatFlags: %d, mBitsPerChannel: %d"
            i,                                                    // 8
            (char*)&format4cc,
            asbds[i].mFormatFlags,
            asbds[i].mBitsPerChannel);
    }
```

Listing 3.3   **Continued**

```
free (asbds);                                          // 9

[pool drain];
return 0;
}
```

Look over the commented callouts to better understand this example:

1. To use the property called kAudioFileGlobalInfo_AvailableStream-
   DescriptionsForFormat, you have to pass Core Audio a structure called
   AudioFileTypeAndFormatID (getting this property seems to be the only use for
   the struct). This structure has two members, a file type and a data format, both of
   which you can set with Core Audio constants found in the documentation or the
   AudioFile.h and AudioFormat.h headers. For starters, let's use an AIFF file with
   PCM, as you created in the previous chapter.

2. As before, you prepare an OSStatus to receive result codes from your Core Audio
   calls. You also prepare a UInt32 to hold the size of the info you're interested in,
   which you have to negotiate before actually retrieving the info.

3. Just as when you retrieved an audio file's property in Listing 1.1, getting a global
   info property requires you to query in advance for the size of the property and to
   store the size in a pointer to a UInt32. The global info calls take a specifier, which
   acts like an argument to the property call and depends on the property you're asking for (the docs for the properties describe what kind of specifier, if any, they
   expect). In the case of kAudioFileGlobalInfo_AvailableStream-
   DescriptionsForFormat, you provide the AudioFileTypeAndFormatID.

4. The AudioFileGetGlobalInfoSize calls tells you how much data you'll receive
   when you actually get the global property, so you need to malloc some memory
   to hold the property.

5. With everything set up, you call AudioFileGetGlobalInfo to get the
   kAudioFileGlobalInfo_AvailableStreamDescriptionsForFormat, passing
   in the AudioFileTypeAndFormatID and the size of the buffer you've set up,
   along with a pointer to the buffer itself.

6. The docs tell you that the property call provides an array of AudioStream-
   BasicDescriptions, so you can figure out the length of the array by dividing
   the data size by the size of an ASBD. That enables you to set up a for loop to
   investigate the ASBDs.

7. The docs stated that the three ASBD fields that get filled in are mFormatID,
   mFormatFlags, and mBitsPerChannel. It's handy to log the format ID, but to
   make it legible, you have to convert it out of the four-character code numeric format and into a readable four-character string. You do this with an endian swap

because the UInt32 representation will reorder the bits from their original pseudo-string representation.

8. To pretty print the mFormatId's endian-swapped representation, you can use the format string %4.4s to force NSLog (or printf) to treat the pointer as an array of 8-bit characters that is exactly four characters long. The mFormatFlags and mBitsPerChannel members are a bit field and numeric value, so just print them as ints for now.

9. Because you malloc()'d memory to hold the ASBD array, you need to be sure to free() it when you're done with it so you don't leak.

So what's the result of this? Bring up the console pane (Shift-⌘-C) and run the program. You should see the following results:

```
0: mFormatId: lpcm, mFormatFlags: 14, mBitsPerChannel: 8
1: mFormatId: lpcm, mFormatFlags: 14, mBitsPerChannel: 16
2: mFormatId: lpcm, mFormatFlags: 14, mBitsPerChannel: 24
3: mFormatId: lpcm, mFormatFlags: 14, mBitsPerChannel: 32
```

This tells you that AIFFs can handle only a small amount of variety in PCM formats, differing only in bit depth. The mFormatFlags are the same for every ASBD in the array. But what do they mean? The flags are a bit field, so with a value of 14, you know that the bits for 0x2, 0x4, and 0x8 are enabled (because 0x2 + 0x4 + 0x8 = 0xE, which is 14 in decimal). At this point, you need to consult the documentation for the AudioStreamBasicDescription flags or the CoreAudioTypes.h header file to figure out what those bit flags represent. Because the bits 0x2, 0x4, and 0x8 are set, this PCM format is equivalent to kAudioFormatFlagIsBigEndian | kAudioFormatFlagIsSignedInteger | kAudioFormatFlagIsPacked.

This confirms what we said in the last chapter about the AIFF format being limited to accepting only big-endian PCM. Let's test that hypothesis. Make the following change to callout 1 in Listing 3.3:

```
fileTypeAndFormat.mFileType = kAudioFileWAVEType;
```

This time, you get much different results:

```
0: mFormatId: lpcm, mFormatFlags: 8, mBitsPerChannel: 8
1: mFormatId: lpcm, mFormatFlags: 12, mBitsPerChannel: 16
2: mFormatId: lpcm, mFormatFlags: 12, mBitsPerChannel: 24
3: mFormatId: lpcm, mFormatFlags: 12, mBitsPerChannel: 32
4: mFormatId: lpcm, mFormatFlags: 9, mBitsPerChannel: 32
5: mFormatId: lpcm, mFormatFlags: 9, mBitsPerChannel: 64
```

This shows that WAV files take a different style of PCM. The 0x2 bit of mFormatFlags is never set, which means that kAudioFormatFlagIsBigEndian is always false; that, in turn, means that WAV files always use little-endian PCM. Also, the last two results set the 0x1 bit, `kAudioFormatFlagIsFloat`, meaning that the format is not limited to just integer samples.

The last chapter also mentioned that the Core Audio Format, CAF, is pretty much content agnostic, so it's instructive to see what happens when you query about putting PCM data into that file format. Change the file type:

```
fileTypeAndFormat.mFileType = kAudioFileCAFType;
```

Then build and run again. This time, you get 11 file-and-data-format combinations:

```
0: mFormatId: lpcm, mFormatFlags: 14, mBitsPerChannel: 8
1: mFormatId: lpcm, mFormatFlags: 14, mBitsPerChannel: 16
2: mFormatId: lpcm, mFormatFlags: 14, mBitsPerChannel: 24
3: mFormatId: lpcm, mFormatFlags: 14, mBitsPerChannel: 32
4: mFormatId: lpcm, mFormatFlags: 11, mBitsPerChannel: 32
5: mFormatId: lpcm, mFormatFlags: 11, mBitsPerChannel: 64
6: mFormatId: lpcm, mFormatFlags: 12, mBitsPerChannel: 16
7: mFormatId: lpcm, mFormatFlags: 12, mBitsPerChannel: 24
8: mFormatId: lpcm, mFormatFlags: 12, mBitsPerChannel: 32
9: mFormatId: lpcm, mFormatFlags: 9, mBitsPerChannel: 32
10: mFormatId: lpcm, mFormatFlags: 9, mBitsPerChannel: 64
```

This shows CAF taking a variety of formats, using both integer and floating-point samples (signaled by bit 0x1 being set) and signed and unsigned integers. It supports all but one of the formats provided by AIFF and WAV.

But enough about PCM—what about compressed audio? Leave the file format as CAF, but change the `mFormatID` to one of the other values listed in "Audio Data Format Identifiers" (in the Core Audio Data Types Reference). For example, we all love our iTunes, so let's look at the AAC format used on the iTunes Store:

```
fileTypeAndFormat.mFormatID = kAudioFormatMPEG4AAC;
```

Build and run this, and you get a single result:

```
0: mFormatId: aac , mFormatFlags: 0, mBitsPerChannel: 0
```

This doesn't tell you a lot, but at least you know that AAC is a valid payload for a CAF file. Don't freak out about the 0 bits per channel. This doesn't mean there's no data; it means that the format uses a variable bit rate, so you shouldn't try to set the bits per channel value.

AAC can be carried in a few different formats. You're probably used to seeing it in .m4a files, which is represented by the file format constant `kAudioFileM4AType`. On the other hand, AAC isn't a valid payload for an .mp3 file, which can carry only MP3 data (technically, MPEG-1 and MPEG-2 Layer 3, hence the name). So let's try one last `AudioFileTypeAndFormatID` pairing:

```
fileTypeAndFormat.mFileType = kAudioFileMP3Type;
fileTypeAndFormat.mFormatID = kAudioFormatMPEG4AAC;
```

When you run this, the program dies on the first `assert()`, right after the call to `AudioFileGetGlobalInfoSize()`. Set a breakpoint right before that, and you'll see that the `OSStatus audioErr` has been set to `1718449215`, as in Figure 3.1.

```
14      audioErr = AudioFileGetGlobalInfoSize
15          (kAudioFileGlobalInfo_AvailableStreamDescriptionsForFormat,
16          sizeof (fileTypeAndFormat),
17          &fileTypeAndFormat,
18          &infoSize);
        assert (audioErr == noErr);
20               OSStatus      audioErr      1718449215   [] 0
21      AudioStreamBasicDescription *asbds = malloc (infoSize);
```

Figure 3.1   fmt? status returned from `AudioFileGetGlobalInfoSize`

What the heck is that? It's another four-character code. Add the following before the `assert()` to tease it out:

```
if (audioErr != noErr) {
    UInt32 err4cc = CFSwapInt32HostToBig(audioErr);
    NSLog (@"audioErr = %4.4s",  (char*)&err4cc);
}
```

Run it again, and you'll find that the error is the four-character code, `fmt?`. This is defined in `AudioFile.h` as the value of `kAudioFileUnsupportedDataFormatError`. Of course, this is exactly what you should have expected: You can't put AAC data in an MP3 file; if you try to do so, Core Audio returns an error.

If you like, take a few minutes to try different pairings of file type and data formats, using constants from both "Built-In Audio File Types" from the Audio File Services Reference and "Audio Data Format Identifiers" in the Core Audio Data Types Reference (both are accessible from Xcode's documentation viewer). You'll find that arbitrary pairings generally don't work, that some file formats take only a single audio data format, and that CAF will let you get away with just about anything.

Hopefully, you'll come away from this example with an understanding of just how different file formats and data formats are, and how Core Audio works with both. This example didn't make use of `AudioStreamPacketDescriptions` or magic cookies; you'll see both of those in the next chapter.

Canonical Formats

With support for so many formats, what's the best? That's a silly question: So many formats exist because each is designed for different uses. Among the compressed formats, AAC is great for audio fidelity (particularly for music) at high compression rates, but for maximum fidelity, you can use Apple Lossless, which reproduces its source audio per-fectly. On the other end of the bandwidth scale, the iLBC (Internet Low-Bandwidth Codec) is optimized for speech over potentially unreliable Internet connections, making it well suited for VoIP or in-game chat purposes. And none of these is appropriate for editing, where you're better served by the low CPU overhead and losslessness of PCM, provided you have enough RAM and disk space.

That said, every platform has a number format it's most efficient at using for a given task. In Core Audio, we call this format *canonical,* in that it forms the baseline from which all other audio formats deviate. Any value not explicitly set by the `AudioStreamBasicDescription` defaults to the value of the canonical format.

In Core Audio's engines, all audio format conversions are one-way, in that they all convert data to (or from) the canonical format. Converting between two other formats requires converting from the input format into the canonical format and then converting from the canonical format into the output format.

Each platform actually has two canonical formats, the `AudioSampleType`, which is used for I/O situations, and the `AudioUnitSampleType`, introduced in Snow Leopard and iOS, which is used in audio units and for digital signal processing.

On Mac OS X, the `AudioSampleType` is a 32-bit float. The `AudioUnitSampleType` is also a 32-bit float, but the channels must be noninterleaved. You can find the `mFormatFlags` definitions in the `CoreAudioTypes.h` header file in the `CoreAudio.framework`:

```
kAudioFormatFlagsCanonical           = kAudioFormatFlagIsFloat |
        kAudioFormatFlagsNativeEndian | kAudioFormatFlagIsPacked,

kAudioFormatFlagsAudioUnitCanonical = kAudioFormatFlagIsFloat |
        kAudioFormatFlagsNativeEndian | kAudioFormatFlagIsPacked |
        kAudioFormatFlagIsNonInterleaved,
```

On iOS, the `AudioSampleType` is 16-bit integer. The `AudioUnitSampleType` is an 8.24-bit fixed-point number, with 8 bits to the left of the radix point[1] and 24 bits to the right. Here's what that looks like in the `CoreAudioTypes.h` file in the iPhone SDK frameworks:

```
kAudioFormatFlagsCanonical           = kAudioFormatFlagIsSignedInteger |
        kAudioFormatFlagsNativeEndian | kAudioFormatFlagIsPacked,

kAudioFormatFlagsAudioUnitCanonical = kAudioFormatFlagIsSignedInteger |
        kAudioFormatFlagsNativeEndian | kAudioFormatFlagIsPacked |
        kAudioFormatFlagIsNonInterleaved | (kAudioUnitSampleFractionBits <<
        kLinearPCMFormatFlagsSampleFractionShift),
```

---

[1] The term *decimal point* applies only in base 10. The generic term is *radix point*.

Core Audio uses audio converters to convert data between formats and codecs to translate data in various compression schemes. Simpler frameworks, such as Audio Queue Services, use these tools behind the scenes to convert whatever data a file contains into a canonical format. When you're supplying samples directly to the audio engines (Audio Units and OpenAL) directly, it's advantageous to use the canonical formats, if you can; you'll save yourself some data conversions and, therefore, have more CPU cycles to use elsewhere.

Processing Audio with Audio Units

This entire chapter has considered Core Audio's concepts of how audio data is represented. Now it turns to the idea of how that data is processed.

As discussed in Chapter 1, "Overview of Core Audio," Core Audio does most of its work at the Audio Units level; the Audio Queue and OpenAL engines are implemented atop audio units.

Each audio unit processes a buffer of samples in some specific way: One captures audio from a mic, the next one downstream performs an effect on those samples, and maybe the next one mixes it with another source. This arrangement is analogous to the patch architecture common in the sound industry. Audio units are connected by audio streams the way audio equipment is patched together with cables.

Just as professional audio equipment has jacks that you plug cables into, audio units have elements, which may have *input scope* or *output scope* to indicate that they either accept or produce data, respectively. To connect two units, you set a property connecting an input element of one unit to the output unit of another.

Mac OS X provides several types of audio units, which can be connected into a workflow called an *audio processing graph*. As packets of audio data are streamed through the graph, each audio unit does its work, in order. You're most likely to encounter these types of units:

- **Effect units.** Perform *digital signal processing*—that is, they change the audio data in some way. They are analogous to hardware effects boxes and outboard signal processors.

- **Instrument units.** Generate audio data representing musical notes, typically from MIDI input, which can itself come from a musical instrument or a software synthesizer.

- **Generator units.** Also generate audio data, but not from a MIDI source. Some units simply generate a signal programmatically, whereas others load data from a network stream or audio file.

- **I/O units.** Provide interfaces to input or output hardware, such as a microphone or a speaker. These are typically implemented on the *Hardware Abstraction Layer* (HAL), the "demilitarized zone" between Core Audio and I/O Kit and the drivers.

- **Converter units.** Reformat audio data back and forth between the canonical for-mats and other formats. These can also merge and split streams, and alter timing and pitch.
- **Mixer units.** Combine audio tracks. There are also splitter units that provide mul-tiple outputs from a single input.
- **Panner units.** Use stereo mixing to create panning effects.
- **Offline effect units.** Perform operations on audio data that cannot be done in real time.

Because it runs on mobile devices with less capable CPUs and embodies an acute awareness of power management, iOS provides only a subset of these units. In fact, iOS 4 doesn't include any instrument, generator, or panner units.

To understand how units and their connections work, consider a hypothetical applica-tion that captures from an input device, such as a microphone, and mixes that audio with some other source, such as playback from a file. For example, this could be a karaoke application that lets the user sing along with favorite songs.

This arrangement consists of four units, as illustrated in Figure 3.2. You start with a generator unit to play audio from a file or the network, along with an I/O unit to get audio from the input hardware. You make connections from the output scope elements of these units to the input scope elements of a mixer unit. Then you connect the output scope element of the mixer unit to the input scope element of an I/O unit to get the mixed audio out to the hardware, such as speakers or headphones. In reality, the process is more involved, as you'll see in Chapters 7, "Audio Units: Generators, Effects, and Rendering," and 8, "Audio Units: Input and Mixing," but that's the basic flow.

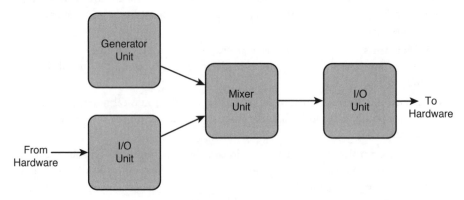

Figure 3.2   Audio unit graph to mix captured and generated sound

On Mac OS X, you can write your own audio units and deploy them in your appli-cation. You can also provide GUIs to adjust the settings of your custom units and make them available to other applications. This isn't possible on iOS, where applications are "sandboxed" and you can't provide functionality for other apps to call into. Chapter 7 talks more about audio units.

The Pull Model

But if you have a bunch of units, how do they work together? Do you just create a bunch of units and push data into them? In Core Audio's pull architecture, it works the opposite way.

With a pull architecture, the framework tells the programmer, "Don't call us—we'll call you." If you have a chain of audio units, the last one (which is probably the I/O unit that will send audio to the speakers or headphones) pulls from the units connected to its input elements, saying, in effect, "Give me something to play." These units call the units upstream from them, and so on. You can get into this arrangement either by writing your own units or by having a unit call into your code with a callback when it needs data.

Callbacks are sometimes called *procs* within Core Audio. In the Audio File Services API, a callback that receives data is a *read proc*, and a callback that produces data is called a *write proc*. Other parts of Core Audio use different terminology: For example, when an audio unit calls into your code for a buffer of samples, it's called a *render callback*. They're different terms but the same idea. Although they're conceptually easy, implementing callbacks can be tricky. You'll create your first callback in the next chapter, in which you create an Audio Queue that calls you back when it has capture data for you to process. Interestingly, callbacks often follow Core Audio's property-oriented design pattern: Instead of calling a "set audio unit callback" function to set up a callback, you set a callback property on the audio unit.

Core Audio's extensive use of callbacks can be convenient. For example, many APIs enable you to register functions as property listeners. When the property changes, the watched API calls the registered function. On the iPhone, for example, a property represents the path that the audio follows to the current output device: the speakers, headphones, or telephone earpiece. If the user pulls out the headphones, this path property changes and the application gets a callback, which gives the code an opportunity to take action, such as pausing playback or recording.

Summary

This chapter built on the theoretical foundation of Chapter 2, "The Story of Sound," to help you understand how the ideas of digital audio are represented in Core Audio's essential data types. Of all the possible digital audio formats you might encounter, you can represent them with `AudioStreamBasicDescriptions`, `AudioStreamPacketDescriptions`, and magic cookies that tell Core Audio how to make sense of each buffer of audio data. You also got a sense of just how far Core Audio's built-in format support goes by using the Audio File Services to inspect the supported audio file types and tell you what kind of data you could put into them. Finally, you looked at the processing side by learning about audio units and their connections and delving into how Core Audio pulls audio through the units.

With this material and Chapter 1's discussion of the common idioms of Core Audio programming—properties, four-character codes, and so on—you're now ready to dig into the specifics of the APIs that Core Audio provides. For many people, the most natural use of an audio framework is to play audio from and record audio to flat files. You already used the Audio File Services for the examples in the first three chapters; in the next chapter, you'll combine it with Audio Queue Services to play and record audio.

II

Basic Audio

4

Recording

The first three chapters explored the nature of digital audio and how it is represented by Core Audio. The next step is processing—actually doing something with the audio. In the next two chapters, we'll start moving samples through Core Audio's recording and playback engines.

To do this, you'll use Audio Queue Services, the highest-level playback and recording API in Core Audio. By the end of the chapter, you may think we're nuts to call a C-based, callback-driven API "high level," but audio queues provide some conveniences that the lower-level APIs don't:

- Unlike with OpenAL and Audio Units, you can use encoded formats such as AAC and MP3 with audio queues.
- By default, Audio Queues call you back on their own thread, which isolates you from some timing challenges with Audio Units.

In this chapter, you'll use Audio Queue Services to record audio from your computer's default input device. (You'll move on to playback in the next chapter.) In real life, playing audio is a much more common scenario than recoding audio. But it's arguably easier to learn how to record audio first. The basic process of moving buffers of packets to and from the audio hardware is the same. Recording makes it easier to get into topics such as file formats and avoids the tricky business of format discovery. It also gives you a way to create audio files to play in the next chapter.

All About Audio Queues

Audio Queue Services uses a fairly simple model to get an audio capture or play-out job done without miring you in the complexities of the audio data, the underlying hardware, or the codecs necessary to put them together.

An audio queue is a simple software interface to a piece of audio hardware. The business end of the hardware is typically a transducer, such as a speaker or a microphone.

Because audio data travels in a constant stream, a queue is the perfect data structure to represent it.

The software end of an audio queue is the nominative queue of buffers. Each buffer is a block of memory that holds the actual data and bookkeeping information about the buffer and its contents.

Figure 4.1 illustrates the Audio Queue architecture. Buffers move from the buffer queue into the audio queue. The buffer is filled with data from the audio hardware and then passed into your callback function. Your callback function sends the audio data "elsewhere" and then puts the buffer at the back of the buffer queue.

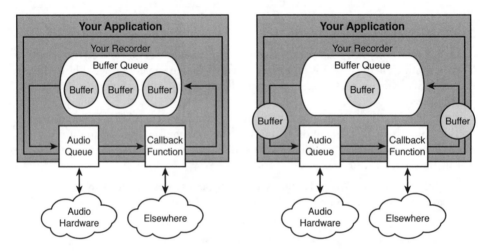

Figure 4.1   The Audio Queue architecture

In Figure 4.1, "Elsewhere" could be functions or methods in your application, in another application, or wherever. For the sake of this example, you're wrapping the data in an audio file and sending it to the filesystem. In your application, the filesystem need not necessarily be involved: You might use the received buffers to perform some kind of analysis (such as for a frequency analyzer or a karaoke game) or send them over the network to a VoIP peer.

Building a Recorder

It's important to see an audio queue for what it is in the grand scheme of things. It's not an API for playing and recording—it's one level lower than that. It's the interface that players and recorders use. Using an audio queue is not like using a recorder—it's like building a recorder.

When you create an audio queue, you provide a callback function that will be called to provide your application with buffers of audio captured from the input device (in the recording case) or to demand that you fill a buffer (for playback).

To try it out, let's do something simple but useful: record from your Mac's default input device and write the captured audio to a file.

When you first use a new API, one of the most sensible things to do is look through the documentation to see what the various calls look like, puzzle out how they work together, and try to understand the implicit design. If you type "AudioQueue" as a search term in Xcode's documentation browser, you'll find about 50 functions and types that contain the string "AudioQueue". Looking through them, you might figure out that there are functions to create audio queues, as with `AudioQueueNewInput()` and `AudioQueueNewOutput()`; control functions, as with `AudioQueueStart()` and `AudioQueueStop()`; parameter and property setters and getters; and so on.

Let's focus on `AudioQueueNewInput()`. It takes the following:

- A format to record to
- A structure representing a callback function
- A pointer to "user data," which is provided to the callback
- A Core Foundation run loop to use for the callbacks
- A Core Foundation run loop "mode" for callbacks
- "Flags" that must be set to `0`
- A pointer to receive a newly created `AudioQueueRef`

With this, you can anticipate some of what a recording queue example app needs to provide:

- A user data pointer that includes everything your callback function needs to do its work, such as the file to write to. The C convention is to define a `struct` for this, although in an Objective-C class, you could also use instance variables and pass `self` as the user data pointer.
- The callback function to process incoming audio. The docs link to `AudioQueueInputCallback`, which provides the function signature that this function must use so that you can copy and paste that directly into your code.
- A main function that does the following:
  - Sets up the audio format to use and the file to record into
  - Creates an audio queue
  - Starts the queue
  - Stops the queue
  - Does cleanup work, such as closing the file
- Convenience functions for tasks that can be modularized and reused in future code.

Create a new command-line tool project in Xcode,[1] add the `AudioToolbox` framework to the default target, and sketch out these sections with comments or #pragma mark macros, as shown in Listing 4.1. Comments to this "skeleton" listing show you where you'll be inserting each code listing as you go.

Listing 4.1   Outline of an Audio Queue–Based Recorder Program

```
#include <AudioToolbox/AudioToolbox.h>

#pragma mark user data struct
// Insert Listing 4.3 here

#pragma mark utility functions
// Insert Listing 4.2 here
// Insert Listings 4.20 and 4.21 here
// Insert Listing 4.22 here
// Insert Listing 4.23 here



#pragma mark record callback function
// Replace with Listings 4.24-4.26
static void MyAQInputCallback(void *inUserData,
                    AudioQueueRef inQueue,
                    AudioQueueBufferRef inBuffer,
                    const AudioTimeStamp *inStartTime,
                    UInt32 inNumPackets,
                    const AudioStreamPacketDescription *inPacketDesc)
{
}

#pragma mark main function
int    main(int argc, const char *argv[])
{
    // Set up format
    // Insert Listings 4.4-4.7 here

    // Set up queue
    // Insert Listings 4.8-4.9 here

    // Set up file
    // Insert Listings 4.10-4.11 here
```

---

[1] From here on out, you won't need Foundation's conveniences such as `NSLog()`, so in the downloadable sample code, this and all subsequent Mac command-line projects use the Core Foundation template.

Listing 4.1   **Continued**

```
    // Other setup as needed
    // Insert Listings 4.12-4.13 here

    // Start queue
    // Insert Listings 4.14-4.15 here

    // Stop queue
    // Insert Listings 4.16-4.18 here


}
```

That's not so scary right? Full listings of Core Audio applications can be daunting, but often they have a lot of little tasks that are reasonably comprehensible in isolation.

A CheckError() Function

Let's start with a convenience function to give you better information when you get a bad OSStatus return value. In the first few chapters, you used an assert() to check that the value was equal to noErr, but you didn't do anything to inspect the value if it wasn't. The return codes do vary from call to call and error to error; even if you want the app to quit, you'll help yourself immensely by actually inspecting the value.

However, the return values you get from Core Audio are somewhat unpredictable. Some are four-character codes that are easy enough to puzzle out from a log message, but others are just constant integer values. It would be nice to have a logging function that could tell the difference.

For the first convenience function (shown in Listing 4.2), you'll write just that. Look at the bytes of the error code. If all of them appear to be characters, treat them as a C string; otherwise, log the code as an integer. Here's the function, which you can place after #pragma mark utility functions in Listing 4.1.

Listing 4.2   **Logging OSStatus Error Codes**

```
static void CheckError(OSStatus error, const char *operation)
{
    if (error == noErr) return;

    char errorString[20];
    // See if it appears to be a 4-char-code
    *(UInt32 *)(errorString + 1) = CFSwapInt32HostToBig(error);
    if (isprint(errorString[1]) && isprint(errorString[2]) &&
        isprint(errorString[3]) && isprint(errorString[4])) {
        errorString[0] = errorString[5] = '\'';
        errorString[6] = '\0';
    } else
```

Listing 4.2   **Continued**

```
            // No, format it as an integer
            sprintf(errorString, "%d", (int)error);

        fprintf(stderr, "Error: %s (%s)\n", operation, errorString);

        exit(1);
}
```

This function uses the function isprint() from the standard C library (in ctype.h) to test whether each of the 4 bytes of error consists of plausible characters. If so, an errorString is created with those 4 bytes, using single quotes, and a null-terminator; if not, errorString is created by converting the integer value to a C string. In either case, the function uses the errorString and operation, a string parameter that represents what you were doing when the error occurred, to log an error message to standard out. After that, the application terminates with a nonzero (error) status.

To call this, you wrap your Core Audio calls with the CheckError() function and an operation string that represents the purpose of the call. As a simple example, consider the last Core Audio call from the CAToneFileGenerator example in Chapter 2, "The Story of Sound" (see "// 16" in Listing 2.1). In that example, you wrote this:

```
audioErr = AudioFileClose(audioFile);
assert (audioErr == noErr);
```

With the convenience function, you can now write this:

```
CheckError (AudioFileClose(audioFile), "Couldn't close audio file");
```

And if that fails, you log an error like this before terminating:

```
Error: Couldn't close audio file ('wht?')
```

If you look through the Audio File Services Reference in the Xcode documentation or the AudioFile.h header file, you'll see that wht? is kAudioFileUnspecifiedError. On the other hand, if the result isn't a four-character code, the value in parentheses simply is an integer, such as (-50), where -50 is the generic paramErr from MacErrors.h.

You'll continue to use this handy function throughout the rest of the book.

Creating and Using the Audio Queue

Here you begin coding the application, leaving placeholders for convenience functions as you discover you need them.

The main tasks for the main() function are to create an audio queue to capture input from the default device, let it run until the user stops it, and then clean everything up. From looking at the API documentation, you know that you'll be doing a lot of the work in a callback function, not in the `main()` itself. This callback function can take one pointer that provides whatever data you need in the callback, so let's define that at the top of the file, as seen in Listing 4.3.

Listing 4.3   User Info Struct for Recording Audio Queue Callbacks

```
#pragma mark user info struct
typedef     struct     MyRecorder {
    AudioFileID              recordFile;
    SInt64                   recordPacket;
    Boolean                  running;
} MyRecorder;
```

We don't expect you to know why you need these three fields in the struct right away. But a common technique is that you know you need *something* for your callback—you create a struct such as `MyRecorder` and then add to or remove from it as you create the rest of your code. For this example, the callback needs to know the file to write to, an index of the packet it's writing to the output file, and a Boolean to keep track of whether the queue is running.

Now that you've defined the `MyRecorder` struct, you can get to work on the `main()` function that sets up, runs, and tears down the queue. Right off the bat, you need to define a local `MyRecorder` variable, along with an `AudioStreamBasicDescription` to represent the recording format, because you'll need one to set up the queue. Listing 4.4 sets these up.

Listing 4.4   Creating MyRecorder Struct and ASBD for Audio Queue

```
int     main(int argc, const char *argv[])
{
    MyRecorder recorder = {0};
    AudioStreamBasicDescription recordFormat;
    memset(&recordFormat, 0, sizeof(recordFormat));
```

This example shows off Audio Queue's capability to work with encoded formats, which means setting up the `AudioStreamBasicDescription` a little differently. First, in Listing 4.5, you use the `mFormatID` and `mChannelsPerFrame` field to indicate that you want to record as stereo AAC.

Listing 4.5   Setting Format of ASBD for Audio Queue

```
recordFormat.mFormatID = kAudioFormatMPEG4AAC;
recordFormat.mChannelsPerFrame = 2;
```

You also need to define a sample rate. You could hard-code 44,100 Hz as you did in the previous chapters. However, because different input devices have different default sample rates, just imposing a value could force Core Audio to do a sample rate conversion you don't need. If your input device could only capture at 8,000 Hz, forcing the ASBD to use 44,100 Hz would just cause Core Audio to do extra work in resampling the input audio—and it still wouldn't sound any better.

Remind yourself to write a convenience function that will figure out the right sample rate for the selected input device, as in Listing 4.6.

Listing 4.6   **Function for Correct Sample Rate**

```
MyGetDefaultInputDeviceSampleRate(&recordFormat.mSampleRate);
```

For encoded formats, this is really all you need to fill in for the ASBD. You can't know some of the ASBD fields, such as `mBytesPerPacket`, because they might depend on details of the encoding format or might even be variable. For formats other than PCM, fill in what you can and let Core Audio do the rest.

One way to do this is to use `AudioFormatGetProperty()` to fill in a partially completed ASBD. If you use the property `kAudioFormatProperty_FormatInfo` and pass in an ASBD with at least its `mFormatID` set, Core Audio uses what it knows about that codec to fill in whatever other fields it can. As with other property getters and setters, you must provide the size of the pointer you're passing in to the call, so this takes two statements, as seen in Listing 4.7.

Listing 4.7   **Filling in ASBD with AudioFormatGetProperty()**

```
UInt32 propSize = sizeof(recordFormat);
CheckError(AudioFormatGetProperty(kAudioFormatProperty_FormatInfo,
                                  0,
                                  NULL,
                                  &propSize,
                                  &recordFormat),
        "AudioFormatGetProperty failed");
```

Notice that this is the first use of the `CheckError()` convenience function. If Core Audio doesn't recognize the format—perhaps you used some bogus four-character code or you asked for a Mac-only format on iOS—the application terminates with this message:

```
Error: AudioFormatGetProperty failed ('fmt?')
```

Having set up the format, you are now ready to create the recording audio queue. Create a local variable to hold a reference to the queue, and then create it with a single call to `AudioQueueNewInput()`, like in Listing 4.8.

Listing 4.8   **Creating New Audio Queue for Input**

```
AudioQueueRef queue = {0};
CheckError(AudioQueueNewInput(&recordFormat,
                              MyAQInputCallback,
                              &recorder,
                              NULL,
                              NULL,
                              0,
                              &queue),
           "AudioQueueNewInput failed");
```

As mentioned earlier, this function takes a lot of parameters, although only a few of them are typically of interest: You indicate the format to record into (`recordFormat`), a callback function (the yet-to-be-written `MyAQInputCallback`), a pointer with user data to provide to the callback (recorder, which is your `MyRecorder` struct), some `NULL` defaults for run loop behavior, a flags value that is always `0`, and, finally, a pointer to receive the created `AudioQueueRef`.

A side effect of creating the queue is that it can provide you with a more complete `AudioStreamBasicDescription` than the one you set it up with. This happens because some of the fields can't be filled in until Core Audio readies a codec for the queue. You can retrieve this ASBD from the queue by getting the property `kAudioConverterCurrentOutputStreamDescription`. Do this in Listing 4.9.

Listing 4.9   **Retrieving Filled-Out ASBD from Audio Queue**

```
UInt32 size = sizeof(recordFormat);
CheckError(AudioQueueGetProperty(queue,
                          kAudioConverterCurrentOutputStreamDescription,
                          &recordFormat,
                          &size),
           "Couldn't get queue's format");
```

With this more detailed ASBD, you can now create the file into which you record the captured audio. You already used `AudioFileCreateWithURL()` to do this in Chapter 2; it takes a `CFURLRef`, a file type, an ASBD, some flags, and a pointer to receive the created `AudioFileID`. One change is needed for the version in Listing 4.10: Because this example hasn't imported the Foundation framework (and doesn't really need to), you'll stick with the Core Foundation conventions for creating URLs instead of using `NSURL` and the toll-free bridge.

Listing 4.10   Creating Audio File for Output

```
CFURLRef myFileURL = CFURLCreateWithFileSystemPath(kCFAllocatorDefault,
                                    CFSTR("output.caf"),
                                    kCFURLPOSIXPathStyle,
                                    false);
CheckError(AudioFileCreateWithURL(myFileURL,
                            kAudioFileCAFType,
                            &recordFormat,
                            kAudioFileFlags_EraseFile,
                            &recorder.recordFile),
            "AudioFileCreateWithURL failed");
CFRelease(myFileURL);
```

The queue also gives you a *magic cookie.* As covered in Chapter 3, "Audio Processing with Core Audio," a magic cookie is an opaque block of data that contains values that are unique to a given codec and that the ASBD hasn't already accounted for. Some compressed formats use cookies; some don't. Because your code might encounter new formats that use cookies, it's wise to always be able to handle them. AAC is one format that uses magic cookies, so you need to get it from the audio queue and set it on the audio file. But this is a distraction from setting up the audio queue, so Listing 4.11 can just be a call to a convenience function that you'll write later.

Listing 4.11   Calling a Convenience Method to Handle Magic Cookie

```
MyCopyEncoderCookieToFile(queue, recorder.recordFile);
```

With a queue and an audio file set up, you're getting closer. The next item to think about is the buffers that the queue works with. In the recording case, the queue fills these buffers with captured audio and sends them to the callback function. However, you're still responsible for creating these buffers and providing them to the queue before you start. And that begs an interesting question: *How big are the buffers supposed to be?* With constant bit rate encoding, such as PCM, you could multiply the bit rate by a buffer duration to figure out a good buffer size. For example, 44,100 samples/second × 2 channels × 2 bytes/channel × 1 second would mean you'd need 176,400 bytes to hold a second of 16-bit stereo PCM at 44.1 KHz. For a compressed format such as AAC, however, you don't know how effective the compression will be. Therefore, you don't know how big a buffer to allocate.

The audio queue can give you this information, but because it's a big job, you can set it aside with another convenience function that you'll have to come back to. Assume that `MyComputeRecordBufferSize()` will take an ASBD, an audio queue, and a buffer duration in seconds and return an optimal size, and call this in Listing 4.12.

Listing 4.12   Calling a Convenience Function to Compute Recording Buffer Size

```
int bufferByteSize = MyComputeRecordBufferSize(&recordFormat, queue, 0.5);
```

Assuming that works, let's create some buffers and provide them to the queue, an action called *enqueuing*. At the top of the file, define the number of buffers to use. In Core Audio, including Apple's examples, it's common practice to use three buffers. The idea is, one buffer is being filled, one buffer is being drained, and the other is sitting in the queue as a spare, to account for lag.

```
#define kNumberRecordBuffers 3
```

You can use more—you're welcome to recompile this program using a greater value for kNumberRecordBuffers when you're finished writing it—but using less than three could get you in trouble. With two buffers, you'd risk dropouts by not having a spare buffer while the other two are being used. With only one buffer, you'll almost certainly have dropouts because the one buffer the queue needs to record into will be unavailable as your callback processes it.

Now back in main(), you can allocate and enqueue these buffers, as shown in Listing 4.13.

Listing 4.13   Allocating and Enqueuing Buffers

```
int bufferIndex;
for (bufferIndex = 0;
     bufferIndex < kNumberRecordBuffers;
     ++bufferIndex)
{
    AudioQueueBufferRef buffer;
    CheckError(AudioQueueAllocateBuffer(queue,
                                        bufferByteSize,
                                        &buffer),
               "AudioQueueAllocateBuffer failed");
    CheckError(AudioQueueEnqueueBuffer(queue,
                                       buffer,
                                       0,
                                       NULL),
               "AudioQueueEnqueueBuffer failed");
}
```

Now that you have a queue with a set of buffers enqueued, you can start the queue, which starts recording. You do this with a call to AudioQueueStart(), shown in Listing 4.14, which takes the queue to start and an optional start time (use NULL to start immediately).

Listing 4.14   Starting the Audio Queue

```
recorder.running = TRUE;
CheckError(AudioQueueStart(queue,
                           NULL),
           "AudioQueueStart failed");
```

Because you're writing a command-line application, your UI will simply be to stop recording when the user presses a key on the keyboard, a behavior we implement in Listing 4.15.

Listing 4.15   Blocking on stdin to Continue Recording

```
printf("Recording, press <return> to stop:\n");
getchar();
```

When the user is done recording, you need to stop the queue so it can finish its work. You do this with `AudioQueueStop()`, in Listing 4.16.

Listing 4.16   Stopping the Audio Queue

```
printf("* recording done *\n");
recorder.running = FALSE;
CheckError(AudioQueueStop(queue,
                          TRUE),
           "AudioQueueStop failed");
```

You have a little more cleanup to do before `main()` can exit. In some cases, the magic cookie is updated during the recording process. Reset the cookie on the file before closing it. To do this, you can use your yet-to-be-written convenience function again, as shown in Listing 4.17.

Listing 4.17   Recalling the Magic Cookie Convenience Function

```
MyCopyEncoderCookieToFile(queue, recorder.recordFile);
```

Finally, you clean up by disposing of all resources allocated by the audio queue and closing the audio file. Listing 4.18 shows these clean-up calls.

Listing 4.18   Cleaning Up the Audio Queue and Audio File

```
    AudioQueueDispose(queue, TRUE);
    AudioFileClose(recorder.recordFile);
    return 0;
}
```

Now you have the `main()` portion of your application, which sets up and uses an audio queue. If you want to get it to compile, you have to stub out no-op versions of the convenience functions you've referenced (and you have to either put them before `main()` or create forward references). Listing 4.19 shows the stub implementations.

Listing 4.19   **Function Definitions for Convenience Routines**

```
OSStatus MyGetDefaultInputDeviceSampleRate(Float64 *outSampleRate) {}
static int MyComputeRecordBufferSize(
                        const AudioStreamBasicDescription *format,
                        AudioQueueRef queue,
                        float seconds) {}
static void MyCopyEncoderCookieToFile(AudioQueueRef queue,
                        AudioFileID theFile) {}
```

Between these utility functions and the callback function `MyAQInputCallback()`, you have four more pieces to write to get your recorder working. Let's clean up the details of the convenience functions first.

Utility Functions for the Audio Queue

The first bit of work you put off in `main()` was to get a sample rate from the input hardware instead of just hard-coding a value that might not suit the current device. To inspect the current input device, you can use Audio Hardware Services.[2] As with so much of Core Audio, you need to use a property getter. Actually, you'll use two: First, in Listing 4.20, you use `AudioHardwareServiceGetPropertyData()` to get the `kAudioHardwarePropertyDefaultInputDevice` property.

Listing 4.20   **Getting Current Audio Input Device Info from Audio Hardware Services**

```
OSStatus MyGetDefaultInputDeviceSampleRate(Float64 *outSampleRate)
{
    OSStatus error;
    AudioDeviceID deviceID = 0;

    AudioObjectPropertyAddress propertyAddress;
    UInt32 propertySize;
    propertyAddress.mSelector = kAudioHardwarePropertyDefaultInputDevice;
    propertyAddress.mScope = kAudioObjectPropertyScopeGlobal;
    propertyAddress.mElement = 0;
    propertySize = sizeof(AudioDeviceID);
    error = AudioHardwareServiceGetPropertyData(kAudioObjectSystemObject,
```

---

[2] Audio Hardware Services does not exist on iOS. To get the hardware sample rate on iPhone, we use Audio Session Services, which is covered in Chapter 10.

Listing 4.20   **Continued**

```
                                         &propertyAddress,
                                         0,
                                         NULL,
                                         &propertySize,
                                         &deviceID);
    if (error) return error;
```

As you can see, getting a property requires you to specify the audio object to query (the constant kAudioObjectSystemObject, in this case) and an AudioObject PropertyAddress, which contains not just the property you want, but also a scope and an element. For querying general properties of the hardware, as you're doing here, you can request global scope and the master element, which is 0.

> **Note**
>
> This section packs in a bunch of concepts about audio hardware properties, but they're seldom used—it's okay to treat this as boilerplate and not worry about scopes and elements for now. They'll make more sense after you cover Audio Units in Chapter 7, "Audio Units: Generators, Effects, and Rendering," which use a similar metaphor.

Assuming that you got the deviceID from this call, you make another call in Listing 4.21 to AudioHardwareServiceGetPropertyData. This time, you pass in the deviceID and request the kAudioDevicePropertyNominalSampleRate property.

Listing 4.21   **Getting Input Device's Sample Rate**

```
    propertyAddress.mSelector = kAudioDevicePropertyNominalSampleRate;
    propertyAddress.mScope = kAudioObjectPropertyScopeGlobal;
    propertyAddress.mElement = 0;
    propertySize = sizeof(Float64);
    error = AudioHardwareServiceGetPropertyData(deviceID,
                                                &propertyAddress,
                                                0,
                                                NULL,
                                                &propertySize,
                                                outSampleRate);

    return error;
}
```

The next utility function to write is the one that retrieves the magic cookie from an audio queue and provides it to an audio file. You have to do this for encoded formats such as AAC, in which the ASBD by itself is not sufficient to describe the audio stream. This is a pretty straightforward task: Get the magic cookie property (if any) from the queue and set it on the audio file. Listing 4.22 shows these steps.

Listing 4.22   **Copying Magic Cookie from Audio Queue to Audio File**

```
static void MyCopyEncoderCookieToFile(AudioQueueRef queue, AudioFileID theFile)
{
    OSStatus error;
    UInt32 propertySize;

    error = AudioQueueGetPropertySize(queue,
                              kAudioConverterCompressionMagicCookie,
                              &propertySize);

    if (error == noErr && propertySize > 0)
    {
    Byte *magicCookie = (Byte *)malloc(propertySize);
    CheckError(AudioQueueGetProperty(queue,
                                  kAudioQueueProperty_MagicCookie,
                                  magicCookie,
                                  &propertySize),
            "Couldn't get audio queue's magic cookie");

    CheckError(AudioFileSetProperty(theFile,
                                  kAudioFilePropertyMagicCookieData,
                                  propertySize,
                                  magicCookie),
            "Couldn't set audio file's magic cookie");
    free(magicCookie);
    }
}
```

As you can see, you copy over the magic cookie by first using `AudioQueueGet`
`PropertySize()` to get the size of the `kAudioConverterCompressionMagicCookie`
property from the queue. If the size is 0, no cookie exists and you're done. Otherwise,
you need to `malloc()` a byte buffer to hold the cookie, copy it to the buffer with
`AudioQueueGetProperty()`, and then set the property on the file with
`AudioFileSetProperty()`, sending the byte buffer as the property's value.

> **Note**
>
> The property constants that represent the magic cookie in the Audio Queue Services and
> Audio File Services APIs are different. They might be the same four-character-code, but to
> be safe, make sure you're using `kAudioQueueProperty`-style constants when getting
> or setting queue properties, and use `kAudioFileProperty`-style constants with file
> properties.

The last utility function is `MyComputeRecordBufferSize()`, which figures out how
big a buffer you need to hold a certain duration of audio in a given format. `main()` uses

this to allocate the buffers it enqueues on the audio queue. The logic is somewhat involved, so Listing 4.23 gives you the code first and then the text explains how it works.

Listing 4.23   **Computing Recording Buffer Size for an ASBD**

```
static int MyComputeRecordBufferSize(
                              const AudioStreamBasicDescription *format,
                              AudioQueueRef queue,
                              float seconds)
{
    int packets, frames, bytes;

    frames = (int)ceil(seconds * format->mSampleRate);

    if (format->mBytesPerFrame > 0)                              // 1
        bytes = frames * format->mBytesPerFrame;
    else
    {
        UInt32 maxPacketSize;
        if (format->mBytesPerPacket > 0)                         // 2
            // Constant packet size
            maxPacketSize = format->mBytesPerPacket;
        else
        {
            // Get the largest single packet size possible
            UInt32 propertySize = sizeof(maxPacketSize);         // 3
            CheckError(AudioQueueGetProperty(queue,
                        kAudioConverterPropertyMaximumOutputPacketSize,
                        &maxPacketSize,
                        &propertySize),
                    "Couldn't get queue's maximum output packet size");
        }
        if (format->mFramesPerPacket > 0)
            packets = frames / format->mFramesPerPacket;         // 4
        else
            // Worst-case scenario: 1 frame in a packet
            packets = frames;                                    // 5

        // Sanity check
        if (packets == 0)
            packets = 1;
        bytes = packets * maxPacketSize;                         // 6
    }
    return bytes;
}
```

Let's dig into the code a little more so you can better understand what's happening. Start with `// 1` and follow along through the code:

1. You first need to know how many frames (one sample for every channel) are in each buffer. You get this by multiplying the sample rate by the buffer duration. If the ASBD already has an `mBytesPerFrame` value, as in the case for constant bit rate formats such as PCM, you can trivially get the needed byte count by multiplying `mBytesPerFrame` by the frame count.

2. If that's not the case, you need to work at the packet level. The easy case for this is a constant packet size, indicated by a nonzero `mBytesPerPacket`.

3. In the hard case, you get the audio queue property `kAudioConverterPropertyMaximumOutputPacketSize`, which gives you an upper bound to work with. Either way, you have a `maxPacketSize`, which you'll need soon.

4. But how many packets are there? The ASBD might provide a `mFramesPerPacket` value; in that case, you divide the frame count by `mFramesPerPacket` to get a packet count (packets).

5. Otherwise, assume the worst case of one frame per packet.

6. Finally, with a frames-per-packet value (which you force to be nonzero, just to be safe) and a maximum size per packet, you can multiply the two to get a maximum buffer size.

Those are the convenience functions. You can probably see why you wanted to factor them out of `main()`, to avoid distraction from the earlier discussion of setting up and starting the audio queue. As a bonus, you can reuse these functions in your future projects.

At this point, you can build and run the example project, although it won't actually do anything; it's missing the callback from the audio queue. Let's finish that next.

The Recording Audio Queue Callback

When you created the audio queue with `AudioQueueNewInput()`, you passed in a function pointer to `MyAQInputCallback`, along with a user data pointer to `recorder`, which is the `MyRecorder` struct that we created in `main()`. The callback is called every time the queue fills one of the buffers with freshly captured audio data; the callback function must do something interesting with this data. As long as the callback function is an empty stub, the program will run and the buffers will be delivered, but nothing interesting will happen because you're not doing anything with the buffers. You need to take each buffer you receive from the queue and write it to the audio file.

Let's begin in Listing 4.24 by casting the user data pointer back to a reference to a `MyRecorder` struct.

Listing 4.24   Header for Audio Queue Callback and Casting of User Info Pointer

```
static void MyAQInputCallback(void *inUserData,
                    AudioQueueRef inQueue,
                    AudioQueueBufferRef inBuffer,
                    const AudioTimeStamp *inStartTime,
                    UInt32 inNumPackets,
                    const AudioStreamPacketDescription *inPacketDesc)
{
    MyRecorder *recorder = (MyRecorder *)inUserData;
```

Now you're ready to write the audio data to the file. The audio data is provided by the callback parameter `inBuffer` (an `AudioQueueBufferRef`), with three other parameters providing a starting time stamp, a number of packets, and a pointer to packet descriptions. The latter two parameters are relevant only for variable bit rate formats, such as the AAC format you're using. Fortunately, these parameters, along with the values you set aside in the `MyRecorder` struct, provide everything you need to call `AudioFileWritePackets()`:

- A file, which you put in the `MyRecorder` struct
- A Boolean indicating whether you want to cache the data you're writing (you don't want to, in this case)
- The size of the data buffer to write, which you get from the `inBuffer` parameter's `mAudioDataByteSize`
- Packet descriptions, provided by the callback's `inPacketDesc` parameter
- An index to which packet in the file to write, which is a running count that you keep track of in recorder's `recordPacket` field
- The number of packets to write, provided by the callback's `inNumPackets` parameter
- A pointer to the audio data, which is the `inBuffer mAudioData` pointer

Listing 4.25 makes the call to `AudioFileWritePackets()` and then updates the index of where to write packets in the file (so that it's not repeatedly writing to index 0).

Listing 4.25   Writing Captured Packets to Audio File

```
    if (inNumPackets > 0)
    {
        // Write packets to a file
        CheckError(AudioFileWritePackets(recorder->recordFile,
                                FALSE,
                                inBuffer->mAudioDataByteSize,
                                inPacketDesc,
                                recorder->recordPacket,
                                &inNumPackets,
```

Listing 4.25   **Continued**

```
                                         inBuffer->mAudioData),
                    "AudioFileWritePackets failed");

        // Increment the packet index
        recorder->recordPacket += inNumPackets;
    }
```

Now that you've used the buffer, you send it back to the queue (you re-enqueue it) in Listing 4.26 so it can be filled with newly captured audio data.

Listing 4.26   **Re-enqueuing a Used Buffer**

```
    if (recorder->running)
        CheckError(AudioQueueEnqueueBuffer(inQueue,
                                           inBuffer,
                                           0,
                                           NULL),
                    "AudioQueueEnqueueBuffer failed");
}
```

With this, you have completed your recording audio queue. To try it, launch System Preferences and go to the Sound panel. Make sure you have a working audio input device selected, such as an internal laptop microphone or an external USB microphone. Back in Xcode, bring up the Console window from the Run menu (Shift-⌘-R). Now build and run the application. You'll see something like the following output:

```
Loading program into debugger,…¶
Program loaded.
run
[Switching to process 2748]
Running,…¶
Recording, press <return> to stop:
```

At this point, the application is recording from your default audio input device.[3] Talk, sing, snap your fingers—do whatever you like to make some sound. When you've had enough, press the Return key. The program ends and displays the following message:

```
* recording done *
```

So where's the sound? Recall that you set up CFURLRef to create the audio file output.caf. This file path is relative to the executable, so in Xcode 4, you can find it

---

[3] Use System Preferences to set your default input device and check the input levels, if you haven't already.

alongside your project's derived data. Open the Organizer window, click the Projects tab and click the Recorder project. In the right pane, notice the Derived Data path and click the circled arrow next to it. This opens the project's derived data in the Finder, as shown in Figure 4.2. From here, you can dig down into Build/Products/Debug to find the executable and the `.output.caf` file that contains your recording. You can play the file by selecting it and pressing the spacebar to preview it in Finder, or drag it to QuickTime Player or any other audio app that handles the CAF format.

Figure 4.2   Location of output.caf captured audio file in the Finder

Summary

In this chapter, you used an audio queue to capture audio from the default input device and write it to a file. Setting up the audio queue required you to work through a number of tasks, including figuring out a good size for the queue's buffers, discovering the input device's sample rate, and retrieving the magic cookie for the format so that you could provide it to the audio file. In more general terms, the essentials of working with an audio queue are to enqueue some buffers, start the queue, and handle the buffers in the callback

You can do a few more interesting tasks with an audio queue. One of the best is level metering, which you can use to provide a user interface that shows the loudness or softness of the audio being captured. Using this feature involves working with two properties of the audio queue. First, you set the property `kAudioQueueProperty_EnableLevelMetering` on the queue, passing in the value 1 as a `UInt32` to enable metering. Then you make repeated calls—perhaps five or ten per second—to get the `kAudioQueueProperty_CurrentLevelMeter` or `kAudioQueueProperty_CurrentLevelMeterDB` property from the queue. The value for these properties is an array (one member per channel in the queue) of `AudioQueueLevelMeterState` values, with the `Float32` values provided either in a 0-for-silence/1-for-maximum range, or as decibel values. You could then use these values to draw a custom view to visualize the audio power levels.

In the next chapter, you'll reverse this process and use an audio queue to play back audio, such as the file you just recorded. You'll use the same concept of providing buffers to a queue, but this time, instead of your callback receiving buffers full of capture data, you'll get empty buffers that you'll need to fill with audio from the file. You'll still be based in this queue metaphor, but you'll be using it quite differently.

5

Playback

In the previous chapter, you learned how to record audio with an Audio Queue, the highest level of Core Audio's engine APIs. An audio queue uses a queue of buffers to process a stream of audio: Your application sets up the queue by providing it with these buffers, and the queue sends a buffer to a callback function in your code when it's time for you to act on it.

All this applies to recording, but it also applies to playback, which is the other use of an audio queue. The difference is one of responsibility: Instead of the recording queue delivering you buffers of newly captured audio, a playback queue gives you empty buffers that you are expected to fill with audio to be played out.

In this chapter, you'll learn how to use playback audio queues by building an application that reads audio from any Core Audio–supported file and plays it through a queue. You'll find some of the same challenges as in the last chapter, such as estimating buffer sizes and managing magic cookies, along with some new concerns unique to playback, such as having to take responsibility for the AudioStreamPacketDescriptions that describe buffers of compressed audio data.

Defining the Playback Application

As with the recording example, you can prepare for writing a playback application by sizing up the relevant APIs in the documentation. To create a playback audio queue, you use the function `AudioQueueNewOutput()`. This function takes almost the same list of parameters as the input version used in the last chapter:

- An `AudioStreamBasicDescription`, describing the audio format being provided to the queue
- An `AudioQueueOutputCallback` function pointer to a callback function you will write
- A user data pointer to provide to the callback
- A Core Foundation run loop on which to call the callback
- A Core Foundation run loop mode for the callback

- An unused flags parameter that must always be 0
- A pointer to receive the created AudioQueueRef

The only difference between this and the recording case is the function pointer to the callback. The AudioQueueOutputCallback declares a different signature that takes only three parameters:

- The user data pointer
- The queue that is performing the callback
- An AudioQueueBufferRef to fill with data

Given this, you can again sketch the outline of your application. In Xcode, create another Command Line Tool project, add AudioToolbox.framework to the target, and outline the program as shown in Listing 5.1.

Listing 5.1   **Outline of an Audio Queue–Based Playback Program**

```
#include <AudioToolbox/AudioToolbox.h>

#pragma mark user data struct
// Insert Listing 5.2 here

#pragma mark utility functions
// Insert Listing 4.2 here
// Insert Listing 5.14 here
// Insert Listing 5.15 here

#pragma mark playback callback function
// Replace with Listings 5.16-5.19
static void MyAQOutputCallback(void *inUserData,
                               AudioQueueRef inAQ,
                               AudioQueueBufferRef inCompleteAQBuffer)
{
}

#pragma mark main function
int    main(int argc, const char *argv[])
{
    // Open an audio file
    // Insert Listings 5.3-5.4 here

    // Set up format
    // Insert Listing 5.5 here
```

Listing 5.1 **Continued**

```
    // Set up queue
    // Insert Listings 5.6-5.10 here

    // Start queue
    // Insert Listing 5.11-5.12 here

    // Clean up queue when finished
    // Insert Listing 5.13 here


}
```

With the exception of the callback function's signature, this is identical to the previous chapter's example. The other big difference is that the comment "open audio file" appears before you set up the audio format and queue. That's because, instead of choosing a format to record to, you need to discover the format of the file you want to play and set up your queue accordingly.

Before you get started setting up your queue, copy over the `CheckError()` function from the last chapter (see Listing 4.2) and paste it into the `#pragma mark utility functions` section. Again, you will use this function to log any Core Audio errors before terminating the program.

Setting Up a File-Playing Audio Queue

As is usually the case with Core Audio's callback patterns, you get a single user data pointer to pass back to your callback function. You usually want to define a custom struct for this pointer so that you can pass multiple values into the callback. The callback reads from an audio file and passes audio packets to the queue. As such, this struct needs to keep track of the file to read from and where you are in the file. It also needs to keep track of whether you should still be playing (that is, whether you've reached the end of the file). Also, as we developed the example, we found that we also needed the struct to have a reference to the array of packet descriptions read from the file and written to the queue because this is set up in `main()` but used in the callback. Listing 5.2 gives the user info `struct`.

Listing 5.2 **User Info Struct for Playback Audio Queue Callbacks**

```
#pragma mark user info struct
typedef struct MyPlayer {
    AudioFileID                   playbackFile;
    SInt64                        packetPosition;
    UInt32                        numPacketsToRead;
    AudioStreamPacketDescription  *packetDescs;
    Boolean                       isDone;
} MyPlayer;
```

Now you can start writing the `main()` function, in Listing 5.3, starting with a variable of this type that you can set up.

Listing 5.3   Declaration of main() Function and Allocation of a MyPlayer Structure

```
int    main(int argc, const char *argv[])
{
    MyPlayer player = {0};
```

Next, you need to find the audio file you're working with. Use a `#define` at the top of the file to create a string with the full path to an audio file on your hard drive. It can be in any of the formats Core Audio understands, such as `.mp3`, `.aac`, `.m4a`, `.wav`, `.aif`, and so on. However, Core Audio cannot read files in the iTunes "protected" format (`.m4p`).

```
#define kPlaybackFileLocation    CFSTR("/Users/username/Music/iTunes/iTunes
Music/Artist Name/Album Name/Song Name.m4a")
```

To hearken back to your work on the recording audio queue, you can use the `output.caf` you recorded in Chapter 4, "Recording," which will be in a long "DerivedData" path something like this:

```
#define kPlaybackFileLocation    CFSTR("/Users/username /Library/Developer/
Xcode/DerivedData/CH04_Recorderdvninfofohfiwcgyndnhzarhsipp/
Build/Products/Debug/output.caf")
```

Either way, back in `main()`, use `AudioFileOpen()` (which you saw in Chapter 1, "Overview of Core Audio") to get an `AudioFileID` and assign it to the `playbackFile` in the player struct. Listing 5.4 shows this call.

Listing 5.4   Opening an Audio File for Input

```
CFURLRef myFileURL = CFURLCreateWithFileSystemPath(
                          kCFAllocatorDefault,
                          kPlaybackFileLocation,
                          kCFURLPOSIXPathStyle,
                          false);
CheckError(AudioFileOpenURL(myFileURL,
                          kAudioFileReadPermission,
                          0,
                          &player.playbackFile),
          "AudioFileOpenURL failed");
CFRelease(myFileURL);
```

Now that you've opened the audio file, you can inspect its properties. In Listing 5.5, you need to get the format of the file's audio as an `AudioStreamBasicDescription` so you can set up a playback queue with that format.

Listing 5.5   **Getting the ASBD from an Audio File**

```
AudioStreamBasicDescription dataFormat;
UInt32 propSize = sizeof(dataFormat);
CheckError(AudioFileGetProperty(player.playbackFile, kAudioFilePropertyDataFormat,
                       &propSize, &dataFormat),
          "Couldn't get file's data format");
```

Now that you have the `dataFormat`, you're ready to create the audio queue for play-back with the `AudioQueueNewOutput()` function, as shown in Listing 5.6.

Listing 5.6   **Creating a New Audio Queue for Output**

```
AudioQueueRef queue;
CheckError(AudioQueueNewOutput(&dataFormat,
                         MyAQOutputCallback,
                         &player,
                         NULL,
                         NULL,
                         0,
                         &queue),
          "AudioQueueNewOutput failed");
```

Again, this is just like how you set up the recording queue, except that the callback function (`MyAQOutputCallback`) has a much different signature. You'll write the call-back later; all that's needed now is a no-op implementation, which you sketched out earlier.

Setting Up the Playback Buffers

The next few steps all involve setting up the buffers that the queue uses. This is an involved process because you have to account for the encoding characteristics of the audio in the file you're opening: whether it's compressed or uncompressed, variable or constant bit rate, and so on.

Part of the challenge here comes from working with packets, which wasn't a concern with LPCM and which you basically just passed from queue to file in the last chapter. To refresh your memory, *a packet is a collection of frames, which, in turn, are collections of samples.* Because the frame size is variable in a packet, you can't just encounter a buffer of audio data and know what to do with it, as you can with LPCM, in which every frame has a fixed size. With encoded formats such as MP3 and AAC, you need an array of `AudioStreamPacketDescriptions` to provide a map of the contents of the audio buffer, to tell you where each packet begins and what's in it.

To be able to allocate the buffers the queue will use, you need to inspect the file and its audio encoding to figure out how big of a data buffer you'll need and how many packets you will be reading on each callback. This will be a distraction from setting up the audio queue, so put it aside as a utility function that you'll write a little later. Listing 5.7 calls this yet-to-be written convenience function.

Listing 5.7   Calling a Convenience Function to Calculate Playback Buffer Size and Number of Packets to Read

```
UInt32 bufferByteSize;
CalculateBytesForTime(player.playbackFile,
                      dataFormat,
                      0.5,
                      &bufferByteSize,
                      &player.numPacketsToRead);
```

As you can see, this function takes the file to read, the ASBD, and a buffer duration in seconds, and populates variables representing an appropriate buffer size and how many packets of audio you will want to read from the file in each callback. You'll see how this function works later.

Now you can set up the `packetDescs` member of the `MyPlayer` struct, in Listing 5.8. This is the array of packet descriptions that map out the contents of each audio buffer you read from the file. Whether you need it depends on whether the audio format is variable bit rate (which uses packet descriptions) or constant (which doesn't).

Listing 5.8   Allocating Memory for Packet Descriptions Array

```
bool isFormatVBR = (dataFormat.mBytesPerPacket == 0 ||
                    dataFormat.mFramesPerPacket == 0);
if (isFormatVBR)
    player.packetDescs = (AudioStreamPacketDescription*)
        malloc(sizeof(AudioStreamPacketDescription) *
               player.numPacketsToRead);
else
    player.packetDescs = NULL;
```

You're almost ready to create and use the buffers, but first you have to set up the magic cookie on the queue. As with recording, the audio format might have some magic cookie data that you need to preserve. For playback, you read the magic cookie as a property of the audio file and write it to the queue. But let's put that off for a bit by just having Listing 5.9 call a utility function that you'll come back to write later.

Listing 5.9   Calling a Convenience Method to Handle Magic Cookie

```
MyCopyEncoderCookieToQueue(player.playbackFile, queue);
```

Now that the queue has been configured and you know how big your buffers need to be, you can create and enqueue some buffers. Start with a `#define` at the top of the file of how many buffers you want to use; again, 3 is often an appropriate value—you have one buffer being played, one filled, and one in the queue to account for lag:

```
#define kNumberPlaybackBuffers    3
```

Back in main(), you're ready to allocate and enqueue the buffers. This process is different than in Chapter 4. For recording, you sent empty buffers to the queue and received filled buffers in the callback. In the playback case, the situation is reversed: You get empty buffers in the callback and need to fill them with audio to be played. That leads to an important consideration here in main(): You don't only need to allocate the buffers; you need to fill them with real data because the queue will start by playing whatever you have primed it with. So how do you get real data into the first three buffers? You can call the callback method with the newly created buffers, as seen in Listing 5.10.

Listing 5.10   **Allocating and Enqueuing Playback Buffers**

```
AudioQueueBufferRef    buffers[kNumberPlaybackBuffers];
player.isDone = false;
player.packetPosition = 0;
int i;
for (i = 0; i < kNumberPlaybackBuffers; ++i)
{
    CheckError(AudioQueueAllocateBuffer(queue,
                                        bufferByteSize,
                                        &buffers[i]),
        "AudioQueueAllocateBuffer failed");

    MyAQOutputCallback(&player, queue, buffers[i]);

    if (player.isDone)
        break;
}
```

As in the recording example, you create new buffers with AudioQueueAllocate Buffer(), passing in the queue, the buffer size, and a pointer to receive the created buffer. Then you fill the buffer by manually calling your yet-to-be-written callback. You might wonder why you're not enqueuing the buffers in this loop. Your callback will have to do because the queue will be sending it drained buffers to fill and enqueue. You can count on that enqueuing behavior here, too.

The callback also must check to see whether it has exhausted all the audio in the file. If so, it sets the isDone variable in the MyPlayer struct. If that happens when you're priming the queue, stop filling buffers—there's no more data available for them. Of course, that would happen for only a tiny file, less than 1.5 seconds (3 buffers × 0.5 seconds each).

Starting the Playback Queue

At this point, the audio queue has three buffers of audio data ready to play. You can now start the queue with `AudioQueueStart()`, as shown in Listing 5.11. As it starts playing, the queue plays the contents of each buffer and calls the callback function `MyAQOutputCallback()` to refill the buffer with new audio from the file. The `main()` function doesn't need to do anything here but wait for the end of the audio.

Listing 5.11   **Starting the Playback Audio Queue**

```
CheckError(AudioQueueStart(queue,
                           NULL),
           "AudioQueueStart failed");

printf("Playing...\n");
do
{
    CFRunLoopRunInMode(kCFRunLoopDefaultMode,
                       0.25,
                       false);
} while (!player.isDone);
```

When this loop exits, you're done reading audio from the file. However, some buffers in the queue might still have data to be played out. With three 0.5-second buffers, continuing playback for another 2 seconds ensures that everything in the queue gets played. Listing 5.12 provides this wait.

Listing 5.12   **Delaying to Ensure Queue Plays Out Buffered Audio**

```
CFRunLoopRunInMode(kCFRunLoopDefaultMode, 2, false);
```

When you're done, Listing 5.13 cleans up the queue as before, by stopping the queue and cleaning up the queue and the audio file.

Listing 5.13   **Cleaning Up the Audio Queue and Audio File**

```
    player.isDone = true;
    CheckError(AudioQueueStop(queue,
                              TRUE),
               "AudioQueueStop failed");
    AudioQueueDispose(queue, TRUE);
    AudioFileClose(player.playbackFile);
    return 0;
}
```

That finishes the `main()` function. As before, you created a queue, allocated and enqueued some buffers, and started the queue. Again, you've set aside a few to-dos: handling the magic cookie and calculating a buffer size, and writing the callback that reads audio from the file and puts it in a buffer. Let's move on to tackle these issues.

Playback Utility Functions

The `main()` function depends on three convenience functions. The first, `CheckError()`, is the same as in Chapter 4, and you probably already copied it over.

Handling the Magic Cookie

As in the recording example, you need to attend to the magic cookie, an opaque block of data that represents encoding-specific values that can't be represented in the `AudioStreamBasicDescription`. When you open the audio file, you can get the file's magic cookie (if any) as a property of the file. Listing 5.14 reads the cookie from the file, and then sets it as a property of the playback queue so that the queue has everything it needs to know about the audio you will be sending to it.

Listing 5.14 **Copying Magic Cookie from Audio File to Audio Queue**

```
static void MyCopyEncoderCookieToQueue(AudioFileID theFile,
                                       AudioQueueRef queue ) {
    UInt32 propertySize;
    OSStatus result = AudioFileGetPropertyInfo (theFile,
                                kAudioFilePropertyMagicCookieData,
                                &propertySize,
                                NULL);
    if (result == noErr && propertySize > 0)
    {
        Byte* magicCookie = (UInt8*)malloc(sizeof(UInt8) * propertySize);
        CheckError(AudioFileGetProperty (theFile,
                                kAudioFilePropertyMagicCookieData,
                                &propertySize,
                                magicCookie),
                "Get cookie from file failed");
        CheckError(AudioQueueSetProperty(queue,
                                kAudioQueueProperty_MagicCookie,
                                magicCookie,
                                propertySize),
                "Set cookie on queue failed");
        free(magicCookie);
    }
}
```

This is exactly the reverse of the cookie copier from the recording example in Chapter 4. This time, you get the cookie property from the file and set it on the queue. At this point, you're probably getting comfortable with getting and setting properties in the various Core Audio APIs, right?

Calculating Buffer Size and Expected Packet Count

The last utility function is one to help figure out a buffer size for your queue, which also tells you how many packets you can expect to read into each buffer. As was the case with recording, this is the hairiest part of the code, so Listing 5.15 presents the entire function, followed by discussion of its key points.

Listing 5.15   **Calculating Buffer Size and Maximum Number of Packets That Can Be Read into the Buffer**

```
void CalculateBytesForTime (AudioFileID inAudioFile,
                            AudioStreamBasicDescription inDesc,
                            Float64 inSeconds,
                            UInt32 *outBufferSize,
                            UInt32 *outNumPackets)
{
    UInt32 maxPacketSize;                                      // 1
    UInt32 propSize = sizeof(maxPacketSize);
    CheckError(AudioFileGetProperty(inAudioFile,
                            kAudioFilePropertyPacketSizeUpperBound,
                            &propSize,
                            &maxPacketSize),
            "Couldn't get file's max packet size");

    static const int maxBufferSize = 0x10000;                 // 2
    static const int minBufferSize = 0x4000;                  // 2

    if (inDesc.mFramesPerPacket) {                            // 3
        Float64 numPacketsForTime = inDesc.mSampleRate /
                            inDesc.mFramesPerPacket * inSeconds;
        *outBufferSize = numPacketsForTime * maxPacketSize;
    } else {                                                  // 4
        *outBufferSize = maxBufferSize > maxPacketSize ?
                        maxBufferSize : maxPacketSize;
    }

    if (*outBufferSize > maxBufferSize &&                     // 5
        *outBufferSize > maxPacketSize)
        *outBufferSize = maxBufferSize;
```

Listing 5.15   **Continued**

```
    else {
        if (*outBufferSize < minBufferSize)
            *outBufferSize = minBufferSize;
    }
    *outNumPackets = *outBufferSize / maxPacketSize;           // 6
}
```

Now let's step through the code to see what's going on. Start with the `// 1` comment and follow along with the numbered paragraphs that follow:

1. You first get the maximum packet size for the file's encoding type, which is available from the audio file property `kAudioFilePropertyPacketSizeUpperBound`.

2. You set up two constants as fail-safe values: a `maxBufferSize` of 64 KB and a `minBufferSize` of 16 KB.

3. If the ASBD tells how many frames are in a packet, calculating the buffer size is simple: You can calculate how many packets elapse in the given number of seconds and multiply that by the maximum packet size to get a sufficiently large buffer.

4. On the other hand, if you don't have an `mFramesPerPacket` value, you need to pick an arbitrarily "large enough" value, which is the greater of `maxBufferSize` and `maxPacketSize`. In the absolute worst case, at least the buffer will be large enough to hold one packet.

5. The second `if-else` applies a few boundary checks. If the calculated buffer size (`outBufferSize`) is larger than both the `maxBufferSize` and the `maxPacketSize`, you clamp it to the `maxBufferSize`. You also must check to see that it's not smaller than the `minBufferSize`.

6. Finally, with an `outBufferSize` calculated, you can divide it by the `maxPacketSize` to figure out how many packets can be safely read from the file on each callback.

This completes the utility functions. Assuming that you stubbed out the callback function `MyAQOutputCallback()`, the program should now compile. Of course, it won't do anything interesting yet—the callback doesn't yet provide the crucial step: reading data from the file and sending it to the queue.

The Playback Audio Queue Callback

You've done a lot of setup work to make it easier for the callback function to do its business. All you need to do here is read packets from the file and write them to the queue. But that's harder than it looks, thanks to having to allocate appropriately sized data buffers and figure out how many packets you can safely read on each pass. Nevertheless, you're ready to go, so start by casting the user data object back to the `MyPlayer` struct, as in Listing 5.16.

Listing 5.16   Header for Audio Queue Callback and Casting of User Info Pointer

```
static void MyAQOutputCallback(void *inUserData,
                               AudioQueueRef inAQ,
                               AudioQueueBufferRef inCompleteAQBuffer)
{
    MyPlayer *aqp = (MyPlayer*)inUserData;
    if (aqp->isDone) return;
```

Note

If you set the `isDone` flag, you should return without doing any work. This keeps you from trying to read past the end of the file. You actually set `isDone` later in the callback function.

Next, use `AudioFileReadPackets()` to read from the file. This call, shown in Listing 5.17, provides the following information:

- The file to read from
- A cache flag
- A pointer to receive the number of bytes actually read
- A pointer to a buffer to hold packet descriptions
- The index of the first packet you want to read
- A pointer to a maximum number of packets to read (which will be replaced by the number of packets actually read when the function returns)
- A pointer to a buffer to receive the audio data

Listing 5.17   Reading Packets from Audio File

```
UInt32 numBytes;
UInt32 nPackets = aqp->numPacketsToRead;
CheckError(AudioFileReadPackets(aqp->playbackFile,
                                false,
                                &numBytes,
                                aqp->packetDescs,
                                aqp->packetPosition,
                                &nPackets,
                                inCompleteAQBuffer->mAudioData),
           "AudioFileReadPackets failed");
```

You did some work in `main()`, which, in turn, depended on `CalculateBytesFor Time()` to set up the `packetDescs` buffer, but its purpose bears repeating: In variable bit rate codecs, this array of packet descriptions makes it possible to parse the audio data that you read into mAudioData. The queue wouldn't be capable of finding and decoding the packets without the data this array provides. On the other hand, for constant bit rate codecs, the packet descriptions aren't needed and the packetDescs pointer is null.

As a result of calling AudioFileReadPackets(), a block of audio data is read into the buffer's mAudioData and an array of packet descriptions (if needed) are read into the MyPlayer struct's packetDescs, whose length is copied into the pointer nPackets.

If you successfully read any audio data, you can now enqueue it for playback, via Listing 5.18.

Listing 5.18   **Enqueuing Packets for Playback**

```
if (nPackets > 0)
{
    inCompleteAQBuffer->mAudioDataByteSize = numBytes;
    AudioQueueEnqueueBuffer(inAQ,
                            inCompleteAQBuffer,
                            (aqp->packetDescs ? nPackets : 0),
                            aqp->packetDescs);
    aqp->packetPosition += nPackets;
}
```

Notice that the AudioFileReadPackets() call reads the audio data directly into the AudioQueueBufferRef provided by the callback's parameter. All you need to do to perform AudioQueueEnqueueBuffer() is to provide the packet descriptions array, if any, which you read into the MyPlayer struct. After you've queued the audio for playback, you advance the packetPosition so that the next AudioFileReadPackets() gets the next set of packets from the file.

On the other hand, what if AudioFileReadPackets() didn't get any packets? Listing 5.19 takes that as a sign that you have reached the end of the file.

Listing 5.19   **Stopping Audio Queue Upon Reaching End of File**

```
    else
    {
        CheckError(AudioQueueStop(inAQ,
                                  false),
                   "AudioQueueStop failed");
        aqp->isDone = true;
    }
}
```

There's a subtle difference in this use of AudioQueueStop() compared to its use in the last chapter: the second variable is false for the player but was true for the recorder. This parameter, inImmediate, determines whether the queue should stop processing immediately. Stopping the queue immediately was fine for the recorder, but it's not fine for playback. When you reach the end of the file, you might have up to a second and a half of audio still in the queue being processed. You don't want to cut that off, so you must allow the queue to play through its remaining buffers. Recall that you put a 2-second delay in `main()` to put off disposing the queue, which is enough time for the queue to fully play out.

Now that you've completed the callback function, you have a complete audio queue player ready to go. Build and run to listen to Core Audio play your specified audio file.

Features and Limits of Queue-Based Playback

So what else can you do with a playback audio queue? Chapter 4 mentioned the level-metering properties (`kAudioQueueProperty_EnableLevelMetering`, `kAudioQueueProperty_CurrentLevelMeter`, and `kAudioQueueProperty_CurrentLevelMeterDB`), which can provide a visible level meter of the power level of the audio you're playing (or perhaps some other sort of visualization).

Along with properties, audio queues support *parameters*. In Core Audio, the difference between properties and parameters is that properties are generally used to set up a software object (an audio file, audio queue, audio unit, and so on) and have values that can be of any type. By contrast, parameters typically represent values of interest to the end user and might change while the object is being used. Parameters are always floating-point numbers. Audio queues support a single parameter—and only for playback—but it's a good one: `kAudioQueueParam_Volume`. This parameter can be set in the range from `0.0` (total silence) to `1.0` (maximum volume, although still constrained by the overall system volume). It's fairly straightforward to add a volume control to your audio player when you have a GUI: You can use an `NSSlider` (or a `UISlider` on iOS) with a range of `0.0` to `1.0`; when its value changes, your event-handling code just resets the queue's `kAudioQueueParam_Volume` to the new slider value.

The example in this chapter plays audio from a file, but you could use the queue for different kinds of audio applications as well; it's just a matter of changing where the samples you provide to the queue come from. For example, you could use the square-, sawtooth-, or sine-wave generator code in Chapter 2, "The Story of Sound," to fill the sample buffer in the callback (you'd need to make other changes, of course, such as setting the queue's format to LPCM). Or, if you wanted to build a net radio client, you would use a networking framework (Cocoa's URL Loading System, Core Services' `CFNetwork`, or even BSD sockets) to get a stream of data from a server and then use the Audio File Stream Services API to generate packets from that stream, which you could then send to the queue.

The Audio Queue does a lot for you that isn't immediately obvious, such as quietly handling decompression from encoded formats such as AAC to the PCM stream actually needed at Core Audio's lower levels. It also eliminates threading concerns that will become apparent in later chapters: By default, your callbacks are performed on one of the queue's internal threads instead of on Core Audio's real-time threads that prohibit blocking calls. Put another way, it's okay for a queue callback to perform a potentially lengthy call such as reading from a file, even though that's not okay in an audio unit call-back (see Chapters 7, "Audio Units: Generators, Effects, and Rendering," and 8, "Audio Units: Input and Mixing").

But as Audio Queue giveth, Audio Queue also taketh away. Think about the fact that the program uses three buffers of 0.5 seconds each. This means the program has a maximum latency of at least 1.5 seconds: When an audio sample is read from the drive, the user won't hear it until all the buffers already in the queue and all the samples in the current buffer are played out. You can mitigate this by using smaller buffers (try changing the buffer size in the example from 0.5 to a smaller value), but the penalty is more frequent callbacks. Still, the nature of using a queue of buffers inherently introduces latency. For many applications, that's fine: The user doesn't know when the samples came off the hard drive or over the network. But if you're creating an application in which sound is created in direct response to user actions, as is the case with games and virtual instruments, you might want to opt for the lower latencies offered by audio units (Chapters 7 and 8) or OpenAL (Chapter 9, "Positional Sound").

Summary

So that's playback with an audio queue. In some ways, it's similar to recording with a queue: You allocate some buffers, enqueue them, and receive them back in a callback function when it's time for your application to do something with them. But as you worked through the example, you saw that the playback case is different in a lot of ways, most significantly in the degree to which you're responsible for managing the memory needed for the array of packet descriptions that the audio file reads into. Another big difference is that you can stop the recording buffer immediately when you're done with it, but for playback, you must delay for a few seconds to let any audio currently in the queue's buffers play out.

As mentioned in the last section, an Audio Queue takes care of encoding and decoding compressed formats. For example, in the last chapter, you indicated that you wanted to record into AAC, and that's what you got in your callbacks, which you then wrote to the file. But it's not as if the microphone picked up data already in AAC; the queue must have done the compression for you. Similarly, in this chapter, you can read a file encoded with any codec that Core Audio understands, hand the bytes to Audio Queue, and get the audio played out. As with input from the mic, output to the speakers can *only* be PCM, so clearly, you're picking up a compressed-to-PCM decoding for free by using the queue.

Now, what if you had some audio in an encoded format and you wanted to work with its PCM representation in some way (say, to run the raw samples through some kind of analysis), but you didn't necessarily want to play it? Or what if you just wanted to convert a file from one format to another? You wouldn't want to have to create an audio queue just to pick up the bonus of the decoding. Fortunately, you don't have to. Audio conversion has its own distinct API. In the next chapter, you'll see how to use it to do your own format conversions.

6

Conversion

Chapter 2, "The Story of Sound," discussed the difference between audio file formats (.mp3, .aif, .caf, and so on) and stream formats (LPCM, AAC, and so on). The last few chapters focused on the stream formats of the audio that you either recorded or played back. Audio Queue was a big help here because it handled the conversion from LPCM to and from encodings such as AAC.

But what happens when you're interested only in that conversion? If you wanted to compress some LPCM data to AAC, you wouldn't want to have to play it through an audio queue. You should rightly expect that there are APIs for doing these kinds of conversions directly.

Core Audio provides several approaches for converting between formats. This chapter starts by looking at Core Audio's command-line utility, afconvert, which provides a convenient converter utility and gives an idea of the scope of Core Audio's support for many file formats and codecs. Next, you'll look at Audio Converter Services, an API in the Audio Toolbox framework that converts buffers of audio between encodings in memory. The example converts an encoded file to an LPCM equivalent. To do this, you read from a source file, convert, and write to the target file. Because you often use conversion services in concert with file I/O, the chapter concludes by rewriting the example with Extended Audio File Services, which combines file I/O and audio conversion into a single step.

The afconvert Utility

Core Audio provides /usr/bin/afconvert, a command-line utility for converting between file formats and audio encodings. You can get help on its basic use with the --help flag:

```
$ afconvert --help
Usage:
afconvert [option...] input_file [output_file]
    Options may appear before or after the direct arguments.
```

```
    If output_file is not specified, a name is generated
    programmatically and the file is written into the same
    directory as input_file.
afconvert input_file [-o output_file [option...]]...
    Output file options apply to the previous output_file.
    Other options may appear anywhere.

General options:
[...]
```

The help text is quite long and doesn't even describe all the various supported formats. To see those, you need to use either the `--help-formats` or the `-hf` flags. When you ask for the formats, you'll see each file format described by its name, its recognized filename extensions, and the possible data formats. The data formats are either four-character codes or all-capital-letter strings that describe an LPCM format by its endianness, value type, and sample size in bits (in a format described in `afconvert`'s help text). For example, consider the WAVE format:

```
'WAVE' = WAVE (.wav)
          data_formats: UI8 LEI16 LEI24 LEI32 LEF32 LEF64 'ulaw'
                        'alaw'
```

This file format can work with six LPCM formats (unsigned 8-bit samples and little-endian ints and floats at various bit depths), along with the very old μ-law and α-law encodings. Compare this to the MP3 file format, which can contain only MP3 data:

```
'MPG3' = MPEG Layer 3 (.mp3, .mpeg, .mpa)
          data_formats: '.mp3'
```

On the other hand, the Core Audio Format (`.caf`) is a more or less universal container, capable of holding any data format that Core Audio itself supports. Look at all the formats it supports:

```
'caff' = Apple CAF (.caf)
          data_formats: '.mp1' '.mp2' '.mp3' 'QDM2' 'QDMC' 'Qclp'
                        'Qclq' 'aac ' 'aach' 'aacl' 'alac' 'alaw'
                        'dvi8' 'ilbc' 'ima4' I8 BEI16 BEI24 BEI32
                        BEF32 BEF64 LEI16 LEI24 LEI32 LEF32 LEF64
                        'ms\x00\x02' 'ms\x00\x11' 'ms\x001' 'samr'
                        'ulaw'
```

If you want to try `afconvert`, go into Terminal and use the `cd` command to change to a directory with a file you want to convert, such as an album directory in your iTunes

Music folder.[1] Let's assume you have a music file encoded with AAC or MP3 and you want to decompress it to LPCM. To use `afconvert`, you need to provide a source file, conversion settings, and an output file. To keep things simple, we'll just convert the data format to 16-bit little-endian ints. You specify the data format with the `-d` argument, so the command will look like this:

```
$ afconvert "My Song Name.m4a" -d LEI16 output.caf
```

This command creates `output.caf`, which you can then play with QuickTime Player or iTunes, or just preview by selecting it in the Finder and pressing the spacebar. With QuickTime or iTunes, you should be able to do a Get Info (⌘-I) to inspect the data format and verify that you actually get 16-bit little-endian integer LPCM in your output file, as in Figure 6.1. Notice also that the use of the CAF file format was inferred by the filename extension of the target file; if you had specified `output.aif`, then `afconvert` would have created an AIFF file instead.

Figure 6.1   Inspecting the output.caf file created by afconvert

A number of other specifiers described by the `--help` output enable you to change various properties, including these:

- The number of channels in your output file (when converting stereo to mono, for example)
- The sample rate or overall bit rate
- The quality or other properties on encoders that support them

Because `afconvert` is a command-line utility, it is highly useful for converting multiple files, often as part of a shell script, makefile, or other automated process.

---

[1] You can speed up this process by typing `cd<space>` in Terminal and then using the Finder to locate the folder you want to navigate to and drag it to the Terminal window. The full path to the folder appears in your command line—for example, `cd /Users/cadamson/Music/iTunes/ iTunes\ Music/Podcasts/MacBreak\ Weekly`.

Using Audio Converter Services

What if you want to include audio conversion in your own application? For that, you need to make your own calls to Audio Converter Services. Following Core Audio conventions, this C API groups its functions with a common prefix. If you type "AudioConverter" into the Xcode documentation search field, you should see about ten matching functions and a handful of `structs` and types. Among these, you may be able to pick out some lifecycle functions for creating and destroying converters, including `AudioConverterNew()`, `AudioConverterReset()`, and `AudioConverterDispose()`. You might also find property setters and getters and two functions that perform conversions, including `AudioConverterConvertBuffer()` and `AudioConverterFill ComplexBuffer()`. A look at the former shows that it is appropriate only for PCM-to-PCM conversions. To convert to or from compressed formats, you'll want to understand `AudioConverterFillComplexBuffer()`.

Looking at the documentation for `AudioConverterFillComplexBuffer()`, you need to provide six parameters:

- A previously created `AudioConverterRef`, which is the converter "object" itself
- A callback function that conforms to `AudioConverterComplexInputDataProc` and provides the input data for the conversion
- A user data pointer
- The maximum size of the output buffer, as a packet count
- A pointer to an output buffer, where the converted data is received
- A pointer to an array of packet descriptions, if needed for the output buffer (if converting to a variable bit rate format)

Some of this should seem familiar after the audio queue chapters, particularly the array of packet descriptions that goes hand-in-hand with the buffer of audio data that the converter produces. What's surprising is the need for a callback: Instead of passing in the data to convert, you pass in a callback function pointer, which is called repeatedly to provide data to convert until the converted buffer is full. Take a look at the `AudioConverterComplexInputDataProc` that defines the callback, and you'll find that it takes the following:

- A reference to the `AudioConverterRef` that is requesting data to convert
- The minimum number of packets the converter wants
- A pointer to a buffer to fill with input data
- A pointer to populate with an array of `AudioStreamPacketDescriptions`, if needed by the format
- A user-data pointer

For the first example in this chapter, you'll duplicate what we were able to do with afconvert: convert an encoded file, such as an MP3 or AAC song from the iTunes Library, in a .caf container file. You'll need to use Audio File Services to read data from one file, do a conversion on some of its packets in memory, and write the result to another file.

Create a new command-line tool in Xcode, add the AudioToolbox framework, and sketch out the program with #pragma marks and the known function headers, as shown here in Listing 6.1.

Listing 6.1   **Outline of an Audio Converter Program**

```
#include <AudioToolbox/AudioToolbox.h>

#pragma mark user data struct
// Insert Listing 6.2 here

#pragma mark utility functions
// Insert Listing 4.2 here
// Insert Listings 6.7-6.15 here

#pragma mark converter callback function
OSStatus MyAudioConverterCallback(AudioConverterRef inAudioConverter,
                UInt32 *ioDataPacketCount,
                AudioBufferList *ioData,
                AudioStreamPacketDescription **outDataPacketDescription,
                void *inUserData)
{
}

#pragma mark main function
int    main(int argc, const char *argv[])
{
    // Open input file
    // Insert Listing 6.3 here

    // Get input format
    // Insert Listing 6.4 here

    // Set up output file
    // Insert Listing 6.5 here

    // Perform conversion
    // Insert Listing 6.6 here

}
```

As with the examples in Chapters 4, "Recording," and 5, "Playback," trust us when we present the user data struct. In your own programs, you'll find yourself adding to and removing from this struct as you figure out what data your callback functions need. For the sake of simplicity, we're skipping ahead and giving you the struct up front in Listing 6.2.

Listing 6.2 **User Info Struct for Audio Converter Program**

```
typedef struct MyAudioConverterSettings
{
    AudioStreamBasicDescription inputFormat;
    AudioStreamBasicDescription outputFormat;

    AudioFileID                 inputFile;
    AudioFileID                 outputFile;

    UInt64                      inputFilePacketIndex;
    UInt64                      inputFilePacketCount;
    UInt32                      inputFilePacketMaxSize;
    AudioStreamPacketDescription *inputFilePacketDescriptions;

    void *sourceBuffer;

} MyAudioConverterSettings;
```

In this struct, you keep track of the data formats (as `AudioStreamBasic Descriptions`) of the input and output streams and references to the input and output files. You also have a counter of the current packet you're reading, the total number of packets in the input file, the maximum size of an input packet, and a pointer to an array of `AudioStreamPacketDescriptions`, which you read from the input file every time you read in more data (which goes into `sourceBuffer`).

Setting Up Files for Conversion

Let's set up the file stuff in `main()`, in preparation for the calls to Audio Converter Services. Because this doesn't directly involve the converter APIs, covering it moves pretty quickly.

First, copy over the `CheckError()` convenience function (Listing 4.2) that you've been using for the last few chapters. Then, at the top of the file, `#define` the full path to the file you want to convert. This is probably an MP3 or AAC in your iTunes Library, or maybe it's just an audio file on your desktop, if you want to keep the path simpler.

```
#define kInputFileLocation    CFSTR("/Insert/Path/To/Audio/File.xxx")
```

The `main()` function in Listing 6.3 starts by allocating a `MyAudioConverterSettings` and opening an `AudioFileID` for the input file, saving the `AudioFileID` to the settings struct.

Listing 6.3   Creating a MyAudioConverterSettings Struct and Opening a Source Audio File for Conversion

```
int    main(int argc, const char *argv[])
{
    MyAudioConverterSettings audioConverterSettings = {0};
    CFURLRef inputFileURL =
      CFURLCreateWithFileSystemPath(kCFAllocatorDefault,
                                    kInputFileLocation,
                                    kCFURLPOSIXPathStyle,
                                    false);
    CheckResult (AudioFileOpenURL(inputFileURL,
                                  kAudioFileReadPermission,
                                  0,
                                  &audioConverterSettings.inputFile),
                "AudioFileOpenURL failed");
    CFRelease(inputFileURL);
```

With the input file opened, you want to get an AudioStreamBasicDescription from it so that you know the format of the source audio. You've done this before; you just call AudioFileGetProperty() to retrieve the kAudioFilePropertyData Format, as in Listing 6.4.

Listing 6.4   Getting ASBD from an Input Audio File

```
UInt32 propSize = sizeof(audioConverterSettings.inputFormat);
CheckResult (AudioFileGetProperty(audioConverterSettings.inputFile,
                                  kAudioFilePropertyDataFormat,
                                  &propSize,
                                  &audioConverterSettings.inputFormat),
            "Couldn't get file's data format");
```

You want two more properties: the total number of packets in the source file and the size of the largest possible packet. The former lets you know how many reads to perform, and the latter enables you to allocate a suitably large buffer for AudioFileReadPackets(). Listing 6.5 shows how to get these properties.

Listing 6.5   Getting Packet Count and Maximum Packet Size Properties from Input Audio File

```
// get the total number of packets in the file
propSize = sizeof(audioConverterSettings.inputFilePacketCount);
CheckResult (AudioFileGetProperty(audioConverterSettings.inputFile,
                                  kAudioFilePropertyAudioDataPacketCount,
                                  &propSize,
                                  &audioConverterSettings.inputFilePacketCount),
            "couldn't get file's packet count");
```

Listing 6.5 **Continued**

```
// get size of the largest possible packet
propSize = sizeof(audioConverterSettings.inputFilePacketMaxSize);
CheckResult(AudioFileGetProperty(audioConverterSettings.inputFile,
                            kAudioFilePropertyMaximumPacketSize,
                            &propSize,
                            &audioConverterSettings.inputFilePacketMaxSize),
            "couldn't get file's max packet size");
```

Now you're ready to set up the output file. Create an ASBD to describe a common LPCM format: 16-bit samples, two channels (stereo), big-endian packed samples— nothing fancy.[2] Pass this ASBD to `AudioFileCreateWithURL()` to create the file and get an `AudioFileID` (see Listing 6.6).

Listing 6.6 **Defining Output ASBD and Creating an Output Audio File**

```
audioConverterSettings.outputFormat.mSampleRate = 44100.0;
audioConverterSettings.outputFormat.mFormatID = kAudioFormatLinearPCM;
audioConverterSettings.outputFormat.mFormatFlags =
    kAudioFormatFlagIsBigEndian | kAudioFormatFlagIsSignedInteger |
    kAudioFormatFlagIsPacked;
audioConverterSettings.outputFormat.mBytesPerPacket = 4;
audioConverterSettings.outputFormat.mFramesPerPacket = 1;
audioConverterSettings.outputFormat.mBytesPerFrame = 4;
audioConverterSettings.outputFormat.mChannelsPerFrame = 2;
audioConverterSettings.outputFormat.mBitsPerChannel = 16;

CFURLRef outputFileURL =
    CFURLCreateWithFileSystemPath(kCFAllocatorDefault,
                            CFSTR("output.aif"),
                            kCFURLPOSIXPathStyle,
                            false);
CheckResult (AudioFileCreateWithURL(outputFileURL,
                            kAudioFileAIFFType,
                            &audioConverterSettings.outputFormat,
                            kAudioFileFlags_EraseFile,
                            &audioConverterSettings.outputFile),
            "AudioFileCreateWithURL failed");
CFRelease(outputFileURL);
```

Now you have the input and output files set up and you have everything ready to start reading, converting, and writing. Because this is a complex process, you'll put it into

---

[2] You filled out all the fields for a PCM format such as this one in Listing 2.1. Also, Listing 3.1 covers the contents of the ASBD.

its own function, Convert(), which you'll write next. For now, Listing 6.7 finishes main() by calling this Convert() and cleaning up the files when finished.

Listing 6.7   Calling a Convenience Convert() Function and Closing Files

```
    fprintf(stdout, "Converting...\n");
    Convert(&audioConverterSettings);

cleanup:
    AudioFileClose(audioConverterSettings.inputFile);
    AudioFileClose(audioConverterSettings.outputFile);
    return 0;
}
```

Calling Audio Converter Services

You're now ready to write the Convert() function, which goes in the utility functions part of the program, before being called from main(). This function is all about making a repeated set of calls to AudioConverterFillComplexBuffer(), which fills a packet buffer that can then be sent to AudioFileWritePackets(). What's strange about this arrangement is that you don't explicitly do any file reading in this function; that's provided by a callback function that you have to write next.

First, create an audio converter via the AudioConverterNew() function, shown in Listing 6.8, that takes as parameters ASBDs to describe the input and output formats and a pointer to populate with a new AudioConverterRef.

Listing 6.8   Creating an Audio Converter

```
void Convert(MyAudioConverterSettings *mySettings)
{
    // Create the audioConverter object
    AudioConverterRef     audioConverter;
    CheckResult (AudioConverterNew(&mySettings->inputFormat,
                                   &mySettings->outputFormat,
                                   &audioConverter),
                 "AudioConveterNew failed");
```

Next, you have some math to do: You have to figure out how big of a packet descriptions array you need to allocate. You had a similar task in Chapter 5; again, you have to juggle multiple contingencies here: whether the format is variable bit rate, whether the buffer is big enough to hold at least one packet, and so on. You address the hard case—determining the sizes for the variable bit rate—first, in Listing 6.9.

Listing 6.9   Determining the Size of a Packet Buffers Array and Packets-per-Buffer Count for Variable Bit Rate Data

```
UInt32 packetsPerBuffer = 0;
UInt32 outputBufferSize = 32 * 1024; // 32 KB is a good starting point
UInt32 sizePerPacket = mySettings->inputFormat.mBytesPerPacket;
if (sizePerPacket == 0)
{
    UInt32 size = sizeof(sizePerPacket);
    CheckResult(AudioConverterGetProperty(audioConverter,
                      kAudioConverterPropertyMaximumOutputPacketSize,
                      &size,
                      &sizePerPacket),
              "Couldn't get kAudioConverterPropertyMaximumOutputPacketSize");

    if (sizePerPacket > outputBufferSize)
        outputBufferSize = sizePerPacket;

    packetsPerBuffer = outputBufferSize / sizePerPacket;
    mySettings->inputFilePacketDescriptions = (AudioStreamPacketDescription*)
        malloc(sizeof(AudioStreamPacketDescription) * packetsPerBuffer);
}
```

The variable bit rate data is signaled by an ASBD with `mBytesPerPacket == 0`. In this case, you get the maximum packet size from the converter. You then compare this to the default buffer size (32 KB) and take the larger of the two, which ensures that you can fit at least one packet in the buffer. You then need to attend to the packet descriptions array; you can determine how many packets will fit in the buffer and allocate enough space to hold this many `AudioStreamPacketDescriptions`.

For constant bit rate data, things are a lot easier. You don't need to handle any `AudioStreamPacketDescriptions`, and calculating the `packetsPerBuffer` count is trivial. Listing 6.10 shows this "else" case.

Listing 6.10   Determining Packets per Buffer for Constant Bit Rate Data

```
else
{
    packetsPerBuffer = outputBufferSize / sizePerPacket;
}
```

In either case, you know how big of a buffer you need to receive the converted audio data, so you `malloc()` it next, in Listing 6.11.

Listing 6.11   Allocating Memory for Audio Conversion Buffer

```
UInt8 *outputBuffer = (UInt8 *)malloc(sizeof(UInt8) * outputBufferSize);
```

With buffers and a converter allocated, you're ready to start a `while` loop to convert and write data. You need one more local variable outside the loop, though: a counter to remember where you are in the output file. Listing 6.12 sets this up.

Listing 6.12   **Loop to Convert and Write Data**

```
UInt32 outputFilePacketPosition = 0;
while(1)
{
```

`AudioConverterFillComplexBuffer()` fills an `AudioBufferList` struct with its converted data, so you need to get one ready for the call (see Listing 6.13).

Listing 6.13   **Preparing an AudioBufferList to Receive Converted Data**

```
AudioBufferList convertedData;
convertedData.mNumberBuffers = 1;
convertedData.mBuffers[0].mNumberChannels =
    mySettings->inputFormat.mChannelsPerFrame;
convertedData.mBuffers[0].mDataByteSize = outputBufferSize;
convertedData.mBuffers[0].mData = outputBuffer;
```

Now you're ready to make the `AudioConverterFillComplexBuffer()` call, in Listing 6.14. You use a pointer to pass in the number of packets you're prepared to receive; in return, you get the number of converted packets that are actually in the buffer.

Listing 6.14   **Calling AudioConverterFillComplexBuffer()**

```
UInt32 ioOutputDataPackets = packetsPerBuffer;
OSStatus error = AudioConverterFillComplexBuffer(audioConverter,
                    MyAudioConverterCallback,
                    mySettings,
                    &ioOutputDataPackets,
                    &convertedData,
                    (mySettings->inputFilePacketDescriptions ?
                     mySettings->inputFilePacketDescriptions : nil));
if (error || !ioOutputDataPackets)
{
    break;     // This is the termination condition
}
```

As described in the overview, this call takes an `AudioConverterRef`, a function pointer to the yet-to-be-written callback function, a "user data" pointer for the callback, the packets count, a pointer to receive the converted data, and a pointer to receive an array of packet descriptions (which is `nil` for constant bit rate formats because they don't need or use packet descriptions).

If the call fails or `0` packets are converted, you `break` out of the `while` loop. However, if it succeeds, you can write the converted data to the output file, as in Listing 6.15.

Listing 6.15   Writing Converted Data to an Audio File

```
// Write the converted data to the output file
CheckResult (AudioFileWritePackets(mySettings->outputFile,
                        FALSE,
                        ioOutputDataPackets,
                        NULL,
                        outputFilePacketPosition /
                            mySettings->outputFormat.mBytesPerPacket,
                        &ioOutputDataPackets,
                        convertedData.mBuffers[0].mData),
            "Couldn't write packets to file");
outputFilePacketPosition += (ioOutputDataPackets *
                        mySettings->outputFormat.mBytesPerPacket);
```

In `AudioFileWritePackets()`, you provide the file to write to, a cache setting, the size to write, an array of packet descriptions (`NULL` here because the PCM output file is a constant bit rate and, therefore, doesn't use packet descriptions), the index of the first packet to write, the number of packets being written, and the buffer of audio data that you received from the audio converter.

After the packets are written to the file, you update the output position by multiplying the number of packets written by the number of bytes in each PCM packet.

And that's it for the converter loop.

The `while(1)` will `break` when `AudioConverterFillComplexBuffer()` gets `0` packets. Then the loop exits. All you need to do at that point is dispose of the converter, as in Listing 6.16.

Listing 6.16   Cleaning up the Audio Converter

```
    }
    AudioConverterDispose(audioConverter);
}
```

Aside from juggling a bunch of parameters between the two important functions and another round of figuring out the right buffer size, interacting with the converter isn't too rough. All that's left now is to implement the `MyAudioConverterCallback` that supplies input packets to the converter.

Implementing the Converter Callback

In the `Convert()` function, you did some buffer-sizing math that didn't appear to have an immediate payoff: for variable bit rate input files, you allocated memory for a packet descriptions array, but you passed `NULL` for the packet descriptions in `AudioFileWrite Packets()`. What's up with that, you might wonder? You don't need packet descriptions for output because the output format is constant bit rate PCM. The packet descriptions are used when you read from the input file in the converter's callback function.

Begin the callback in Listing 6.17 by casting the user data object back to the `MyAudioConverterSettings` struct. You also can take this opportunity to zero out the audio buffer, in case a failure occurs and you don't read into it successfully.

Listing 6.17 Converter Callback Function Header, User Info Cast, and Zeroing of Audio Buffers

```
OSStatus MyAudioConverterCallback(AudioConverterRef inAudioConverter,
                 UInt32 *ioDataPacketCount,
                 AudioBufferList *ioData,
                 AudioStreamPacketDescription **outDataPacketDescription,
                 void *inUserData)
{
    MyAudioConverterSettings *audioConverterSettings =
        (MyAudioConverterSettings *)inUserData;

    ioData->mBuffers[0].mData = NULL;
    ioData->mBuffers[0].mDataByteSize = 0;
```

> **Note**
>
> It's okay to assume that the `AudioBufferList` has only one buffer; it was created in the `while()` loop of `Convert()`.

Next, you'll do some math in Listing 6.18 to figure out how many packets to read. `ioDataPacketCount` initially is the `packetsPerBuffer` that you calculated in `Convert()`, but as you reach the end of the input, fewer packets than this might be left. Reset `ioDataPacketCount` to the number of packets left to read. If this is 0, let the callback return without reading any data. This condition breaks the `while()` loop back in `Convert()`.

Listing 6.18 Determining How Many Packets Can Be Read from the Input File

```
// If there are not enough packets to satisfy request,
// then read what's left
if (audioConverterSettings->inputFilePacketIndex + *ioDataPacketCount >
            audioConverterSettings->inputFilePacketCount)
```

Listing 6.18   Continued

```
    *ioDataPacketCount = audioConverterSettings->inputFilePacketCount -
            audioConverterSettings->inputFilePacketIndex;

if(*ioDataPacketCount == 0)
    return noErr;
```

If you do have data to read, you need to prepare a buffer to receive the audio data. You `free()` any old buffer that the settings struct points to (because any data in it has already been consumed by this point) and allocate a new buffer large enough to hold the number of packets you intend to read. Listing 6.19 shows this operation.

Listing 6.19   Allocating a Buffer to Fill and Convert

```
if (audioConverterSettings->sourceBuffer != NULL)
{
    free(audioConverterSettings->sourceBuffer);
    audioConverterSettings->sourceBuffer = NULL;
}

audioConverterSettings->sourceBuffer = (void *)calloc(1, *ioDataPacketCount *
                        audioConverterSettings->inputFilePacketMaxSize);
```

With the buffer allocated, you're ready to read some packets from the source file into it, as in Listing 6.20.

Listing 6.20   Reading Packets into the Conversion Buffer

```
UInt32 outByteCount = 0;
OSStatus result = AudioFileReadPackets(audioConverterSettings->inputFile,
                        true,
                        &outByteCount,
                        audioConverterSettings->inputFilePacketDescriptions,
                        audioConverterSettings->inputFilePacketIndex,
                        ioDataPacketCount,
                        audioConverterSettings->sourceBuffer);
#ifdef MAC_OS_X_VERSION_10_7
    if (result == kAudioFileEndOfFileError && *ioDataPacketCount) result = noErr;
#else
    if (result == eofErr && *ioDataPacketCount) result = noErr;
#endif
 else if (result != noErr) return result;
```

The `if-else` here handles a case you haven't seen yet. If the read takes you to the end of the file, the return value of `AudioFileReadPackets()` is an end-of-file constant—either `kAudioFileEndOfFileError` on Lion or `eofErr` on earlier versions of OS X. Either way, although it's not noErr, it's also not an error that's so bad you want to cause an early termination. If you reach the end of file and get a nonzero packet count, act like it wasn't an error by resetting the result to noErr.

Finally, in Listing 6.21, you update the MyAudioConverterSettings struct with the new position in the source file and the data you read from the source file (and its size), both of which go into the AudioBufferList member. If you received an array of packet descriptions, you also copy those over to the struct. The converter needs the data, data size, and packet descriptions array (if any) to parse the audio data and perform its conversion.

Listing 6.21   **Updating the Source File Position and AudioBuffer Members with the Results of Read**

```
audioConverterSettings->inputFilePacketIndex += *ioDataPacketCount;
ioData->mBuffers[0].mData = audioConverterSettings->sourceBuffer;
ioData->mBuffers[0].mDataByteSize = outByteCount;
if (outDataPacketDescription)
    *outDataPacketDescription =
        audioConverterSettings->inputFilePacketDescriptions;
return result;
}
```

Whew! That was a lot of work, but now you're done!

To review:

- In main(), you opened an input file, inspected its format and packet-sizing proper-ties, and created an output file with a PCM format of your choice.

- You then wrote a Convert() function to repeatedly set up an AudioBufferList to transfer packets and call AudioConverterFillComplexBuffer() to convert the compressed input data to PCM. You then wrote this to the output file with AudioFileWritePackets().

- The input to the converter comes from a callback function that you wrote, which repeatedly read from the input file and provided audio data and packet descriptions to a passed-in AudioBufferList.

Does it work? Build and run to find out.

Assuming that you've provided a valid path to an audio file that Core Audio can read, the program takes a few seconds to perform the conversion and writes an uncompressed AIFF file to output.aif. The file is relative to wherever the executable is on the filesys-tem, which means you should find it in your project's derived data folder. Figure 6.2 shows the path to output.aif, in this case.

With this PCM data in an AIFF container, many applications on your Mac are capa-ble of playing this audio file, including QuickTime Player and iTunes. You can even drop it into a Safari or Firefox window, or just select it and press spacebar in the Finder to lis-ten to it.

Figure 6.2　Location of output.aif as written
by CH06_AudioConverter program

Converting with Extended Audio File Services

You might be discouraged by having to do so much work with buffer wrangling and callbacks just to convert audio from one format to another. You might even be tempted to just call /usr/bin/afconvert with an NSTask if you ever need to do a conversion from within a Cocoa application.

Part of the problem comes from the fact that you're operating at a fairly low level—and with Core Audio's very modular APIs, at that. The Audio Converter is meant to work with any source, such as files, network audio, or even synthesized audio that's created entirely within your own code. As a result, the common interface for exchanging data has to be data buffers, and that can mean a lot of buffer wrangling.

Still, the most common case for audio format conversion involves files on at least one end, and Core Audio does have an API to make this easier. The Extended Audio File Services combine the Audio File Services and Audio Converter Services into a simplified API. Specifically, they combine file I/O and format conversion into a single action. You read from a compressed file and get buffers of uncompressed PCM. Going in the other direction, you send PCM to a write function, and compressed audio is written to the filesystem.

Let's start by making a copy of the example program so you can simplify it by using an Extended Audio File. Create a new command-line tool and add AudioToolbox.framework to the target, as always.

Listing 6.22 shows an outline of the revised program. Notice that there's no stubbed-out callback function. With Extended Audio Files, you don't need one.

Listing 6.22   **Outline of an Extended Audio File Converter Program**

```
#include <AudioToolbox/AudioToolbox.h>

#pragma mark user data struct
    // Insert Listing 6.23 here

#pragma mark utility functions
    // Insert Listing 4.2 here
    // Insert Listings 6.28-6.34 here

#pragma mark main function
int    main(int argc, const char *argv[])
{
    // Open input file
    // Insert Listing 6.24 here

    // Set up output file
    // Insert Listings 6.25-6.26 here

    // Perform conversion
    // Insert Listing 6.27 here

}
```

As always, start by copying over the CheckError() function from Listing 4.2.

Now look at the state struct. You don't need this for passing state to a callback function because you won't be using any callback APIs; still, it is a convenient container to pass data from main() to Convert(). So what do you need to pass? With ExtAudioFile, the format you're converting from becomes completely opaque. All the fields in the struct that dealt with the input file's data format, packet sizing, and so on can thus all go away. All you need are the PCM ASBD and references to the two files, as shown in Listing 6.23.

Listing 6.23   **Struct for Passing ASBD and Audio File References**

```
typedef struct MyAudioConverterSettings
{
    AudioStreamBasicDescription outputFormat;
    ExtAudioFileRef             inputFile;
    AudioFileID                 outputFile;
} MyAudioConverterSettings;
```

Notice that the input file is no longer an AudioFileID, but rather an ExtAudioFileRef. The two are not interchangeable; any code you reuse from the first example requires a different function call anytime you find a reference to inputFile.

Let's move on to `main()`, where you start by creating an extended audio file, in Listing 6.24.

Listing 6.24   **Opening an Extended Audio File for Input**

```
int    main(int argc, const char *argv[])
{
    MyAudioConverterSettings audioConverterSettings = {0};

    // Open the input with ExtAudioFile
    CFURLRef inputFileURL =
        CFURLCreateWithFileSystemPath(kCFAllocatorDefault,
                                      kInputFileLocation,
                                      kCFURLPOSIXPathStyle,
                                      false);
    CheckResult(ExtAudioFileOpenURL(inputFileURL,
                                    &audioConverterSettings.inputFile),
                "ExtAudioFileOpenURL failed");
```

Here the change is to create `inputFile` with `ExtAudioFileOpenURL()` instead of `AudioFileOpenURL()`. This is where using extended audio files starts to pay off. Previously, we needed to inspect the input format and get the packet count and maximum packet size. With extended audio files, you have no visibility into the source data format, so you don't have to worry about any of that.

Let's move on to defining the `outputFormat` and creating the output file, in Listing 6.25, which is exactly as before.

Listing 6.25   **Setting the Output Audio Data Format and Creating an Audio File**

```
audioConverterSettings.outputFormat.mSampleRate = 44100.0;
audioConverterSettings.outputFormat.mFormatID = kAudioFormatLinearPCM;
audioConverterSettings.outputFormat.mFormatFlags =
    kAudioFormatFlagIsBigEndian | kAudioFormatFlagIsSignedInteger |
    kAudioFormatFlagIsPacked;
audioConverterSettings.outputFormat.mBytesPerPacket = 4;
audioConverterSettings.outputFormat.mFramesPerPacket = 1;
audioConverterSettings.outputFormat.mBytesPerFrame = 4;
audioConverterSettings.outputFormat.mChannelsPerFrame = 2;
audioConverterSettings.outputFormat.mBitsPerChannel = 16;

CFURLRef outputFileURL = CFURLCreateWithFileSystemPath(kCFAllocatorDefault,
                                                       CFSTR("output.aif"),
                                                       kCFURLPOSIXPathStyle,
                                                       false);
CheckResult (AudioFileCreateWithURL(outputFileURL,
                                    kAudioFileAIFFType,
                                    &audioConverterSettings.outputFormat,
```

Listing 6.25   **Continued**

```
                                    kAudioFileFlags_EraseFile,
                                    &audioConverterSettings.outputFile),
                    "AudioFileCreateWithURL failed");
CFRelease(outputFileURL);
```

The PCM `outputFormat` is the only format you care about here because you don't know the `inputFormat`. You do want the extended audio file to produce audio in this same PCM format, though. To do that, set the property `kExtAudioFileProperty_ClientDataFormat` on the extended audio file, as shown in Listing 6.26. In a sense, this is how you say, "When you convert the data, this is the format I'd like to receive."

> **Note**
>
> One important restriction exists: The client data format *must* be PCM. In other words, you can't use a single `ExtAudioFile` to convert between two compressed formats.

Listing 6.26   **Setting the Client Data Format Property on an Extended Audio File**

```
CheckResult(ExtAudioFileSetProperty(audioConverterSettings.inputFile,
                                    kExtAudioFileProperty_ClientDataFormat,
                                    sizeof (AudioStreamBasicDescription),
                                    &audioConverterSettings.outputFormat),
                    "Couldn't set client data format on input ext file");
```

At this point, you're done with `main()`, except to call the `Convert()` function as before and to clean up the files. Listing 6.27 wraps up the `main()` function.

Listing 6.27   **Calling the Conversion Function and Closing the Extended Audio File**

```
    fprintf(stdout, "Converting...\n");
    Convert(&audioConverterSettings);

cleanup:
    ExtAudioFileDispose(audioConverterSettings.inputFile);
    AudioFileClose(audioConverterSettings.outputFile);
    return 0;
}
```

> **Note**
>
> Notice that here you replaced the `inputFile`'s `AudioFileClose()` with a call to `ExtAudioFileDispose()`.

Reading and Converting with Extended Audio Files

Now let's move on to `Convert()`, which actually performs the conversion.

You still need to do a little math to figure out a suitable buffer size to receive data from the input file (the extended audio file) and write to the output file (a plain old audio file, as before). Fortunately, this is massively simplified by the fact that you are dealing with only PCM in the code. Constant bit rate here means that you no longer have to deal with packet descriptions. Plus, allocating the data buffer is much easier because you don't have to do any calculations with a maximum packet size; all packets are exactly one frame each in PCM. Listing 6.28 shows the calculation.

Listing 6.28   **Determining the Size of the Output Buffer and Packets-per-Buffer Count**

```
void Convert(MyAudioConverterSettings *mySettings)
{
    // 32 KB is a good starting point
    UInt32 outputBufferSize = 32 * 1024;
    UInt32 sizePerPacket = mySettings->outputFormat.mBytesPerPacket;
    UInt32 packetsPerBuffer = outputBufferSize / sizePerPacket;
```

This is the same code as before, but you no longer need to check whether `sizePerPacket` is 0; that would indicate a variable bit rate format. Instead, in Listing 6.29, you can easily allocate the data buffer and set up an output file index, as before.

Listing 6.29   **Allocating a Buffer for Receiving Data from an Extended Audio File**

```
UInt8 *outputBuffer = (UInt8 *)malloc(sizeof(UInt8) * outputBufferSize);
UInt32 outputFilePacketPosition = 0; // In bytes
```

You go into a `while` loop to read data from the extended audio file and write it to the output file. You still work with an `AudioBufferList` to provide data to `AudioFileWritePackets()`, but fortunately, an `ExtAudioFileRead()` populates that same struct for you. So in Listing 6.30, let's set one up at the top of the `while`.

Listing 6.30   **Starting Read-Convert-Write Loop and Setting Up an AudioBuffer**

```
while(1)
{
    AudioBufferList convertedData;
    convertedData.mNumberBuffers = 1;
    convertedData.mBuffers[0].mNumberChannels =
        mySettings->outputFormat.mChannelsPerFrame;
    convertedData.mBuffers[0].mDataByteSize = outputBufferSize;
    convertedData.mBuffers[0].mData = outputBuffer;
```

When you used the converter directly, you did the file reading in a callback. There's no need for that when using an extended audio file, so you need a local variable to tell the extended audio file how many frames (equal to packets in this PCM case) you're willing to accept. The function updates this function, to report back how many frames were read. Listing 6.31 performs the actual read from the file.

Listing 6.31   **Reading and Converting with ExtAudioFileRead()**

```
UInt32 frameCount = packetsPerBuffer;
CheckResult(ExtAudioFileRead(mySettings->inputFile,
                             &frameCount,
                             &convertedData),
           "Couldn't read from input file");
```

As you can see, `ExtAudioFileRead()` is a simple call: It takes just an `ExtAudioFileRef`, a pointer to the number of frames to read, and a pointer to an `AudioBufferList` to receive the read-and-converted data.

If you didn't read any frames, you're at the end of the file and can exit `Convert()`, as shown in Listing 6.32.

Listing 6.32   **Terminating If No Frames Are Read**

```
if (frameCount == 0) {
   printf ("Done reading from file\n");
   return;
}
```

If you did read some frames, you write them to the output file as before, with `AudioFileWritePackets()`. Listing 6.33 shows how to write the data.

Listing 6.33   **Writing Converted Audio Data to an Output File**

```
CheckResult (AudioFileWritePackets(mySettings->outputFile,
                                   FALSE,
                                   frameCount,
                                   NULL,
                                   outputFilePacketPosition /
                                    mySettings->outputFormat.mBytesPerPacket,
                                   &frameCount,
                                   convertedData.mBuffers[0].mData),
           "Couldn't write packets to file");
```

You use `frameCount` here where we previously had to count packets. Again, this is okay because you're dealing with only PCM data in the program, and PCM packets *always* contain only one frame.

After you've performed the write, you update the output file's write position and end both the `while` loop and the `Convert()` function, as shown in Listing 6.34.

Listing 6.34   **Advancing Output File Write Position**

```
outputFilePacketPosition +=
    (frameCount * mySettings->outputFormat.mBytesPerPacket);
}
}
```

Build and run this application. You should find that it functions *exactly* the same as the earlier version. When the authors tested the same source file with each version of the program, the generated `output.aif` files were identical, byte for byte. The big win, of course, is that the extended audio file code is about 100 lines shorter. It's also vastly easier to follow because the code works only with PCM, freeing you from the variable bit rate complexities of working with packet description arrays.

Summary

If you've worked through both of these examples, you might wonder why you'd ever want to deal with using Audio Converter Services directly. The answer is obvious: Extended Audio File Services help you only when you're dealing with files. For example, if you find yourself dealing with some other media, such as sending data across a network, an `ExtAudioFile` won't help you.

Fortunately, some other Core Audio APIs also do conversion automatically—you picked up encoded-to-PCM conversion for free when using Audio Queue Services in the previous two chapters—so direct use of the conversion APIs is often optional. It's important to know *how* they work when you encounter those cases, but if you can get Core Audio to do format conversion for you, go ahead and let it do the heavy lifting for you.

At this point, you've made use of much of the Audio Toolbox: In the process of covering Audio Queue Services and Audio Converter Services, you've also been able to work with Audio File Services and Extended Audio File Services. By combining these APIs in different ways—perhaps by looking in the documentation for properties and functions they offer that you haven't exercised directly in the chapters—you can perform a lot of interesting work on audio captured from the mic, played over speakers and headphones, or read from and written to files.

In the next few chapters, you've move further down in the Core Audio stack to the low-level audio "engine" APIs, Audio Units, and OpenAL. These offer lower latency than the audio queue but sometimes require more work on your part to handle issues such as threading and format conversion. In many cases, you'll build on what you've learned so far as you go further into Core Audio. For example, because you usually have to use

PCM in Audio Units and OpenAL, you could push the audio from an MP3 file through those engines by doing an `ExtAudioFileRead()` to convert to PCM in memory. And by now, you're probably getting comfortable with Core Audio's conventions such as property getting and setting and working with callbacks. You'll see these traits even in the low, low level that is Audio Units.

III

Advanced Audio

Audio Units: Generators, Effects, and Rendering

Chapter 1, "Overview of Core Audio," roughly divvied up Core Audio's frameworks into two general groupings: "engine" APIs that process streams of audio through the system, and "helper" APIs that work with audio in different ways, such as performing format conversions or doing file I/O. In Chapters 4, "Recording," and 5, "Playback," you worked with the Audio Queue, a higher-level audio engine API, and in Chapter 9, "Positional Sound," you'll look at OpenAL, which is also a high-level engine. Audio Queues and OpenAL are both implemented atop Audio Units, the code that's arguably the heart of Core Audio. Audio Units are as close to the metal as most developers will ever need to get, and they afford opportunities to work with raw audio that are simply not practical at higher levels of abstraction.

These next two chapters dig deep into Audio Units by showing the many ways you can work with audio at this level. You'll be able to synthesize audio, perform effects on audio streams, capture from the mic, mix multiple streams, and combine all these abilities. You'll also see how working at this level shares many commonalities with higher-level Core Audio programming, but introduces some new responsibilities for handling memory and latency that you will need to keep in mind as you unleash your newfound powers.

Where the Magic Happens

Welcome to the lowest level of functionality Core Audio application developers need: the Audio Units API. The only levels lower than this on Mac OS X are primarily of interest to programmers creating audio device drivers. On iOS, it is not even possible to go lower than Audio Units.

With Audio Units, we get very close to the metal, particularly if your original point of reference before reading this book was passing a file URL to NSSound or AVAudioPlayer and forgetting about it. Here at the audio unit level, you work with callbacks that are called dozens or even hundreds of times a second, with raw samples that can be inspected and manipulated on the fly, and with latencies that are so short they might as well be instantaneous.

Here at the heart of Core Audio, you can do things that are not practical, or simply not possible, with the higher-level abstractions. For example, if you wanted to mix two sounds and play them simultaneously, there is no straightforward way to do so with Audio Queues—you would have to use two queues, and even then, the API offers little control over their mutual synchronization. If you wanted to perform an effect on sound going through a queue, you would have to decompress to PCM first (because encoded formats are generally not receptive to the kinds of mathematical trickery used in creating audio effects), perform your effect, and then stuff the result into the queue—and even then, it wouldn't be easy to chain multiple effects together or share your work with others.

With the power of Audio Units comes a lot of challenge. Most readers likely will find these the hardest chapters of the book and find Audio Units the hardest API to put to work successfully because the nature of Audio Units requires your code to take on so much responsibility. That's why we take our time here: We have prepared four example projects to exercise a lot of different features of Audio Units.

How Audio Units Work

You got an overview of Audio Units in Chapter 3, "Audio Processing with Core Audio" (in the section "Processing Audio with Audio Units"), as a means of explaining the essential model of Core Audio's audio processing model. Of course, that was four chapters ago, so let's refresh.

An audio unit is a software object that performs some sort of work on a stream of audio. For example, some units create streams of audio, others perform effects (such as echoes and reverbs), and a few special units interface with the audio hardware to capture audio from input devices or play it out to devices such as headphones or speakers. To use Audio Units, you create and set up the units you need, create connections between them, and then tell them to start processing.

This arrangement is analogous to audio hardware in the real world. For example, imagine that you have an electric guitar, a distortion box, and an amplifier. None of these does much by itself. But you could connect the guitar (a sound generator) via a cable to the input of the distortion box (which performs audio effects) and then connect its output to the input of the amp (an output device). Flip on the power, strum a G major, and suddenly it's "Hello, Cleveland!"

Notice the purpose of each piece of hardware in this example. As with these analog devices, audio units are grouped into types that describe their purpose. Core Audio provides the following types of audio units:

- **Generator units:** Create a stream of audio from some source, such as files, the network, or memory.
- **Instrument units:** Similar to generator units, produce a stream of synthesized audio from MIDI data.

- **Mixer units:** Combine multiple streams into one or more streams. The mix can be performed in two dimensions (for stereo panning) or in a simulated three-dimensional sound field.

- **Effect units:** Perform some sort of digital signal processing on a stream, usually producing an audible effect such as a reverb, a pitch change, noise filtering, and so on.

- **Converter units:** Perform transformations that are generally not meant to deliver user-audible effects. These include units to convert between different flavors of PCM (to change sample rate or bit depth, for example), adjust playback speed, and so on.

- **Output units:** Interface with audio input and/or output hardware, enabling you to capture audio from input devices and play it out to output devices. The name is somewhat of a misnomer because these are potentially input/output units.

The last of these, the output units, are critical because they make all the other units do their work. As mentioned in Chapter 3, Core Audio works with a pull model: Software objects that need audio samples pull data from other objects. You saw this model at work with Audio Queues: When you start the queue, it starts pulling data from your code by means of callbacks. In Audio Units, an output unit pulls either from another unit or by making a callback into your code.

Consider the earlier analogy, with a guitar, distortion box, and amplifier represented as a generator, effect, and output unit, respectively. In the Core Audio model, the amplifier pulls audio from the effects box, which, in turn, pulls it from the guitar. The physical analogy fails somewhat here—you can't pull sound from the guitar strings—but what if the guitar had a tiny buffer of the last few milliseconds of audio it produced? In that case, the guitar could provide those samples to the effects box on demand, which would apply its distortion effect and hand the changed samples to the amplifier, which would start blasting them out. As the amp used up its samples, it would pull another buffer from the effects box, which would pull from the guitar, and so on.

From here, you can see the possibilities. Imagine that you have not just a guitar, but a whole band—but still only the one amp. In this case, you would need a mixer box with one output going into the amp. Into its first input, you could put the original distortion box and guitar chain; then you could put the singer's mic into another input, the keyboard in another input, and so on. When the amp needed audio, it would pull from the mixer box, which, in turn, would pull from all of its inputs and mix them together, providing the resulting mixed samples to the amp.

Now imagine that you introduce more units into this arrangement wherever it makes sense, such as putting an effect unit after the singer's microphone or putting mics on multiple backup singers, using a second mixer unit to mix their streams into one and delivering that stream to the final mix. The possibilities really are endless.

Sizing Up the Audio Units

Audio units are created by specifying their type, subtype, and manufacturer. You get these by digging through the documentation or the AUComponent.h file. To whet your appetite, Tables 7.1 through 7.7 list every system-provided audio unit on Mac OS X 10.6 (Snow Leopard).

Table 7.1   **Audio Unit Subtypes for Generator Units (Type kAudioUnitType_Generator)**

Subtype	Description
kAudioUnitSubType_ScheduledSoundPlayer	Schedules audio to be played a specified time.
kAudioUnitSubType_AudioFilePlayer	Plays audio from a file.
kAudioUnitSubType_NetReceive	Receives network audio from a corresponding kAudioUnitSubType_NetSend unit on another host or in another application.

Table 7.2   **Audio Unit Subtypes for Instrument Units (Type kAudioUnitType_MusicDevice)**

Subtype	Description
kAudioUnitSubType_DLSSynth	Multi-timbral music synthesizer that accepts MIDI commands. Works with DLS or SoundFont formats.

Table 7.3   **Audio Unit Subtypes for Mixer Units (Type kAudioUnitType_Mixer)**

Subtype	Description
kAudioUnitSubType_MultiChannelMixer	Mixes any number of single- or multi-channel input buses to one output bus.
kAudioUnitSubType_StereoMixer	Mixes any number of mono or stereo input buses to one stereo output.
kAudioUnitSubType_3DMixer	Mixes any number of mono or stereo input buses. Mono inputs can be panned with 3D parameters. Output is one bus of 2 to 8 channels.
kAudioUnitSubType_MatrixMixer	Mixes any number of input and output buses, with any number of channels per bus. Supports highly configurable mapping of inputs and outputs.

Table 7.4   **Audio Unit Subtypes for Panner Units (Type kAudioUnitType_Panner)**

Subtype	Description
kAudioUnitSubType_SphericalHeadPanner	Uses "spherical head" model to produce stereo output.
kAudioUnitSubType_VectorPanner	Uses pan between adjacent channels in 3D space to create surround output.
kAudioUnitSubType_SoundFieldPanner	Uses "sound field" model to produce stereo output.
kAudioUnitSubType_HRTFPanner	Uses head-related transfer function to produce stereo output.

Table 7.5   **Audio Unit Subtypes for Effect Units (Type kAudioUnitType_Effect)**

Subtype	Description
kAudioUnitSubType_Delay	Adds a digital delay effect.
kAudioUnitSubType_LowPassFilter	Cuts off frequencies above a certain value; lower frequencies pass through.
kAudioUnitSubType_HighPassFilter	Cuts off frequencies below a certain value; higher frequencies pass through.
kAudioUnitSubType_BandPassFilter	Cuts off frequencies above and below certain values; frequencies in between pass through.
kAudioUnitSubType_HighShelfFilter	Provides a "treble" control effect.
kAudioUnitSubType_LowShelfFilter	Provides a "bass" control effect.
kAudioUnitSubType_ParametricEQ	Equalizer effect that allows setting of amplitude (gain), center frequency, and bandwidth.
kAudioUnitSubType_GraphicEQ	Effect that offers a 10- or 31-band graphic equalizer effect.
kAudioUnitSubType_PeakLimiter	Effect to reduce the amplitude of specific frequencies that spike over a certain level.
kAudioUnitSubType_DynamicsProcessor	Adjusts dynamic range of audio, compressing and expanding when source is beyond certain thresholds.
kAudioUnitSubType_MultiBandCompressor	Effect to compress four frequency ranges ("bands"), with difference settings for each.
kAudioUnitSubType_MatrixReverb	Produces a highly-configurable reverb ("echo") effect.

Table 7.5   **Continued**

Subtype	Description
kAudioUnitSubType_SampleDelay	A digital delay like kAudioUnitSubType_Delay, except that the delay is specified as a sample count rather than a number of seconds.
kAudioUnitSubType_Pitch	Effect to alter the pitch of the source audio.
kAudioUnitSubType_AUFilter	Adjusts gain for five bands of frequencies.
kAudioUnitSubType_NetSend	Sends audio across network or between applications; corresponding generator unit subtype is kAudioUnitSubType_NetReceive.
kAudioUnitSubType_Distortion	Produces a distortion effect.
kAudioUnitSubType_RogerBeep	Produces a beep, similar to someone releasing the button of a walkie-talkie, when the input level drops below a given threshold for a specified amount of time.

Table 7.6   **Audio Unit Subtypes for Converter Units (Type kAudioUnitType_ FormatConverter)**

Subtype	Description
kAudioUnitSubType_AUConverter	Uses Audio Converter Services to perform LPCM conversions (sampler rate, bit depth, etc.)
kAudioUnitSubType_Varispeed	Changes playback speed. Pitch-shifts audio as a result: faster playback raises pitch, slower playback lowers it.
kAudioUnitSubType_TimePitch	Similar to Varispeed, but allows for independent control of playback speed and pitch, allowing it to play faster without changing pitch.
kAudioUnitSubType_DeferredRenderer	Pulls input from a thread other than the caller.
kAudioUnitSubType_Splitter	Splits one input bus into two identical output buses.
kAudioUnitSubType_Merger	Merges two input buses into one output bus.

Table 7.7   **Audio Unit Subtypes for Output Units (Type kAudioUnitType_Output)**

Subtype	Description
kAudioUnitSubType_GenericOutput	Output unit not tied to audio hardware; can be used to perform software rendering of audio in connected units.
kAudioUnitSubType_SystemOutput	Output to the device used for alerts and other UI sounds
kAudioUnitSubType_DefaultOutput	Output to the device selected in System Preferences:Sound
kAudioUnitSubType_HALOutput	Input from and output to any supported audio device.

As you can see, there's an extraordinary amount of audio processing power just in the Apple-provided units. Also keep in mind that applications such as Logic and Garage Band and third-party developers can provide additional own audio units to further extend Core Audio's capabilities.[1]

Some of the features provided by audio units are quite advanced and used for specific audio needs. For now, we'll take things slow and add complexity (and more units) as we go.

Your First Audio Units

Let's begin with a fairly basic exercise to get started with Audio Units. You'll use one generator unit and one output unit: one unit to create sound and another to deliver it to the user.

For this example, we want an output unit and a generator unit. For output, Table 7.7 shows a DefaultOutputUnit that sends samples to the output device specified in the "Sound" system preference. That's just what we need. As for generators, Table 7.1 offers AUAudioFilePlayer, described as "a unit that obtains and plays audio data from a file." Let's use that one.

Figure 7.1 shows the units and their relationships graphically.

Drawing a graph of units in this way this leads to an important helper API: Audio Processing Graph Services, often just called AUGraph. Although you can work with individual audio units, you often need to coordinate the activities of a group of units and their relationships. An AUGraph provides exactly these features. This makes it easy to create connections between audio units—which are wrapped by AUNodes in the graph— and start and stop the entire collection of units at one time. You'll use AUGraphs throughout this chapter, but keep in mind that its use is just a convenience: The calls to the graph and its nodes always have equivalent operations that work on individual units.

[1] Note that most of Apple's "standard" units are not available on iOS. Chapter 10 looks at Audio Units on iOS.

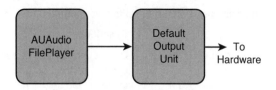

Figure 7.1   Audio Unit graph of a simple file player

To start building this example, create a Command Line Tool project in Xcode. You'll need to add `AudioToolbox.framework`, as always, as well as `AudioUnit.framework`, which contains headers for the audio unit-related functions you'll be using.

Start with a roadmap of the program you need to write. As has been the case in previous chapters, you'll call some convenience routines from `main()` to set things up. At this point, you don't need any callback functions, so you don't need to leave a section for them. Still, it'll be convenient later to put your essential variables (it's so tempting to call them instance variables) in a struct that you can pass to your helpers and later use this struct as a user-info object when you need to start writing callbacks. Listing 7.1 shows the skeleton of the program.

Listing 7.1   **Outline of an Audio Unit-Based File Player Program**

```
#include <AudioToolbox/AudioToolbox.h>

#pragma mark user-data struct
// Insert Listing 7.2 here

#pragma mark utility functions
// Insert Listing 4.2 here
// Insert Listings 7.7 - 7.13 here
// Insert Listings 7.14 - 7.17 here

#pragma mark main function
int     main(int argc, const char *argv[])
{
    // Open the input audio file
    // Get the audio data format from the file
    // Insert Listing 7.3 here

    // Build a basic fileplayer->speakers graph
    // Configure the file player
    // Insert Listing 7.4 here

    // Start playing
    // Sleep until the file is finished
    // Insert Listing 7.5 here
```

Listing 7.1   **Continued**

```
    // Cleanup
    // Insert Listing 7.6 here
}
```

As is often the case, you start off by looking at the members you found needed to be in the struct. Given that you're reading from a file, you might have guessed that you're going to use the Audio File Services and, thus, might want to keep track of your input file as an `AudioFileID`. You also want to figure out the audio format of that file's contents, which you track with an `AudioStreamBasicDescription`. When you have those, you can think about your engine: You have two Audio Units managed by an `AUGraph`. You don't need to pass the output unit between functions, but you do need to pass around the file player unit. Listing 7.2 shows the struct to use.

Listing 7.2   **User Info Struct for Audio Unit File Player**

```
typedef struct MyAUGraphPlayer
{
    AudioStreamBasicDescription inputFormat;
    AudioFileID                 inputFile;

    AUGraph graph;
    AudioUnit fileAU;

} MyAUGraphPlayer;
```

For this program to compile, you need to add `AudioToolbox.framework` and `AudioUnit.framework` to your project.

Building the main() Function

Let's go down to `main()`. First, you need to `#define` a file URL to open, which you can put at the top of the source file (of course, your path will be different):

```
#define kInputFileLocation CFSTR("/Users/cadamson/Desktop/my-favorite-song.m4a")
```

Before you begin `main()`, be sure to copy over the `CheckError()` function from Listing 4.2, as always.

The first thing to do in `main()` is to open an input file and get its data format as an `AudioStreamBasicDescription`, as shown in Listing 7.3. You've done this a few times now, with the Audio Queue player in Chapter 5 (see Listings 5.4 and 5.5) and with the audio converter in Chapter 6, "Conversion" (see Listings 6.4 and 6.5): It's just a one-line call to `AudioFileOpenURL()`, followed by getting `kAudioFilePropertyDataFormat` via `AudioFileGetProperty()`.

Listing 7.3   **Opening an Audio File and Getting Data Format from It**

```
int    main(int argc, const char *argv[])
{
    CFURLRef inputFileURL = CFURLCreateWithFileSystemPath(
                                kCFAllocatorDefault,
                                kInputFileLocation,
                                kCFURLPOSIXPathStyle,
                                false);
    MyAUGraphPlayer player = {0};
// Open the input audio file
    CheckError(AudioFileOpenURL(inputFileURL,
                                kAudioFileReadPermission,
                                0,
                                &player.inputFile),
               "AudioFileOpenURL failed");
    CFRelease(inputFileURL);
// Get the audio data format from the file
    UInt32 propSize = sizeof(player.inputFormat);
    CheckError(AudioFileGetProperty(player.inputFile,
                                    kAudioFilePropertyDataFormat,
                                    &propSize,
                                    &player.inputFormat),
               "Couldn't get file's data format");
```

Next, set up the audio unit graph and the file-playing audio unit. These are big jobs, so let's set them aside for a minute and write them in convenience functions called `CreateMyAUGraph()` and `PrepareFileAU()`, as shown in Listing 7.4.

Listing 7.4   **Calling Convenience Functions to Set up AUGraph and Prepare a File Player Unit**

```
// Build a basic fileplayer->speakers graph
CreateMyAUGraph(&player);

// Configure the file player
Float64 fileDuration = PrepareFileAU(&player);
```

Notice that you need `PrepareFileAU()` to return the file's duration; we need to know how long to keep `main()` around before we let the application terminate. We can calculate that in `PrepareFileAU()` because you have to do some related calculations on the stream format anyway.

After you've created the `AUGraph`, it's a simple matter to start it playing: Call `AUGraphStart()`, as shown in Listing 7.5. Now you don't need to interact with the graph; just let the program sleep until you've played out all the audio.

Listing 7.5   **Starting an AUGraph**

```
// Start playing
CheckError(AUGraphStart(player.graph),
        "AUGraphStart failed");

// Sleep until the file is finished
usleep ((int)(fileDuration * 1000.0 * 1000.0));
```

With the file done, you can close down the AUGraph. This consists of three steps (shown in Listing 7.6), which might make more sense after you've written the function to set up the graph. When you create an AUGraph, you open the graph to create the audio units, initialize it to allocate resources and prepare to stream, and then start it. So at the end of the program, you perform corresponding shutdown steps in reverse order: stop, uninitialize, and close. You also need to close the audio file.

Listing 7.6   **Stopping and Cleaning Up an AUGraph**

```
cleanup:
    AUGraphStop (player.graph);
    AUGraphUninitialize (player.graph);
    AUGraphClose(player.graph);
    AudioFileClose(player.inputFile);

    return 0;
}
```

So that's main(). It's pretty insubstantial—you've just moved the creation of the AUGraph and the file player audio unit to helper functions. Let's deal with those now.

Creating an Audio Unit Graph

Setting up an audio unit graph consists of a series of steps whose order is important. When you create an AUGraph off the top of your head and you get errors, it's often because you've skipped or misordered the steps, leaving your nodes and units either uninitialized or not created at all. The proper order follows:

1. Create the AUGraph.
2. Create nodes.
3. Open the graph.
4. *Optional:* Get audio units from nodes if you need to access any of the units directly.
5. Connect nodes.
6. Initialize the AUGraph.
7. Start the AUGraph.

You begin with the easy step, creating the AUGraph, as shown in Listing 7.7.

Listing 7.7   **Creating an AUGraph**

```
void CreateMyAUGraph(MyAUGraphPlayer *player)
{
    // Create a new AUGraph
    CheckError(NewAUGraph(&player->graph),
               "NewAUGraph failed");
```

Next, you need to create the nodes of the graph. The process for this is a somewhat unusual legacy of the old Component Manager, which dates back to the original MacOS and QuickTime. The Component Manager supports the runtime discovery of software components, which are similar to plug-ins, in that they provide some discrete, classifiable functionality. Components have types and subtypes that indicate their use, along with a manufacturer. It's also possible for multiple components of a given type/subtype/manufacturer combination to be present on an end user's system, so the Component Manager's discovery process is built around matching a component description and iterating over the results until the caller finds a suitable component.

In this case, the component type and subtype for an audio unit are constants defined in the AUComponent.h header file and described in the Audio Unit Component Services documentation. Combining those with a constant to indicate Apple as the manufacturer, you can create a component that matches the default output audio unit, as shown in Listing 7.8.

Listing 7.8   **Creating a Default Output AUGraph Node**

```
// Generate description that matches output device (speakers)
    AudioComponentDescription outputcd = {0};
    outputcd.componentType = kAudioUnitType_Output;
    outputcd.componentSubType = kAudioUnitSubType_DefaultOutput;
    outputcd.componentManufacturer = kAudioUnitManufacturer_Apple;

// Adds a node with above description to the graph
AUNode outputNode;
CheckError(AUGraphAddNode(player->graph,
                          &outputcd,
                          &outputNode),
        "AUGraphAddNode[kAudioUnitSubType_DefaultOutput] failed");
```

In this code, the appearance of the AudioComponentDescription type indicates that you are using the Audio Component Manager semantics, which were introduced in Mac OS X 10.6. For earlier versions of Mac OS X, you need to use the legacy Component

Manager API—but beware that it is deprecated on Snow Leopard and absent on Lion. iOS also uses the newer API and has never supported the older Component Manager.[2]

When you have the component description, you create a new graph node with `AUGraphAddNode()`. At this point, the node merely exists within the graph; it has no connection to other nodes and no real functionality yet. You can go ahead and create your other node, the file player, shown in Listing 7.9.

Listing 7.9   Creating a File Player AUGraph Node

```
// Generate description that matches a generator AU of type:
// audio file player
    AudioComponentDescription fileplayercd = {0};
    fileplayercd.componentType = kAudioUnitType_Generator;
    fileplayercd.componentSubType = kAudioUnitSubType_AudioFilePlayer;
    fileplayercd.componentManufacturer = kAudioUnitManufacturer_Apple;

// Adds a node with above description to the graph
AUNode fileNode;
CheckError(AUGraphAddNode(player->graph,
                          &fileplayercd,
                          &fileNode),
           "AUGraphAddNode[kAudioUnitSubType_AudioFilePlayer] failed");
```

As you can see, the only difference in this code is the type and subtype used in the component description.

These are the only nodes you need for your graph, so you can now open the graph in Listing 7.10.

Listing 7.10   Opening an AUGraph

```
// Opening the graph opens all contained audio units but does
// not allocate any resources yet
CheckError(AUGraphOpen(player->graph),
           "AUGraphOpen failed");
```

Opening the `AUGraph` opens the audio units contained within each of the nodes. Doing this enables you to get and set properties on the units and to create connections between the nodes, but you can't allocate any resources yet.

A node is used only for managing relationships within the graph. All the cool stuff mentioned earlier (processing streams, performing effects, and so on) happen within the audio units themselves. The nodes act like a wrapper around them. If you need to work

---

[2] The later section "Adding Your Code to the Audio Rendering Process" addresses other issues involving the deprecation of the Component Manager.

directly with a unit, you can get the unit from its containing node via
`AUGraphNodeInfo()`, which takes a graph and a node as its first two parameters and
uses its third and fourth parameters to provide pointers to a component description and
the audio unit (you can `NULL` out either of these parameters if you don't want them).
You'll need to configure the file player unit later and tell it which file—and how much
of it—to play, so you should get a pointer to it now (shown in Listing 7.11).

Listing 7.11   **Retrieving an AudioUnit from an AUNode**

```
// Get the reference to the AudioUnit object for the
// file player graph node
CheckError(AUGraphNodeInfo(player->graph,
                           fileNode,
                           NULL,
                           &player->fileAU),
           "AUGraphNodeInfo failed");
```

The `fileAU` is of type `AudioUnit`, which is `typedef`'ed as a `ComponentInstance`
on Mac OS X 10.5 (and, therefore, is compatible with the legacy Component Manager
APIs) and as an `AudioComponentInstance` on version 10.6 and up and on iOS. As
long as your code uses the `AudioUnit` type, the distinction is largely irrelevant and your
source will compile for the various SDKs.

The next step is an important one: You want to connect the file player node to the
output node. With an `AUGraph`, you use a one-line call to `AUGraphConnectNode`
`Input()`, as shown in Listing 7.12.

Listing 7.12   **Connecting Nodes in an AUGraph**

```
// Connect the output source of the file player AU to
// the input source of the output node
CheckError(AUGraphConnectNodeInput(player->graph,
                                   fileNode,
                                   0,
                                   outputNode,
                                   0),
           "AUGraphConnectNodeInput");
```

This function takes five parameters: an `AUGraph`, a source node, a source output number, a destination node, and a destination output number. These numbers refer to the
buses, or *elements*, of the audio units inside the nodes.[3] The idea is that every audio unit
has an arbitrary number of buses running into and out of it. In many cases, there is a

---

[3] The APIs generally use the term *element*, but many Core Audio developers, including ourselves,
find *bus* more descriptive and memorable. We call them *buses* throughout the rest of the book.

single bus that goes through the unit. But in the case of something like a mixer unit, there could be many input buses (numbered 0 through n), and a single output bus. This arrangement is shown in Figure 7.2.

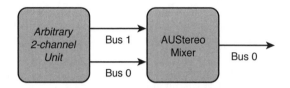

Figure 7.2   Mixing two buses down to one with a mixer unit

The input/output units have a special convention for buses: Bus 0 represents device output, and bus 1 represents device input. In this case, you connect bus 0 (the only one) of the file player unit to bus 0 of the output node to send the audio stream out to the audio hardware.

With the graph created and connections made, you finish the graph setup by initializing the graph via AUGraphInitialize(), as shown in Listing 7.13.

Listing 7.13   **Initializing an AUGraph**

```
    // Now initialize the graph (causes resources to be allocated)
    CheckError(AUGraphInitialize(player->graph),
            "AUGraphInitialize failed");
}
```

Unlike AUGraphOpen(), the initialize step is potentially expensive because it allows units to allocate needed resources such as RAM or file handles. When a graph is initialized, it is potentially ready to be started. In this case, though, you have to do a little more work to set up the file player unit.

Setting Up the File Player Audio Unit

You've created a graph with a file player node connected to a default output node. The only thing left to do is to customize the file player node so that it knows what to play. You have an AudioFileID opened, but you've done nothing to associate the player unit with this file. How do you do that?

This question will go unanswered if you comb through the documentation in Xcode or on the Apple website. Sometimes documentation on constants (such as kAudioUnitSubType_AudioFilePlayer) will give you what you need, but that's not the case here. The only documentation on using the file player unit is a 100-line comment in the AudioUnitProperties.h header file. Yes, *really*. It starts on line 2445 in the 10.6 headers and on line 2487 of the 10.7 headers. Here's an excerpt:

```
#pragma mark AUAudioFilePlayer
/*!
    @enum          Apple AUAudioFilePlayer Property IDs
    @abstract      The collection of property IDs for Apple
                   AUAudioFilePlayer
    @discussion    This audio unit lets you schedule regions
                   of audio files for future playback,
                   with sample-accurate timing.

                   The unit is a subclass of
                   AUScheduledSoundPlayer and inherits all of
                   its behavior. In particular, this unit
                   implements the
                   kAudioUnitProperty_ScheduleStartTimeStamp
                   and kAudioUnitProperty_CurrentPlayTime
                   properties. Instead of scheduling slices
                   (buffers) of audio to be played (via
                   kAudioUnitProperty_ScheduleAudioSlice),
                   however, you schedule regions of audio files
                   to be played. The unit reads and converts
                   audio file data into its own internal
                   buffers. It performs disk I/O on a
                   high-priority thread shared among all
                   instances of this unit within a process.
                   Upon completion of a disk read, the unit
                   internally schedules buffers for playback.
```

Reading through these docs, you can puzzle out how to initialize the file player unit:

- Provide a list of `AudioFileIDs` to play by setting the unit's `kAudioUnitProperty_ScheduledFileIDs` property.

- Define a region to play with the `kAudioUnitProperty_ScheduledFileRegion` property.

- Prime the player by setting the `kAudioUnitProperty_ScheduledFilePrime` property.

- Provide a start time with the `kAudioUnitProperty_ScheduleStartTimeStamp` property.

The last of these is actually inherited from the related `AUScheduledSoundPlayer` unit, so that's even more stealth documentation in the header file to read. Having fun yet?

Nevertheless, you have the information you need to initialize the file player unit in its convenience method. The first step is easy: Just set the scheduled file IDs property to your `AudioFileID`, as shown in Listing 7.14.

Listing 7.14   **Scheduling an AudioFileID with the AUFilePlayer**

```
double PrepareFileAU(MyAUGraphPlayer *player)
{

    // Tell the file player unit to load the file we want to play
    CheckError(AudioUnitSetProperty(player->fileAU,
                                    kAudioUnitProperty_ScheduledFileIDs,
                                    kAudioUnitScope_Global,
                                    0,
                                    &player->inputFile,
                                    sizeof(player->inputFile)),
            "AudioUnitSetProperty[kAudioUnitProperty_ScheduledFileIDs] failed");
```

Notice that `AudioUnitSetProperty()` has similar semantics to the property setters
in previous chapters, such as those for audio files and audio queues. The first two parameters are the unit you're working with and the ID of the property to set, and the last two
are a `void*` to the property value and the size of the value. In between there are two
unique fields: scope and bus. The *scope* identifies what part of the audio unit the property
applies to: input (to the unit), output (from the unit), or global. The *bus* (technically
called an element, but almost always called a bus in practice) refers to a numbered stream
flowing into or out of the unit. In some cases, the scope and/or the bus might not matter. For the scheduled ID property, the scope is global and the bus is meaningless, so you
use `kAudioUnitScope_Global` and 0, respectively.

Next, you schedule a region of the file to play (see Listing 7.15). The stealth documentation states that this requires setting up a `ScheduledAudioFileRegion` structure
and setting that as a property on the audio unit.

Listing 7.15   **Setting a ScheduledAudioFileRegion for the AUFilePlayer**

```
UInt64 nPackets;
UInt32 propsize = sizeof(nPackets);
CheckError(AudioFileGetProperty(player->inputFile,
                                kAudioFilePropertyAudioDataPacketCount,
                                &propsize,
                                &nPackets),
        "AudioFileGetProperty[kAudioFilePropertyAudioDataPacketCount] failed");

// Tell the file player AU to play the entire file
ScheduledAudioFileRegion rgn;
memset (&rgn.mTimeStamp, 0, sizeof(rgn.mTimeStamp));
rgn.mTimeStamp.mFlags = kAudioTimeStampSampleTimeValid;
rgn.mTimeStamp.mSampleTime = 0;
rgn.mCompletionProc = NULL;
rgn.mCompletionProcUserData = NULL;
rgn.mAudioFile = player->inputFile;
```

Listing 7.15   Continued

```
rgn.mLoopCount = 1;
rgn.mStartFrame = 0;
rgn.mFramesToPlay = nPackets * player->inputFormat.mFramesPerPacket;

CheckError(AudioUnitSetProperty(player->fileAU,
                                kAudioUnitProperty_ScheduledFileRegion,
                                kAudioUnitScope_Global,
                                0,
                                &rgn,
                                sizeof(rgn)),
           "AudioUnitSetProperty[kAudioUnitProperty_ScheduledFileRegion] failed");
```

Start by getting the packet count, which enables you to calculate the
ScheduledAudioFileRegion's mFramesToPlay member. The ScheduledFileRegion
contains an AudioTimeStamp structure, which you use to indicate that playback should
begin at time stamp 0.[4] The ScheduledAudioFileRegion structure also enables you to
set up a callback function (along with the typical user info object) that will be called
when the file is fully read from disk and scheduled to play from RAM. You can null out
those fields, as our main() just usleep()s for a set duration instead of expecting a callback. The remaining fields set the AudioFileID to play, specify how many times to loop
through the file, set a starting frame, and establish a count of the number of frames to
play (which you calculate by multiplying the packet count by the frames-per-packet
count). With this structure fully initialized, you can set it as the
kAudioUnitProperty_ScheduledFileRegion property of the file player unit.

A separate property, kAudioUnitProperty_ScheduleStartTimeStamp, tells the
unit when to start playing after the unit (or the graph containing it) has started. A special
value of -1 is defined as meaning "start on the next render cycle," which effectively
means "as soon as possible," instead of matching time stamp values with the
ScheduledAudioFileRegion. For your needs here, Listing 7.16 suffices.

Listing 7.16   Setting the Scheduled Start Time for AUFilePlayer

```
// Tell the file player AU when to start playing (-1 sample time
// means next render cycle)
AudioTimeStamp startTime;
memset (&startTime, 0, sizeof(startTime));
startTime.mFlags = kAudioTimeStampSampleTimeValid;
startTime.mSampleTime = -1;
```

---

[4] The semantics of the starting timestamp are inherited from the AUScheduledSoundPlayer and
are too involved to get into here... the grisly details are in the AudioUnitProperties.h
comments.

Listing 7.16   **Continued**

```
CheckError(AudioUnitSetProperty(player->fileAU,
                                kAudioUnitProperty_ScheduleStartTimeStamp,
                                kAudioUnitScope_Global,
                                0,
                                &startTime,
                                sizeof(startTime)),
           "AudioUnitSetProperty[kAudioUnitProperty_ScheduleStartTimeStamp]");
```

That completes the work of configuring the `AUFilePlayer` audio unit. All that's left is to calculate a playback time in seconds, which the `main()` function uses to determine how long to `usleep()` to allow the file to play out in its entirety, as shown in Listing 7.17.

Listing 7.17   **Calculating File Playback Time in Seconds**

```
    // File duration
    return (nPackets * player->inputFormat.mFramesPerPacket) /
           player->inputFormat.mSampleRate;
}
```

At this point, you can build and run the program; it should play the file from your hard drive and exit when playback is complete.

Now that you've had your first experience with audio units, you might be a little skeptical. After all, you haven't accomplished anything that you couldn't already do with a playback audio queue (as in Chapter 5), although the two approaches have different complexities: Using the queue made you read from the file in callbacks, whereas the file player unit is totally fire-and-forget but involves some drudgery in setting up the scheduled playback time. Still, it's fair to ask, "Where's the win? What's so much better about operating down at the audio unit level?"

In this example, there's not much advantage over just using Audio Queues (or `NSSound` or `AVAudioPlayer`), but you're only getting started. In the next example, you'll start doing things that aren't possible in the higher-level APIs.

Speech and Effects with Audio Units

A few more system-supplied audio units exist than the ones listed in the Apple Core Audio Overview document and Tables 7.1 through 7.7. One that's particularly interesting is a speech synthesis audio unit that ships as part of the Speech Synthesis Manager. Ordinarily, you use this framework by directly calling functions such as `SpeakCFString()`, or even use the Cocoa `NSSpeechSynthesizer` class without worrying about how the sound gets out to the speakers. But by getting the speech synthesizer's audio unit and putting into your own `AUGraph`, you gain the capability to manipulate the sound at will.

For this second example, create another command-line tool project in Xcode. You need to add `AudioToolbox.framework` and `AudioUnit.framework` again, along with `ApplicationServices.framework`, which provides the headers for the Speech Synthesis Manager.

Building Blocks of the Speech Synthesis Graph

You'll build this example in two stages. You'll use an `#ifdef` to write the first version; then you switch to the more elaborate second version. Listing 7.18 shows an outline of what you're going to write.

Listing 7.18   **Outline of a Speech Synthesis Audio Unit Program**

```
#include <AudioToolbox/AudioToolbox.h>
#include <ApplicationServices/ApplicationServices.h>

// #define PART_II

#pragma mark user-data struct
// Insert Listing 7.19 here

#pragma mark utility functions
// Insert Listing 4.2 here

void CreateMyAUGraph(MyAUGraphPlayer *player) {
// Insert Listing 7.21 here
#ifdef PART_II
// Insert Listings 7.24 - 7.26 here
#else
// Insert Listing 7.22 here
#endif
}

// Replace with listing 7.23
void PrepareSpeechAU(MyAUGraphPlayer *player)
{
}

#pragma mark main function
// Replace with listing 7.20
int    main(int argc, const char *argv[])
{
    // Build a basic speech->speakers graph
    // Configure the speech synthesizer
    // Start playing
    // Sleep a while so the speech can play out
    // Cleanup
}
```

The #ifdef-#else-#endif is in the CreateMyAUGraph function, which you'll use to lay out the nodes differently in Parts 1 and 2 (I mean, PART_II) of the exercise.

As usual, you'll use a custom struct to pass your essential pointers. In this example, you want to keep track of your AUGraph and the speech synthesis audio unit. Listing 7.19 shows the fields you'll need for the MyAUGraphPlayer struct.

Listing 7.19   **User Info Struct for Speech Synthesis Audio Unit Program**

```
typedef struct MyAUGraphPlayer
{
    AUGraph graph;
    AudioUnit speechAU;

} MyAUGraphPlayer;
```

Notice that, this time, you aren't interested in an AudioStreamBasicDescription. You could get it as a property of the speech synthesizer unit (specifically, the kAudioUnitProperty_StreamFormat property of bus 0 of its output scope) if you particularly wanted to inspect it, but you don't need to in this case. Moreover, the system audio units all default to a canonical LPCM format that's compatible with one another, meaning that you don't set the stream format properties on your units unless you have a specific need to do so.

You're going to defer all the AUGraph and speech synthesizer setup to utility functions, so the main() function is straightforward. You did most of these tasks in the previous example, so Listing 7.20 has nothing new.

Listing 7.20   **main() Function for Speech Synthesis Audio Unit Program**

```
int    main(int argc, const char *argv[])
{
    MyAUGraphPlayer player = {0};

    // Build a basic speech->speakers graph
    CreateMyAUGraph(&player);

    // Configure the speech synthesizer
    PrepareSpeechAU(&player);

    // Start playing
    CheckError(AUGraphStart(player.graph), "AUGraphStart failed");

    // Sleep a while so the speech can play out
    usleep ((int)(10 * 1000. * 1000.));
```

Listing 7.20   **Continued**

```
cleanup:
    AUGraphStop (player.graph);
    AUGraphUninitialize (player.graph);
    AUGraphClose(player.graph);

    return 0;
}
```

Before starting into the graph, copy over the `CheckError()` function from
Listing 4.2.

Creating a Speech Synthesis AUGraph

Creating a graph requires the same steps as in the example for the file player: Create a
graph, describe and create nodes, open the graph, get units out of the nodes (if you need
to access the units directly), connect the nodes, and initialize the graph. The first few
steps, shown in Listing 7.21, are much like what you did before.

Listing 7.21   **Setting Up AUGraph and AUNodes for Speech Synthesis**

```
void CreateMyAUGraph(MyAUGraphPlayer *player)
{
    // Create a new AUGraph
    CheckError(NewAUGraph(&player->graph),
            "NewAUGraph failed");

    // Generates a description that matches our output
    // device (speakers)
    AudioComponentDescription outputcd = {0};
    outputcd.componentType = kAudioUnitType_Output;
    outputcd.componentSubType = kAudioUnitSubType_DefaultOutput;
    outputcd.componentManufacturer = kAudioUnitManufacturer_Apple;

    // Adds a node with above description to the graph
    AUNode outputNode;
    CheckError(AUGraphAddNode(player->graph,
                            &outputcd,
                            &outputNode),
            "AUGraphAddNode[kAudioUnitSubType_DefaultOutput] failed");

    // Generates a description that will match a generator AU
    // of type: speech synthesizer
    AudioComponentDescription speechcd = {0};
    speechcd.componentType = kAudioUnitType_Generator;
    speechcd.componentSubType = kAudioUnitSubType_SpeechSynthesis;
    speechcd.componentManufacturer = kAudioUnitManufacturer_Apple;
```

Listing 7.21   **Continued**

```
// Adds a node with above description to the graph
AUNode speechNode;
CheckError(AUGraphAddNode(player->graph,
                         &speechcd,
                         &speechNode),
           "AUGraphAddNode[kAudioUnitSubType_SpeechSynthesis] failed");

// Opening the graph opens all contained audio units, but
// does not allocate any resources yet
CheckError(AUGraphOpen(player->graph),
           "AUGraphOpen failed");

// Gets the reference to the AudioUnit object for the
// speech synthesis graph node
CheckError(AUGraphNodeInfo(player->graph,
                           speechNode,
                           NULL,
                           &player->speechAU),
           "AUGraphNodeInfo failed");
```

This is almost identical to the previous example, except that the generator unit is of subtype kAudioUnitSubType_SpeechSynthesis.

What's left is to connect the units (see Listing 7.22). This is the part that you'll change later in this section, so this is where you use the #ifdef to switch the parts of the example that get compiled.

Listing 7.22   **Connecting Units in the Speech Synthesis Graph**

```
#ifdef PART_II
#else
    // Connect the output source of the speech synthesis AU
    // to the input source of the output node
    CheckError(AUGraphConnectNodeInput(player->graph,
                                       speechNode,
                                       0,
                                       outputNode,
                                       0),
               "AUGraphConnectNodeInput");

    // Now initialize the graph (causes resources to be allocated)
    CheckError(AUGraphInitialize(player->graph),
               "AUGraphInitialize failed");

#endif
}
```

Again, this is exactly identical to the previous section: You connect bus 0 of the speech node to bus 0 of the output node, which allows the generated audio to go out to the hardware. Figure 7.3 shows this arrangement.

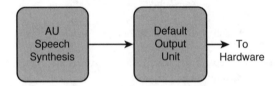

Figure 7.3   Audio Unit graph of simple speech synthesizer

The graph is ready; now you just need your application to start talking.

Setting Up a Speech Synthesizer

The Speech Synthesis Manager defines a fairly comprehensive API for generating synthetic speech from text, with control over variables such as the voice used and the speed of the speech. You can create multiple speakers, each of which uses a single SpeechChannel structure. This "channel" is the key to interacting with your speech synthesis unit: Instead of creating a channel with NewSpeechChannel(), you retrieve the channel that the unit has created for itself and send speech commands through that channel. Listing 7.23 shows how to get the SpeechChannel.

Listing 7.23   **Setting Up Speech Synthesis**

```
void PrepareSpeechAU(MyAUGraphPlayer *player)
{
    SpeechChannel chan;

    UInt32 propsize = sizeof(SpeechChannel);
    CheckError(AudioUnitGetProperty(player->speechAU,
                                    kAudioUnitProperty_SpeechChannel,
                                    kAudioUnitScope_Global,
                                    0,
                                    &chan,
                                    &propsize),
            "AudioUnitGetProperty[kAudioUnitProperty_SpeechChannel] failed");

    SpeakCFString(chan, CFSTR("hello world"), NULL);
}
```

The essential functionality of this short function is to retrieve the kAudioUnitProperty_SpeechChannel property from the speech synthesis audio unit.

When you have that, speech generated with SpeakCFString() or the other Speech Synthesis Manager functions will go through the graph and out to the output unit.

At this point, you're done. Build and run the program to hear the computer say "Hello, world" out the default audio device. Of course, you can change the string in the last line to your favorite catchphrase, a torrent of obscenities, or whatever.

Adding Effects

So far, using a speech synthesis audio unit hasn't done anything for you that you wouldn't have gotten by doing your own NewSpeechChannel() and calling SpeakCFString() without touching Core Audio. But all that's about to change, because you have an AUGraph—you have access to the raw PCM data generated by the synthesizer.

Early in the chapter, you learned about the various kinds of audio units. An important type of audio unit is the effect, which performs a transformation of some sort on audio passing through the unit.

If you insert an effect in between the speech synthesizer unit and the default output unit, it can work with the synthesized data to add an audible effect to the audio. The Core Audio Overview appendix lists a number of system-supplied effect units. One that's fairly easy to use is AUMatrixReverb, which you'll use here. Figure 7.4 shows what this graph looks like.

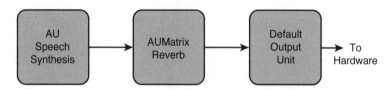

Figure 7.4   Audio Unit graph of speech synthesizer with reverb effect

The code you'll write for this is what you #define'd as PART_II earlier, so this goes between #ifdef PART_II and #else in the CreateMyAUGraph() function. First, you create the reverb unit, as shown in Listing 7.24.

Listing 7.24   **Creating an AUMatrixReverb AUGraph Node**

```
#ifdef PART_II
    // Generate a description that matches the reverb effect
    AudioComponentDescription reverbcd = {0};
    reverbcd.componentType = kAudioUnitType_Effect;
    reverbcd.componentSubType = kAudioUnitSubType_MatrixReverb;
    reverbcd.componentManufacturer = kAudioUnitManufacturer_Apple;
```

Listing 7.24   **Continued**

```
// Adds a node with the above description to the graph
AUNode reverbNode;
CheckError(AUGraphAddNode(player->graph,
                         &reverbcd,
                         &reverbNode),
          "AUGraphAddNode[kAudioUnitSubType_MatrixReverb] failed");
```

Syntactically, this is like all the other units you've created: You set up an `AudioComponentDescription` and pass it to `AUGraphNode()` to create a matching `AUNode` in the `AUGraph`. Notice, however, that you're now using `kAudioUnitType_ Effect` for the `componentType` and `kAudioUnitSubType_MatrixReverb` for the `componentSubType`.

Now connect the nodes in a different order, as shown in Listing 7.25. In the earlier example, you connected the `AUSpeechSynthesis` unit to the `DefaultOutputUnit`. To run the synthesized audio through the effect, you connect `AUSpeechSynthesis` to the `AUMatrixReverb` and then connect the `AUMatrixReverb` to the `DefaultOutputUnit`.

Listing 7.25   **Connecting AUNodes to Send Synthesized Speech Through a Reverb Effect**

```
// Connect the output source of the speech synthesizer AU to
// the input source of the reverb node
CheckError(AUGraphConnectNodeInput(player->graph,
                                   speechNode,
                                   0,
                                   reverbNode,
                                   0),
           "AUGraphConnectNodeInput (speech to reverb) failed");

// Connect the output source of the reverb AU to the input
// source of the output node
CheckError(AUGraphConnectNodeInput(player->graph,
                                   reverbNode,
                                   0,
                                   outputNode,
                                   0),
           "AUGraphConnectNodeInput (reverb to output) failed");
```

All these units generate and/or receive only a single stream, so they all use bus 0.

The reverb unit can take some properties to determine its behavior. Again, the only documentation is in `AudioUnitProperties.h`, where a handful of Apple Audio Unit–specific properties are defined. The `kAudioUnitProperty_ReverbRoomType` property takes a number of values enumerated as constants, with a `kReverbRoomType_` type of naming scheme. In Listing 7.26, you set your reverb for a big room full of echo.

Listing 7.26   **Configuring the AUMatrixReverb**

```
// Get the reference to the AudioUnit object for the reverb
// graph node
AudioUnit reverbUnit;
CheckError(AUGraphNodeInfo(player->graph,
                           reverbNode,
                           NULL,
                           &reverbUnit),
           "AUGraphNodeInfo failed");

// Now initialize the graph (this causes the resources to be
// allocated)
CheckError(AUGraphInitialize(player->graph),
           "AUGraphInitialize failed");

// Set the reverb preset for room size
UInt32 roomType = kReverbRoomType_LargeHall;
CheckError(AudioUnitSetProperty(reverbUnit,
                                kAudioUnitProperty_ReverbRoomType,
                                kAudioUnitScope_Global,
                                0,
                                &roomType,
                                sizeof(UInt32)),
           "AudioUnitSetProperty[kAudioUnitProperty_ReverbRoomType] failed");
```

Again, you need to retrieve the audio unit from the AUNode before you can set properties on it. You do this with AUGraphNodeInfo(). You also need to initialize the AUGraph for setting the property to have any effect, meaning that AudioUnitSetProperty() needs to come after AUGraphInitialize().

Uncomment the #define PART_II and then build and run this version of the code. This time, your speech sounds like it's echoing through a large hall. You can change the value of the room type to see what the speech synthesizer sounds like in a kReverbRoomType_MediumChamber or a kReverbRoomType_Cathedral.

Before moving on to the next project, there's a very useful technique you can use with complex AUGraphs, like the one in this example. The CAShow() function logs (to standard output) a list of all the nodes in the graph, along with the connections between them and the stream format used in each of those connections. To try it, just add a CAShow(player->graph); call to the bottom of CreateMyAUGraph(). When you run the program again, you'll see the graph logged out to Xcode's debug area, like this:

```
AudioUnitGraph 0xAC3E000:
  Member Nodes:
    node 1: 'auou' 'def ' 'appl', instance 0x8ac3e04d O I
    node 2: 'augn' 'ttsp' 'appl', instance 0x810000 O I
    node 3: 'aufx' 'mrev' 'appl', instance 0x8ac3e04e O I
```

```
Connections:
  node   2 bus   0 => node   3 bus   0 [ 2 ch,   44100 Hz, 'lpcm'
      (0x00000029) 32-bit little-endian float, deinterleaved]
  node   3 bus   0 => node   1 bus   0 [ 2 ch,   44100 Hz, 'lpcm'
      (0x00000029) 32-bit little-endian float, deinterleaved]
CurrentState:
  mLastUpdateError=0, eventsToProcess=F, isRunning=F
```

The three nodes are easily identified by the four-character codes representing their type and subtype, and the connections show the node/bus combination and LPCM formats. CAShow() can really help debug bad connections or stream format mismatches when a graph gets complex.

Adding Your Code to the Audio Rendering Process

So far, everything we've done has involved arranging units, setting a few properties, and letting them do their thing. This is tremendously powerful, particularly when you consider how many system-supplied units there are to play with. Still, we're not really programming, so much as we are *configuring*. It would be straightforward to present an AUGraph in a GUI (maybe looking something like Quartz Composer) and let the user add, configure, and connect units.

What if we wanted to insert our own code into the graph? What if we wanted to provide our own generator or effect? Fortunately, Core Audio lets you do that. In fact, there are several options: you can either set up *render callbacks* into your own code, or you can create your own units. The first option is much easier, whereas creating your own units is mostly going to be of interest to developers who intend to sell them to end-users, which in turn may require licensing and legal agreements with Apple. For this book, let's stick with the approach that involves more code and less lawyers.

The Audio Unit Render Cycle

So far, the effect and output units have needed input audio, which you've supplied by connecting them to other units. But this isn't the only way to use an audio unit. Let's take a deeper look at the audio unit render cycle.

To get any audio unit to perform its work (applying an effect, generating samples, and so on), you can manually call the function AudioUnitRender(). Among its variables, you supply an AudioBufferList, which is a struct that just wraps a variable number of AudioBuffers. The AudioBuffer is a struct with a channel count, a buffer size, and a pointer to a buffer called mData. If mData is not NULL, the unit places its output into this pointer. If mData is NULL, the unit can provide its own buffers. This design enables you to use units in isolation if you need to: You can apply an effect unit to an arbitrary buffer of samples by putting the samples in an `AudioBufferList`'s `mData` and then calling `AudioUnitRender()`, passing in an effect unit, all the other required parameters, and the `AudioBufferList`.

You haven't had to do this manually because the default output unit does it for you, repeatedly calling the unit connected to its bus 0 input scope and sending the resulting samples on to the audio hardware. But there's an interesting application to consider here. What if you wanted to save your reverb-powered speech synthesis from the last section to a file instead of outputting it to the speakers? You could replace the default output unit at the end of the graph with a generic output unit, identified by the subtype `kAudioUnitSubType_GenericOutput`. This output unit is not connected to audio hardware and doesn't do anything by itself. Instead, it gives you access to the end result of an `AUGraph`: You can just call `AudioUnitRender()` on the generic output unit and supply your own buffer. When the function returns, the buffer would contain frames of audio as processed by the graph. You could then write this buffer to a file with Audio File Services or Extended Audio File Services. Because these renders aren't tied to the timing of a hardware output device, you could call `AudioUnitRender()` as fast as possible, thereby writing your file much faster than a real-time play-out would require.

`AudioUnitRender()` provides one end of the render cycle—pulling audio from a unit—but what's happening upstream? You can also get that under your control, if you want. So far, you've connected your units with the function `AUGraphConnectNodeInput()` because you've worked with `AUGraph`s. When you're working with individual units, you have two options. You can set the property `kAudioUnitProperty_MakeConnection` on a unit, which takes as its value an `AudioUnitConnection` struct that specifies the source unit, source output bus number, and destination bus number. Setting this property is identical to calling `AUGraphConnectNodeInput()` on two graph nodes: The destination unit pulls from the source unit when it needs to.

The other way to supply samples to a unit is to set a different property: `kAudioUnitProperty_SetRenderCallback`. This property tells a unit that, instead of getting its input samples from another unit, it will do so by calling into a function that you provide. This enables you to inject your own code into the audio render cycle. Let's play with that.

A Custom Rendering Example

In Chapter 2, "The Story of Sound," you wrote a sine wave to a file by generating the samples programmatically and writing them to a file with Audio File Services. You can use pretty much the same math to generate a sine wave on the fly and then provide those samples to a default output unit to play the sine wave to the speakers in real time.

Create another command-line tool project with the outline in Listing 7.27.

Listing 7.27   **Outline of a Simple Sine Wave Player**

```
#include <AudioToolbox/AudioToolbox.h>

#define sineFrequency 880.0

#pragma mark user-data struct
// Insert Listing 7.28 here

#pragma mark callback function
// Insert Listing 7.34 here

#pragma mark utility functions
// Insert Listing 4.2 here

// Replace with listings 7.30 - 7.32
void CreateAndConnectOutputUnit (MySineWavePlayer *player) {
}

// Replace with listing 7.29
int    main(int argc, const char *argv[])
{
    // Set up output unit and callback
    // Start playing
    // Clean up
}
```

One thing you'll do differently in this example is use the Audio Unit directly instead of through an AUGraph. The reason for this is simple: You have only one unit and no connections, so you don't need a graph. Figure 7.5 shows how simple the arrangement is for this example.

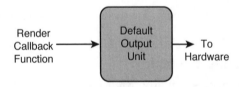

Figure 7.5   Output unit connected to a render callback function

You start with a struct you can pass around. In previous examples, combining variables in a struct was more of a convenience, but now it's a necessity: The point of this exercise is to use a callback function to produce the audio, and you need a single user info pointer to provide anything the callback function needs. As you'll see in Listing 7.28, the render callback needs just two things: the default output audio unit and a counter variable representing the current offset (or phase) in the sine wave.

Listing 7.28   **User Info Struct for Audio Unit Sine Wave Player**

```
typedef struct MySineWavePlayer
{
    AudioUnit outputUnit;
    double startingFrameCount;
} MySineWavePlayer;
```

The `main()` function for the sample is trivial; it defers the setup of the unit to a convenience function, then starts the output unit and lets it go for a few seconds. Listing 7.29 shows `main()` in its entirety.

Listing 7.29   **main() Function for Audio Unit Sine Wave Player**

```
int    main(int argc, const char *argv[])
{
    MySineWavePlayer player = {0};

    // Set up unit and callback
    CreateAndConnectOutputUnit(&player);

    // Start playing
    CheckError (AudioOutputUnitStart(player.outputUnit),
                "Couldn't start output unit");

    // Play for 5 seconds
    sleep(5);
cleanup:

    AudioOutputUnitStop(player.outputUnit);
    AudioUnitUninitialize(player.outputUnit);
    AudioComponentInstanceDispose() (player.outputUnit);

    return 0;
}
```

Because you're going to work directly with the audio unit, you start the output unit directly via `AudioOutputUnitStart()` instead of starting an `AUGraph`. You might notice that the cleanup functions are analogous to how you cleaned up a graph: Instead of using `AUGraphStop()`, `AUGraphUninitialize()`, and `AUGraphClose()`, you perform equivalent actions directly on the unit with `AudioOutputUnitStop()`, `AudioUnitUninitialize()`, and `AudioComponentInstanceDispose()`.

This `main()` also calls the beloved `CheckError()` function, so be sure to copy over Listing 4.2 as usual. Now let's move on to the core of this example.

Creating and Connecting Audio Units

When you worked with `AUGraph`, you described the units you wanted to create and then created graph nodes with `AUGraphAddNode()`. If you needed to work with the actual audio unit wrapped by the node, you'd fetch it with `AUGraphNodeInfo()`. In this example, creating a graph and a node would be extra work, so let's just create the output unit directly. You start your `CreateAndConnectOutputUnit()` in a familiar way, shown in Listing 7.30, by providing an `AudioComponentDescription` that describes the audio unit you want to create. This is identical to what you did in Listings 7.8 and 7.21.

Listing 7.30   **Describing a Default Output Audio Unit**

```
void CreateAndConnectOutputUnit (MySineWavePlayer *player) {
    // Generates a description that matches the output
    // device (speakers)
    AudioComponentDescription outputcd = {0};
    outputcd.componentType = kAudioUnitType_Output;
    outputcd.componentSubType = kAudioUnitSubType_DefaultOutput;
    outputcd.componentManufacturer = kAudioUnitManufacturer_Apple;
```

Getting the Audio Unit itself requires use of some more Audio Component Manager functions. These calls are based on the legacy Component Manager API, which was originally designed to provide a means of discovering and using shared resources. You provide a description of the component you want and then iterate over matches (of which there could be zero, one, or many) until you find the component you want. You perform this iteration with the `AudioComponentFindNext()` function, which uses the odd semantic of having you pass in your last match (`NULL` on your first call), along with your component description. Listing 7.31 shows how to use it to get a component for the default output unit described.

Listing 7.31   **Getting an Audio Unit with AudioComponentFindNext**

```
AudioComponent comp = AudioComponentFindNext(NULL, &outputcd);
if (comp == NULL) {
    printf ("can't get output unit");
    exit (-1);
}
CheckError(AudioComponentInstanceNew(comp,
                                &player->outputUnit),
        "Couldn't open component for outputUnit");
```

Assuming that `AudioComponentFindNext()` finds a matching component, you create your `AudioUnit` by calling `AudioComponentInstanceNew()`.

Now that you have the default output unit, you need to set it up—that is, you need to add your render callback and initialize the unit. You probably won't be surprised to hear that setting up the render callback is a matter of setting a property on the unit, kAudioUnitProperty_SetRenderCallback. The value for this property is an AURenderCallbackStruct whose fields are a function pointer to your callback function and a context object. Assuming that you'll call your callback function SineWaveRenderProc(), Listing 7.32 shows how to set up the callback.

Listing 7.32   **Setting Render Callback on Audio Unit**

```
// Register the render callback
AURenderCallbackStruct input;
input.inputProc = SineWaveRenderProc;
input.inputProcRefCon = &player;
CheckError(AudioUnitSetProperty(player->outputUnit,
                                kAudioUnitProperty_SetRenderCallback,
                                kAudioUnitScope_Input,
                                0,
                                &input,
                                sizeof(input)),
           "AudioUnitSetProperty failed");

// Initialize the unit
CheckError (AudioUnitInitialize(player->outputUnit),
           "Couldn't initialize output unit");
}
```

At this point, your output unit is ready to use. When you start it, it pulls new audio by calling the SineWaveRenderProc() function and sends it on to the speakers. All you need to do is provide that callback function to generate some samples.

The Render Callback Function

A render callback function is called every time a connected audio unit needs samples to play. If you look up the AURenderCallbackStruct in the documentation, you'll find that it links to AURenderCallback, which provides the function signature that a render callback function must use. AURenderCallback is shown in Listing 7.33.

Listing 7.33   **AURenderCallback Definition**

```
typedef OSStatus (*AURenderCallback) (
    void                        *inRefCon,
    AudioUnitRenderActionFlags  *ioActionFlags,
    const AudioTimeStamp        *inTimeStamp,
    UInt32                      inBusNumber,
    UInt32                      inNumberFrames,
    AudioBufferList             *ioData
);
```

The callback function receives six parameters:

- `inRefCon`: Your context (aka, user info) pointer.
- `ioActionFlags`: A bit field describing the purpose of the call. It's often blank (0), and you can look up the possible values as the `AudioUnitRenderActionFlag`'s enum in the documentation or `AUComponent.h`.
- `inTimeStamp`: An `AudioTimeStamp` structure that indicates the timing of this call relative to other calls to your render callback.
- `inBusNumber`: Which bus (aka, element) of the Audio Unit is requesting audio data.
- `inNumberFrames`: The number of frames to be rendered. Notice that this variable is prefixed as "in" instead of "io." That indicates that this isn't a case when you can render fewer frames and indicate that situation by passing back the number of frames actually rendered. Your callback must provide exactly the requested number of frames.
- `ioData`: An `AudioBufferList` struct to be filled with data. You write your samples into the `mData` members of the `AudioBuffers` contained in this struct. The list has a count of how many `AudioBuffers` are present, and each `AudioBuffer` has members for its channel count and byte size. Combined with `inNumberFrames`, you can figure out how much data can be safely written to these data buffers.

The function returns an `OSStatus`, which you can use to signal errors. One unwritten rule of the render callback is that you are expected to perform your work quickly. Core Audio calls your callback on a real-time thread with a hard deadline; if you miss this deadline, you get silence.[5] This also means that you cannot perform any action on a render callback that either is known to take a long time or can take an indeterminate amount of time. Particularly bad ideas for render callback actions include these:

- File I/O
- Network I/O
- Large memory allocations or copies
- Heavy use of Objective-C messaging
- Format conversion (except between flavors of PCM)
- Blocking threads

---

[5] Author Chris puzzled for hours over a render callback that looked right but generated no sound. The problem was that each call generated hundreds of `NSLog()` messages, and the expense of the logging caused the callback to miss the deadline. As soon as he commented out the `NSLog()`, the program started working.

You might rightly object that this precludes many of the things you'd want to do with audio. The next chapter reveals one solution. For now, however, let's keep things simple and fast.

Core Audio Threading

Realizing the limits of Audio Unit render callbacks can give you a new appreciation for all that the Audio Queue did in Chapters 4 and 5. Recall that the playback audio queue in Chapter 5 read samples from a file in its callback; chances are, you used a compressed file such as an .m4a or .mp3. To work with slow I/O and expensive format conversion, the queue must be doing some fancy footwork to not starve the audio unit callback. But where?

One way you can investigate this yourself is to set a breakpoint in the callback functions of your examples, open the Debug Navigator (⌘-5), and inspect the running threads. This chapter's Audio Unit example uses a small number of threads (five, in our Lion experience), and your callback's stack will show that you're being called by the C++ method `HALB_IOThread::Entry`, which calls into a `BufferedAudioConverter`, and calls you with `AudioConverterChain::CallInputProc`. The fact that you're on an I/O thread is the important part: Your code is expected to keep up with the timed system-level activities.

Set a breakpoint in the callback of Chapter 5's example and do a few continues (enough so you hear some audio); you'll see a very different story. There are more threads, and the one that calls you is not an I/O thread, but rather a `GenericRunLoopThread` that calls the C++ method `ClientAudiQueue::CallOutputCallback`. The other threads tell an interesting story: Catch your program at the right time, and you may see a separate `AQConverterThread` calling `AudioConverterFillComplexBuffer` to convert your compressed samples to PCM while the `HP_IOThread` is performing some kind of timed wait. You might gather that the Audio Queue performs indeterminate or long-lasting actions on one thread and then provides a means for the real-time thread to pick up the decompressed data with a quick `memcpy()`. You'll learn how to connect these dots in the next section. For now, keep in mind that not having to worry about threads is what makes the Audio Queue a handy convenience API.

All your render callback needs to do is produce samples representing a sine wave. You did this in Chapter 2, but there's a new catch. In the earlier example, you could just loop through as many waveforms as you needed to satisfy your minimum duration, which made the counting easy. In the callback case, you have to provide an exact number of frames on each call, and this frame count almost certainly won't match a wavelength. Consider Figure 7.6, which shows a sine wave set against hypothetical buffers as a series of dashed boxes: Each one ends at a different offset (or phase) in the sine wave. If you restart the sine wave for each buffer, the discontinuity in the signal creates a "buzz" in the sound wave.

As a result, you need to keep track of where you are in the wave with your context object so that, if the last sample you render is only partway into a wavelength, you can continue from that point on the next callback. With that in mind, Listing 7.34 contains the code for the render callback function.

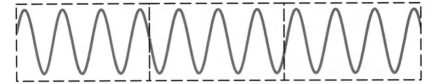

Figure 7.6   Render callback buffers do not align with wavelengths

Listing 7.34   **Render Callback to Produce a Sine Wave**

```
OSStatus SineWaveRenderProc(void *inRefCon,
                      AudioUnitRenderActionFlags *ioActionFlags,
                      const AudioTimeStamp *inTimeStamp,
                      UInt32 inBusNumber,
                      UInt32 inNumberFrames,
                      AudioBufferList * ioData)
{
    MySineWavePlayer *player = (MySineWavePlayer*)inRefCon;

    double j = player->startingFrameCount;
    double cycleLength = 44100. / sineFrequency;
    int frame = 0;
    for (frame = 0; frame < inNumberFrames; ++frame)
    {
        Float32 *data = (Float32*)ioData->mBuffers[0].mData;
        (data)[frame] = (Float32)sin (2 * M_PI * (j / cycleLength));
        // copy to right channel too
        data = (Float32*)ioData->mBuffers[1].mData;
        (data)[frame] = (Float32)sin (2 * M_PI * (j / cycleLength));

        j += 1.0;
        if (j > cycleLength)
            j -= cycleLength;
    }

    player->startingFrameCount = j;
    return noErr;
}
```

This function casts the context pointer to a `MySineWavePlayer` and, from that, sets up local variable `j`, which represents the offset (or phase) in the wave, measured as a frame count. It then sets up a cycle length (or wavelength) by dividing the sample rate (44,100) by a `sineFrequency` (in Listing 7.27, you #define'd this as `880.0`, which is an A on the piano). With this, you have enough info to set up a loop and calculate sine values. Each time you generate a new 32-bit sine value, you copy it to the buffer provided by the `ioBufferList`, using the `frame` counter to figure out the offset in the buffer to write to. Notice that, by default, you have two channels going into the output unit, so you write a sample to the second channel as well. If you wanted only mono sound, you would need to explicitly set an `AudioStreamBasicDescription` on the output unit and specify that you would be sending only one channel.

At the bottom of the loop, the offset count is incremented and reset to 0 if you have exceeded the frame count of a wavelength. When the loop exits, this offset is stored back to your struct as `startingFrameCount` so that you know where to continue the wave on your next callback.

Now you're ready to go. Build and run the program. You should hear 5 seconds of a sine wave from your default output device. It's a nice, steady tone. You can also change the frequency value and rebuild to get different tones, just as you would expect.

One other point you might want to investigate is how often you're being called back, and how many frames are being requested. This is a product of the sampling rate and the size of the buffers: A faster rate or smaller buffers results in more frequent callbacks. As an experiment (see Listing 7.35), you could add a log statement to the top of the callback to see how many frames are being requested, along with the current time.

Listing 7.35   **Logging the Requested Number of Frames and Render Callback Frequency**

```
printf ("SineWaveRenderProc needs %ld frames at %f\n", inNumberFrames,
CFAbsoluteTimeGetCurrent());
```

The output—and there's a lot of it—looks something like this:

```
SineWaveRenderProc needs 512 frames at 304518326.158135
SineWaveRenderProc needs 512 frames at 304518326.169738
SineWaveRenderProc needs 512 frames at 304518326.181346
SineWaveRenderProc needs 512 frames at 304518326.192959
```

The interval between those time stamps is a pretty consistent 0.0116 seconds, meaning that you're being called back every 11.6 milliseconds or so. Keep this in mind when you write your render callbacks; the time intervals involved in render callbacks are several orders of magnitude smaller than what's required by operations such as opening an Internet socket connection or spinning up a stopped hard drive. On the other hand, enjoy the fact that this frequency is on the same order of magnitude as your screen's refresh rate. Virtually no perceivable latency is involved in working with audio units, which means no delay between rendering samples and getting them to the user's ears. For some kinds of applications, that's critically important; musicians couldn't work with tools or virtual instruments that have a noticeable lag between performing actions and hearing sound, and gamers would hate having sounds out of sync with onscreen action.

Summary

This chapter gave you a taste of how audio units work and what you can do with them. As you've seen, the default audio units provide a great deal of functionality without your having to write a lot of signal-processing code: Just connect generator to effect, to output and let 'er rip. When you do want to insert your code into the processing chain, render callbacks give you the opportunity to do so.

Audio Units are the heart of Core Audio, and you're not done with them just yet. In the next chapter, you'll discover how to perform capture with input units, giving you a brief glimpse of the floor of Core Audio and the hardware APIs that lie beneath. Having played with generator, effect, and output units in this chapter, the next one gives you the opportunity to work with mixer units and create far more elaborate AUGraphs.

Audio Units: Input and Mixing

In the previous chapter, you took on Core Audio's ultimate level of responsibility by employing Audio Units in your program. Audio Units are ultimately responsible for all of Core Audio's distinctive audio-processing abilities: low-latency capture and play-out, audio synthesis, effects, and so on. It is the most difficult form of Core Audio programming, both conceptually and in terms of specifics: from managing unit scopes and buses to handling the real-time demands of render callbacks, there are lots of new and frustrating ways for your code to fail.

By the end of this chapter, we hope you'll find that the struggle is worth it. In this chapter, you continue your study of audio units with powerful new capabilities. First, you'll use output units to capture audio from input devices such as microphones and audio–capable cameras. To do this, you'll also get a glimpse of the APIs that provide a consistent Core Audio interface to many different kinds of I/O technologies. You'll also get to push your luck with asynchronicity as you process input and output on different callback threads—and still get the samples from one unit to the another. You'll wrap up by employing mixer units, which combine multiple streams of audio and enable you to mix your many audio sources into something that can be played out a pair of speakers or headphones.

> **Note**
>
> If you thought the chapters leading up to this one were tough, you haven't seen anything yet. This chapter tests your will. For this one, we've had to bring in threading concerns, hardware APIs, and even some C++. *Super gross!* It's okay if you want to read it once for the big picture, then again for the nitty-gritty details. And you might not be able to put these techniques to use yourself until you've actually worked through our big example, because little details and gotchas abound.

Working with I/O Input

So far, the source of the audio in the examples has been either generator units (`AUFilePlayer` and `AUSpeechSynthesis`) or your own sine-wave-generating render callback. Another important way to get sound into an Audio Unit or `AUGraph` is to perform capture from an input device. That's what you'll spend most of this chapter doing.

You might think that capture devices are considered generator units, but combing through the list of system-supplied units reveals that they're not there. Then you might say "Okay, we have output units to go out to speakers or headphones or speakers, so there must be input units, too." But there aren't. In an unfortunate bit of naming, samples from input devices are actually supplied by output units. For this reason, there's an informal tendency to refer to these as I/O units, even though their unit type is literally `kAudioUnitType_Output`.

In this example, you start with a simple graph that captures from the user's default input device and is connected to the generic output unit as usual. Figure 8.1 shows this arrangement.

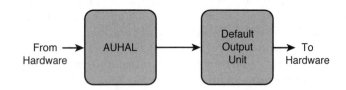

Figure 8.1   A Conceptual AUGraph for play-through of captured audio

Notice that the input audio unit is called AUHAL. That merits a bit of explanation. The *Hardware Abstraction Layer* (HAL) is an abstraction over the underlying I/O details of audio hardware devices. Your input and output devices might include various I/O technologies—a USB microphone, an old FireWire iSight camera with its integrated mic, Line In and Line Out on a sound card—but at the HAL level, you can use a consistent interface to discover devices and their capabilities, get and set properties, and receive or deliver streams of PCM samples. The AUHAL is an *Audio Unit* that provides input to and/or output from a *HAL* device.

For the first part of the example, you'll set up an `AUGraph` that provides a simple play-through from one unit to the other; when the output unit needs samples, the input unit will provide them. This is actually harder than it sounds at first, but at least the outline of the steps is straightforward. Let's set up a command-line tool project in Xcode and add the `AudioToolbox`, `CoreAudio`, and `AudioUnit` frameworks to the target. Listing 8.1 shows the skeleton of the program.

Listing 8.1   **Outline of an AUGraph-Based Play-Through Program**

```
#include <AudioToolbox/AudioToolbox.h>

// #define PART_II

#pragma mark user-data struct
// Replace with Listing 8.3
typedef struct MyAUGraphPlayer
```

Listing 8.1   **Continued**

```
{
#ifdef PART_II
// Insert Listing 8.23 here
#else
#endif
}

#pragma mark - render procs -
// Insert Listings 8.15 - 8.18 here
// Insert Listings 8.21 - 8.22 here

#pragma mark - utility functions -
// Insert Listing 4.2 here

// Replace with Listings 8.4 - 8.14
void CreateInputUnit (MyAUGraphPlayer *player) {
}

// Replace with Listings 8.19 - 8.20
void CreateMyAUGraph(MyAUGraphPlayer *player)
{
#ifdef PART_II
// Insert Listings 8.24 - 8.27 here
#else
#endif
}

// Insert Listing 8.29 here

// Replace with Listing 8.2
int main (int argc, const char * argv[]) {

    // Create the input unit

    // Build a graph with output unit

#ifdef PART_II
// Insert Listing 8.28 here
#else
#endif

    // Start playing

    // And wait

    // Cleanup
}
```

As you can see, this is another example that you will build on later by adding some PART_II features that you can #ifdef around for now. As always, you'll be using the CheckError() function on all your Core Audio calls, so copy Listing 4.2 into your source.

Connecting Input and Output Units

The main() for the program is simple (see Listing 8.2). It calls convenience functions to set up the input unit and the rest of the AUGraph, and then it starts the graph and block until the user presses a key to quit.

Listing 8.2   main() Function for AUGraph Play-Through

```
int main (int argc, const char * argv[]) {

    MyAUGraphPlayer player = {0};

    // Create the input unit
    CreateInputUnit(&player);

    // Build a graph with output unit
    CreateMyAUGraph(&player);

#ifdef PART_II
#endif

    // Start playing
    CheckError (AudioOutputUnitStart(player.inputUnit),
            "AudioOutputUnitStart failed");
    CheckError(AUGraphStart(player.graph),
            "AUGraphStart failed");

    // And wait
    printf("Capturing, press <return> to stop:\n");
    getchar();

cleanup:
    AUGraphStop (player.graph);
    AUGraphUninitialize (player.graph);
    AUGraphClose(player.graph);

}
```

We've set up a separate function to create the input unit here instead of putting it in CreateMyAUGraph(). We've done this to make a point. Although we'd like to think that the output unit pulls from the input unit, this really isn't the case. They're separate I/O units, so the input and output units are started independently and run independently.

This is a problem for AUGraphs as you currently understand them because you need the output unit to pull from *somewhere*. It can't pull directly from the input unit, which is running on a separate timing cycle and might or might not be able to provide samples at a given time. To make things worse, the input unit is going to be providing samples when it's good and ready to, regardless of the state of the output unit or the AUGraph. So when it wants to provide samples to our program, what do we do with them?

Ring Buffers to the Rescue

You need some place for the input unit to leave its samples and for the output unit to collect them from. An ideal tool for this is a *ring buffer*. This is a block of memory that acts like an infinitely long read/write buffer. The input unit can write samples to it whenever it needs to, and the output unit reads from the buffer as necessary. It's called a ring buffer because it wraps around in memory: When you try to read or write past the last address in the buffer, the call wraps around to the beginning.

Many possible implementations exist, but for simple purposes, you can imagine a buffer with two pointers into it: a read pointer and a write pointer. Consider Figure 8.2, which shows the states of a ring buffer at several points. At step ①, the buffer is empty; the write pointer points to the first address of the buffer, and the read pointer is invalid because there is no data in the buffer to read yet. Write some data to the buffer, and suddenly you're at step ②: The read pointer now points to the beginning of the buffer, and the write pointer points to the first free address in the buffer. Write again, and in step ③, the write pointer is further into the buffer. At this point, you could safely read (writePoint - readPoint) bytes from the buffer. Imagine that you read up through the first write, which puts you in step ④, with the read pointer still trailing the write pointer. You could read all the way up to the write pointer, but no further, obviously. For a final step, you'll write a third block of data to the buffer. In this diagram, the address of the write pointer plus the length of the new data is beyond the end of the ring buffer. So, as illustrated in step ⑤, the first part of the block is written to the end of the ring buffer, and the rest of it is written back at the beginning. In terms of memory addresses, it now seems like the write pointer is behind the read buffer, but this is illusory: Further reads advance the read pointer until it reaches the end of the buffer, at which point it wraps around, just as the write pointer did.

Obviously, for this to work, the reading and writing needs to be somewhat coordinated. If you try to read when there's no data available, you get nothing; if you keep writing to the buffer and fill it up (if the write pointer catches up to the read pointer), the reader loses data. A ring buffer is appropriate only when the data in the buffer will be produced and consumed at pretty much the same rate. Picking an appropriate size can be tricky, too. Bigger buffers make collisions less likely, but after a point, you can end up wasting memory.

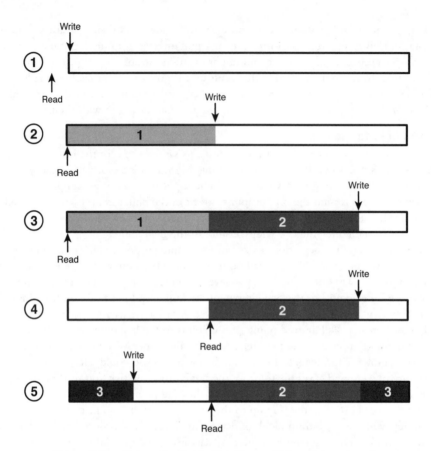

Figure 8.2   States of a ring buffer after multiple writes and reads

Using a Ring Buffer with Audio Units

The ring buffer solves the timing problem. When the input unit has samples from the capture device ready for you, an *input callback* function can copy them to the ring buffer. And when the AUGraph (which, for now, is just the output unit) needs samples to play, it reads from the ring buffer. Figure 8.3 shows this arrangement, displacing the units vertically to try to drive home the point that this is no longer a synchronous pull through a graph. Instead, the input and output units are exchanging samples asynchronously, through the ring buffer.

The Core Audio SDK provides a ring buffer, but not where you might expect to find it. The CARingBuffer is a C++ class, found in Core Audio's Public Utility folder, at

`/Developer/Extras/CoreAudio/PublicUtility.`[1] To use this in your project, drag `CARingBuffer.h` and `CARingBuffer.cpp` to your project. We recommend adding a separate group in your project for this utility code (we called our group CA public utility), and unchecking the Copy Items into Destination Group's Folder button; you'll want to compile the version in the `PublicUtility` folder instead of making a local copy (and, thereby, unintentionally forking it).

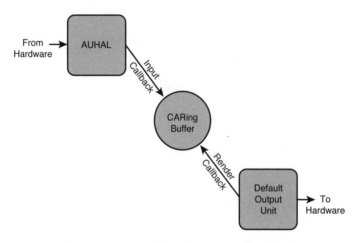

Figure 8.3   An AUGraph for play-through of captured audio

> **Note**
>
> Because you're adding C++ code to the project, you need to change build settings to be able to call into C++ code. The easiest way to do so in this project is to just change the file extension of the `main.c` file to `.cpp` (the standard C++ extension) or `.mm` (the Objective-C++ extension). If you don't want to change the file extension, you can also bring up the file's inspector (Option-⌘-1) and, under the "Identity and Type" section, change the file type to one of the C++-aware file types, such as C++ Source or Objective-C++ Source.

Now that you've added the `CARingBuffer` to your project, you can make use of it in the user data struct that you'll pass between your callback functions (see Listing 8.3).

---

[1] The `CARingBuffer` included with the Core Audio SDK on Mac OS X 10.5 and 10.6 is buggy and can be fixed with an updated version of the class. See Apple Technical Q&A 1665, "CoreAudio PublicUtility—Installing the `CARingBuffer` Update" for an explanation and a link to the corrected code. Lion-based versions of Xcode provide the correct version of `CARingBuffer`, but starting in Xcode 4.3, Xcode does not install the Core Audio `PublicUtility` folder at all. Instead, Apple includes it in the "Audio Tools for Xcode" package, available via Xcode's "More Developer Tools..." menu item. The items in this package can be installed anywhere you like. In the book's downloadable code, we expect `PublicUtility` to be at the old location."

Both the input and render callbacks need to know about the ring buffer so that the former can write to it when capture data is ready and the latter can read from it when it needs to render data out to speakers or headphones. You also need some timing offsets so that, even if callbacks from the devices have different time stamps, you can store and fetch samples in the ring buffer reliably. Beyond this, you use the struct to refer to the AUGraph and its input and output units, the ASBD used throughout the graph, and an AudioBufferList that the input unit can read samples into before copying them to the ring buffer.

Listing 8.3   User Data Struct for Audio Play-Through Program

```
typedef struct MyAUGraphPlayer
{
    AudioStreamBasicDescription streamFormat;

    AUGraph graph;
    AudioUnit inputUnit;
    AudioUnit outputUnit;
#ifdef PART_II
#endif

    AudioBufferList *inputBuffer;
    CARingBuffer *ringBuffer;

    Float64 firstInputSampleTime;
    Float64 firstOutputSampleTime;
    Float64 inToOutSampleTimeOffset;

} MyAUGraphPlayer;
```

As you can see from Listing 8.3, you've got room for a PART_II surprise. (As if "Part I" wasn't complex enough!).

Creating an AUHAL Unit for Input

The first utility function you need to write is one to set up an I/O unit to handle input. Unlike output, you can't make use of the kAudioUnitSubType_DefaultOutput subtype because there's no guarantee that the default output unit also provides input, and there's no "default input" unit as there is for default output. Instead, you create a different kind of I/O unit, an AUHAL, and explicitly connect it to a specific audio device. Let's start by creating this unit in Listing 8.4.

Listing 8.4   **Creating an Audio Unit for Input**

```
void CreateInputUnit (MyAUGraphPlayer *player) {

    // Generates a description that matches audio HAL
    AudioComponentDescription inputcd = {0};
    inputcd.componentType = kAudioUnitType_Output;
    inputcd.componentSubType = kAudioUnitSubType_HALOutput;
    inputcd.componentManufacturer = kAudioUnitManufacturer_Apple;

    AudioComponent comp = AudioComponentFindNext(NULL, &inputcd);
    if (comp == NULL) {
        printf ("Can't get output unit");
        exit (-1);
    }

    CheckError(AudioComponentInstanceNew(comp,
                                          &player->inputUnit),
               "Couldn't open component for inputUnit");
```

As you can see from Listing 8.4, you are using the Audio Component Manager APIs, as we did in Listings 7.31 and 7.32, to describe and find an `AudioUnit`. The other difference from the previous listing is the use of the subtype `kAudioUnitSubType_HALOutput` instead of `kAudioUnitSubType_DefaultOutput`. And yes, asking for a HAL output device to do audio *input* is still badly counterintuitive.

The next step (see Listing 8.5) is to explicitly enable input from the unit. You didn't have to do this for the default output unit, but you do need to do so when you work with AUHAL objects. The property you set is `kAudioOutputUnitProperty_EnableIO`, but there's a twist: For audio input, set this property on bus 1, not the usual bus 0. This is because of an important convention for I/O units: *Bus 1 represents a stream from input hardware, and bus 0 represents a stream to output hardware.* You haven't had to worry much about buses before this because most of the units have had a single bus (number 0) that you could connect to the default output unit to play out to the hardware. For this input-only unit, you need to enable I/O on bus 1 and disable it on bus 0.

Listing 8.5   **Enabling I/O on Input AUHAL**

```
UInt32 disableFlag = 0;
UInt32 enableFlag = 1;
AudioUnitScope outputBus = 0;
AudioUnitScope inputBus = 1;
CheckError (AudioUnitSetProperty(player->inputUnit,
                                  kAudioOutputUnitProperty_EnableIO,
                                  kAudioUnitScope_Input,
                                  inputBus,
                                  &enableFlag,
```

Listing 8.5   **Continued**

```
                                    sizeof(enableFlag)),
            "Couldn't enable input on I/O unit");

CheckError (AudioUnitSetProperty(player->inputUnit,
                                  kAudioOutputUnitProperty_EnableIO,
                                  kAudioUnitScope_Output,
                                  outputBus,
                                  &disableFlag,
                                  sizeof(enableFlag)),
            "Couldn't disable output on I/O unit");
```

At this point, you are still dealing with the AUHAL in the abstract; you have not associated this input unit with any specific audio device. You do that now with Listing 8.6. This uses the `AudioObjectGetPropertyData()` call, which you used in Chapter 4, "Recording" (see Listings 4.20 and 4.21), to figure out your input hardware sample rate. In this case, all you need is the `AudioDeviceID` that identifies the input device currently set in System Preferences.

Listing 8.6   **Getting the Default Audio Input Device**

```
AudioDeviceID defaultDevice = kAudioObjectUnknown;
UInt32 propertySize = sizeof (defaultDevice);
AudioObjectPropertyAddress defaultDeviceProperty;
defaultDeviceProperty.mSelector = kAudioHardwarePropertyDefaultInputDevice;
defaultDeviceProperty.mScope = kAudioObjectPropertyScopeGlobal;
defaultDeviceProperty.mElement = kAudioObjectPropertyElementMaster;

CheckError (AudioObjectGetPropertyData(kAudioObjectSystemObject,
            &defaultDeviceProperty,
            0,
            NULL,
            &propertySize,
            &defaultDevice),
    "Couldn't get default input device");
```

Audio Hardware Devices

We've repeatedly talked about having multiple audio "devices," and you might think that this doesn't really apply to you. After all, if you have a MacBook, you don't have a bunch of different devices, right? Wrong. Even a stock MacBook has two input devices: the built-in internal microphone and a built-in line-in jack. There's also a built-in output, which plays over internal speakers unless headphones are plugged in. On a bigger scale, the Mac Pro has built-in devices for analog line in and line out, digital in and out, and an internal speaker. Check out the Sound system preference panel to see what your computer has to work with.

Now consider that any Mac can gain additional input and/or output devices via serial port connections. A user might plug in a FireWire iSight (an input-only device) or a USB headset (which does input and output). Other software devices also exist, such as the Soundflower driver that provides system audio capture to applications like Audio Hijack Pro by providing a virtual output device that copies off outgoing audio to other applications before sending it on to hardware. Ultimately, you can't make any assumptions about audio capabilities based on Mac model. The safer way is to use the Audio Object API to either detect the default input or output device or iterate over all the devices with the `kAudioHardwarePropertyDevices` property.

One other consideration to keep in mind is that an individual device can be capable of input, output, or both. USB headsets and certain other devices (such as the Griffin iMic) are examples of the latter. An important technical difference arises, in that a single device has one clock servicing its needs, whether input, output, or both. If you discovered and used a device that does both input and output, you wouldn't need to take the asynchronous approach in this chapter because an output unit for this device could safely call `AudioUnitRender()` on its corresponding input unit. This isn't a safe assumption on Mac OS X, but iOS devices *always* have a single input/output device, which makes play-through applications much easier to write, as you'll see in Chapter 10, "Core Audio on iOS."

When you have the `AudioDeviceID`, you set it as the AUHAL property `kAudioOutputUnitProperty_CurrentDevice`, as shown in Listing 8.7. This associates the input audio unit with a specific audio device.

Listing 8.7   **Setting the Current Device Property of the AUHAL**

```
CheckError(AudioUnitSetProperty(player->inputUnit,
                                kAudioOutputUnitProperty_CurrentDevice,
                                kAudioUnitScope_Global,
                                outputBus,
                                &defaultDevice,
                                sizeof(defaultDevice)),
           "Couldn't set default device on I/O unit");
```

You will want to know the `AudioStreamBasicDescription` that the AUHAL produces because you might need to set it as the stream format for other units to use. To do this, get the `kAudioUnitProperty_StreamFormat` property from the AUHAL, as shown in Listing 8.8. Notice again that you work with bus 1, which represents capture data flowing through an I/O unit.

Listing 8.8   **Getting AudioStreamBasicDescription from Input AUHAL**

```
propertySize = sizeof (AudioStreamBasicDescription);
CheckError(AudioUnitGetProperty(player->inputUnit,
                                kAudioUnitProperty_StreamFormat,
                                kAudioUnitScope_Output,
```

Listing 8.8   **Continued**

```
                                    inputBus,
                                    &player->streamFormat,
                                    &propertySize),
                "Couldn't get ASBD from input unit");
```

Look again at that call, because it's a little confusing to see "output" and "input" in adjacent parameters. You address the output scope of the audio unit, meaning the data coming out of the unit. However, you use inputBus (which is 1) to indicate that you want the stream that I/O units use for capture data. The difference is that the scope is input to and output from the *unit*, whereas the bus represents input to and output from the *device* (but only for I/O units). Table 8.1 summarizes the possible combinations of scope and bus and gives their meaning.

Table 8.1   **Scope/Bus Use in I/O Units**

Scope	Bus	Semantics	Property Access
Input	1	Input from hardware to I/O unit	Read-only
Output	1	Output from I/O unit to program or other units	Read/write
Input	0	Input to I/O unit from program or other units	Read/write
Output	0	Output from I/O unit to hardware	Read-only

In fact, you need to make use of this distinction next. The input hardware might be running at a different sample rate than the default provided by the AUHAL. For example, although the default sample rate is 44,100 Hz, the built-in line input on a Mac Pro might run at 88,200. You have different ways to deal with this, but one simple option is to just use the input hardware rate throughout your program, as shown in Listing 8.9. After all, that avoids resampling and loss of quality. So you'll get the ASBD that's going into the AUHAL, copy its value over to the ASBD that the AUHAL is producing, and reset that latter ASBD on the AUHAL's output scope.

Listing 8.9   **Adopting Hardware Input Sample Rate**

```
AudioStreamBasicDescription deviceFormat;
CheckError(AudioUnitGetProperty(player->inputUnit,
                                    kAudioUnitProperty_StreamFormat,
                                    kAudioUnitScope_Input,
                                    inputBus,
                                    &deviceFormat,
                                    &propertySize),
                "Couldn't get ASBD from input unit");

player->streamFormat.mSampleRate = deviceFormat.mSampleRate;
```

Listing 8.9   **Continued**

```
propertySize = sizeof (AudioStreamBasicDescription);
CheckError(AudioUnitSetProperty(player->inputUnit,
                                kAudioUnitProperty_StreamFormat,
                                kAudioUnitScope_Output,
                                inputBus,
                                &player->streamFormat,
                                propertySize),
           "Couldn't set ASBD on input unit");
```

Another task to deal with is providing buffers to receive data from the input unit (detailed in Listing 8.10). This is the `AudioBufferList` structure that you previously received in render callbacks and would provide to `AudioUnitRender()` if you needed to call it manually. Usually, the `AudioBufferList` has been provided because it's been set up by the output unit that then calls your units and renders callbacks. In the capture case, you need to provide your own buffers to receive the captured data because the `ioData` parameter received in the callback function will always be `NULL` for input callbacks. Fortunately, a property called `kAudioDevicePropertyBufferFrameSize` tells how many frames are in the AUHAL's I/O buffers, and you can use that to allocate a suitably large buffer to receive the capture data in the callback.

Listing 8.10   **Calculating Capture Buffer Size for an I/O Unit**

```
UInt32 bufferSizeFrames = 0;
propertySize = sizeof(UInt32);
CheckError (AudioUnitGetProperty(player->inputUnit,
                                 kAudioDevicePropertyBufferFrameSize,
                                 kAudioUnitScope_Global,
                                 0,
                                 &bufferSizeFrames,
                                 &propertySize),
            "Couldn't get buffer frame size from input unit");
UInt32 bufferSizeBytes = bufferSizeFrames * sizeof(Float32);
```

Notice that the frames are assumed to be `Float32` samples, which is the data type of the canonical format that audio units use by default. You can now use this `bufferSizeBytes` in building up an `AudioBufferList` structure, shown in Listing 8.11.

Listing 8.11   **Creating an AudioBufferList to Receive Capture Data**

```
// Allocate an AudioBufferList plus enough space for
// array of AudioBuffers
UInt32 propsize = offsetof(AudioBufferList, mBuffers[0]) + (sizeof(AudioBuffer) *
player->streamFormat.mChannelsPerFrame);
```

Listing 8.11   Continued

```
// malloc buffer lists
player->inputBuffer = (AudioBufferList *)malloc(propsize);
player->inputBuffer->mNumberBuffers = player->streamFormat.mChannelsPerFrame;

// Pre-malloc buffers for AudioBufferLists
for(UInt32 i =0; i< player->inputBuffer->mNumberBuffers ; i++) {
    player->inputBuffer->mBuffers[i].mNumberChannels = 1;
    player->inputBuffer->mBuffers[i].mDataByteSize = bufferSizeBytes;
    player->inputBuffer->mBuffers[i].mData = malloc(bufferSizeBytes);
}
```

The first line in Listing 8.11 uses the little-seen `offsetof()` macro. You might have to look at this carefully to figure out what's going on. An `AudioBufferList` has a fixed-length field (a `UInt32`) for the number of buffers, followed by an array of `AudioBuffers`. The size `AudioBufferList` that you need is the size of everything up to that array (which is what `offsetof()` provides) and then as many `AudioBuffer` pointers as there are channels in the stream format. This means that you can `malloc()` a structure of this exact size and assign the number of buffers. You then loop through the `AudioBuffers`, initializing their members and `malloc()`ing the `mData` buffers that actually receive the sample.

> **Note**
>
> By convention, AUHAL *deinterleaves* multichannel audio. This means that you set up two `AudioBuffers` of one channel each instead of setting up one `AudioBuffer` with `mNumberChannels==2`. A common cause of `paramErr` (`-50`) problems in `AudioUnitRender()` calls is having `AudioBufferLists` whose topology (or arrangement of buffers) doesn't match what the unit is prepared to produce. When dealing at the unit level, you almost always want to do noninterleaved like this.

This buffer provides some memory to receive the data from the input unit. But what do you do with it then? Remember that the original plan was to use a ring buffer to store samples so that the output unit's callback can pick them up. If you look through the `CARingBuffer.h` header, you'll see that it's nicely tuned for working with the data types you're already using—the `Store()` and `Fetch()` functions take `AudioBufferLists`, for example. For now, you just need to create the ring buffer, which you do with the `Allocate()` function, supplying a channel count, bytes per frame, and a buffer size, as shown in Listing 8.12.

Listing 8.12   Creating a CARingBuffer

```
// Alloc ring buffer that will hold data between the
// two audio devices
player->ringBuffer = new CARingBuffer();
```

Listing 8.12   **Continued**

```
player->ringBuffer->Allocate(player->streamFormat.mChannelsPerFrame,
                    player->streamFormat.mBytesPerFrame,
                    bufferSizeFrames * 3);
```

Setting aside the weird C++ syntax that you haven't had to use elsewhere in the book, the other point to notice is that you've created a ring buffer three times the size of the buffer you use for the callbacks. This is kind of a guess; no hard-and-fast rule governs the right size of the ring buffer, except that it has to be large enough that the read and write pointers never collide. In the example, we count on output callbacks occurring more or less as frequently as input callbacks; this means that, every time you write a bufferSizeFrames-sized chunk, you'll soon be reading a chunk of that size. If this weren't the case and you found that you wrote to the buffer more frequently than you read from it, you would want to make the buffer larger. It's an art, not a science.

Now that you have created the input unit, associated it with a device, set up a buffer to receive capture data, and set up a ring buffer to put it in, the last step (beginning with Listing 8.13) is to provide this AUHAL with a callback function to use whenever capture data is available. This is almost identical to the render callback of the last section, except that when you receive data from an I/O unit, you're setting up an input callback.

Listing 8.13   **Setting up an Input Callback on an AUHAL**

```
// Set render proc to supply samples from input unit
AURenderCallbackStruct callbackStruct;
callbackStruct.inputProc = InputRenderProc;
callbackStruct.inputProcRefCon = player;

CheckError(AudioUnitSetProperty(player->inputUnit,
                        kAudioOutputUnitProperty_SetInputCallback,
                        kAudioUnitScope_Global,
                        0,
                        &callbackStruct,
                        sizeof(callbackStruct)),
            "Couldn't set input callback");
```

This uses the same AURenderCallbackStruct that you used for the render callback earlier, providing the name of a callback function and a user data pointer. Here, though, you use a different property: kAudioOutputUnitProperty_SetInputCallback.

The last thing CreateInputUnit() needs to do is initialize the unit (see Listing 8.14). You also initialize the timing offset counters, whose purpose is explained later when you get to the input callback function.

Listing 8.14   Initializing Input AUHAL and Offset Time Counters

```
CheckError(AudioUnitInitialize(player->inputUnit),
          "Couldn't initialize input unit");

player->firstInputSampleTime = -1;
player->inToOutSampleTimeOffset = -1;

printf ("Bottom of CreateInputUnit()\n");
}
```

Setting up an input unit takes about 100 lines of code. In the big picture, you do rely on some techniques that you've seen before: describing and finding a unit, getting and setting stream formats, and getting size properties so that you can allocate suitably large data buffers. And you haven't even written the callback function yet! Let's do that now.

> **Note**
>
> By the way, if you ever want a refresher on this section's topics, take a look at Apple Technical Note 2091, "Device Input Using the HAL Output Audio Unit," in your Xcode documentation bundles or on developer.apple.com.

Writing the Input Callback

After the AUHAL has captured some data from the input device, it uses the input callback you registered to provide that data to your program. It does this by calling the function `InputRenderProc()`, which you set up as part of the callback struct that you set as the AUHAL's `kAudioOutputUnitProperty_SetInputCallback` property. So what do you do in that function? You collect the samples from the unit and send them to your `CARingBuffer` so that the output unit can pick them up later.

The `InputRenderProc()` function in Listing 8.15 has the same signature as the render callback you saw in the previous chapter. As usual, you first must cast the user data object back to your player struct.

Listing 8.15   Signature for an Input Callback Function

```
OSStatus InputRenderProc(void *inRefCon,
                         AudioUnitRenderActionFlags *ioActionFlags,
                         const AudioTimeStamp *inTimeStamp,
                         UInt32 inBusNumber,
                         UInt32 inNumberFrames,
                         AudioBufferList * ioData)
{
    MyAUGraphPlayer *player = (MyAUGraphPlayer*) inRefCon;
```

Now you get to work. When you created the struct, you set up some "offset" time fields. Now you start using them in Listing 8.16. You have these because the input and output units might be using totally different schemes for their time stamps. One might be using real-world "wall clock" time, whereas the other might be counting seconds since your application launched. This matters because the CARingBuffer keeps track of the time stamps of the samples added to it. If they're wildly different, you won't get any sound. You can deal with this by noticing the first time stamp provided by each unit and, when you have both, calculating the difference (or offset) between them.

Listing 8.16   **Logging Time Stamps from Input AUHAL and Calculating Time Stamp Offset**

```
// Have we ever logged input timing? (for offset calculation)
if (player->firstInputSampleTime < 0.0) {
    player->firstInputSampleTime = inTimeStamp->mSampleTime;
    if ((player->firstOutputSampleTime > 0.0) &&
        (player->inToOutSampleTimeOffset < 0.0)) {
        player->inToOutSampleTimeOffset =
            player->firstInputSampleTime - player->firstOutputSampleTime;
    }
}
```

This block of code calculates the offset only if firstOutputSampleTime has also been set, which needs to happen in the output render callback. That means that you also have to do this calculation in the output callback so that, regardless of whether the input or output callback gets called first, you can calculate inToOutSampleTimeOffset as soon as possible.

As mentioned earlier, the point of the input callback is to retrieve the samples from the AUHAL and put them in the ring buffer so that the output unit can read them later. You might think that the samples would be provided as the parameter AudioBufferList *ioData, but this isn't the case: For input samples, this parameter is always NULL. Instead, the callback is just a signal that the captured samples are ready. You still have to retrieve them yourself with AudioUnitRender(), as shown in Listing 8.17.

Listing 8.17   **Retrieving Captured Samples from Input AUHAL**

```
OSStatus inputProcErr = noErr;
inputProcErr = AudioUnitRender(player->inputUnit,
                               ioActionFlags,
                               inTimeStamp,
                               inBusNumber,
                               inNumberFrames,
                               player->inputBuffer);
```

If this succeeded, you can copy the samples over to the ring buffer. The CARingBuffer's Store() method is designed for just this purpose. In fact, its parameter list—an AudioBufferList, a framesToWrite count, and a start time—aligns nicely with the variables you currently have in scope. You sized and allocated an AudioBufferList in the previous section for just this purpose, and the frame count and start time are provided as parameters to the callback, shown in Listing 8.18.

Listing 8.18   **Storing Captured Samples to a CARingBuffer**

```
    if (! inputProcErr) {
        inputProcErr = player->ringBuffer->Store(player->inputBuffer,
                                            inNumberFrames,
                                            inTimeStamp->mSampleTime);
    }

    return inputProcErr;
}
```

That was a lot of explanation but not a lot of work. At this point, you have an input unit that connects to the default input audio device and uses a callback to deliver samples to your application. Your callback puts those samples in a CARingBuffer so that they can be picked up later and played out. Time to build that part.

Building an AUGraph to Play Samples from a CARingBuffer

You can get back to somewhat familiar footing in this part of the play-through application: All examples in the previous chapter involved a default output unit that gets samples either from upstream audio units or from a render callback. In this case, you need to do the latter: The samples you need are in the CARingBuffer, so you need to use a render callback to fetch samples from the ring buffer. Let's start writing CreateMyAUGraph() with Listing 8.19.

Listing 8.19   **Creating an AUGraph for Audio Play-Through**

```
void CreateMyAUGraph(MyAUGraphPlayer *player)
{

    // Create a new AUGraph
    CheckError(NewAUGraph(&player->graph),
            "NewAUGraph failed");

    // Generate a description that matches default output
    AudioComponentDescription outputcd = {0};
    outputcd.componentType = kAudioUnitType_Output;
    outputcd.componentSubType = kAudioUnitSubType_DefaultOutput;
    outputcd.componentManufacturer = kAudioUnitManufacturer_Apple;
```

Listing 8.19   **Continued**

```
AudioComponent comp = AudioComponentFindNext(NULL, &outputcd);
if (comp == NULL) {
    printf ("Can't get output unit"); exit (-1);
}

// Adds a node with above description to the graph
AUNode outputNode;
CheckError(AUGraphAddNode(player->graph,
                          &outputcd,
                          &outputNode),
           "AUGraphAddNode[kAudioUnitSubType_DefaultOutput] failed");
```

You've done everything here already (in Listings 7.8 and 7.21): creating an AUGraph, describing the default output unit, and adding a node matching that description to the graph. Again, this version uses the new Audio Component Manager API, so it compiles for and runs on Mac OS X 10.6 and up; you would need equivalent Component Manager calls to run on 10.5 or earlier.

Now let's finish the graph. You'll leave room in Listing 8.20 to make things more complex later with an #ifdef.

Listing 8.20   **Setting ASBD from Input AUHAL and Render Callback in the Play-Through AUGraph**

```
#ifdef PART_II
#else
    // Opening the graph opens all contained audio units
    // but does not allocate any resources yet
    CheckError(AUGraphOpen(player->graph),
               "AUGraphOpen failed");

    // Get the reference to the AudioUnit object for the
    // output graph node
    CheckError(AUGraphNodeInfo(player->graph,
                               outputNode,
                               NULL,
                               &player->outputUnit),
               "AUGraphNodeInfo failed");

    // Set the stream format on the output unit's input scope
    UInt32 propertySize = sizeof (AudioStreamBasicDescription);
    CheckError(AudioUnitSetProperty(player->outputUnit,
                                    kAudioUnitProperty_StreamFormat,
                                    kAudioUnitScope_Input,
                                    0,
                                    &player->streamFormat,
                                    propertySize),
               "Couldn't set stream format on output unit");
```

Listing 8.20   **Continued**

```
    AURenderCallbackStruct callbackStruct;
    callbackStruct.inputProc = GraphRenderProc;
    callbackStruct.inputProcRefCon = player;

    CheckError(AudioUnitSetProperty(player->outputUnit,
                                    kAudioUnitProperty_SetRenderCallback,
                                    kAudioUnitScope_Global,
                                    0,
                                    &callbackStruct,
                                    sizeof(callbackStruct)),
               "Couldn't set render callback on output unit");

#endif

    // Now initialize the graph (causes resources to be allocated)
    CheckError(AUGraphInitialize(player->graph),
               "AUGraphInitialize failed");

    player->firstOutputSampleTime = -1;
}
```

You use AUGraphOpen() to create the audio units wrapped by the nodes—only one so far—so that you can set properties on the output unit. What properties do you need to set? You might remember that, in setting up the input unit, you took notice of its sample rate, which might be different than the default value in your newly created output unit. You set the kAudioUnitProperty_StreamFormat of the output unit to the ASBD that you stored in player->streamFormat, to keep the two units in sync. If you remember the discussion of scopes and buses as they relate to I/O units, you'll understand why you set this value on bus 0's input scope: Bus 0 represents output to hardware, and the input scope represents what's going into the audio unit. So setting this property is how you tell the output unit, "This is the format you'll be receiving."

The other tasks in this listing are ones you've done before. You describe an output render callback as calling a yet-to-be-written GraphRenderProc() function and set this on the output unit with the kAudioUnitProperty_SetRenderCallback property; as a result, your GraphRenderProc() will be called whenever the output unit needs samples to play out. With that set up, you can initialize the graph and set a flag value for firstOutputSampleTime, to ensure that your callback gets a chance to set it the first time it's called.

Writing the Play-Through App's Render Callback

The task for the render callback is simple: When the output unit needs some samples to play, you retrieve a suitably large set from the `CARingBuffer`, where the input callback has been writing them.

The first task to do in Listing 8.21 is to perform the same offset calculation that you did in Listing 8.16. As a reminder, the reason for this is that the timestamps used by the input and output units might be different. Because the input callback is storing samples into the ring buffer with the time stamps it gets from the input unit, the output unit might need to adjust the time stamps it requests from the ring buffer.

Listing 8.21   **Adjusting Time Stamp Offsets in Render Callback**

```
OSStatus GraphRenderProc(void *inRefCon,
                         AudioUnitRenderActionFlags *ioActionFlags,
                         const AudioTimeStamp *inTimeStamp,
                         UInt32 inBusNumber,
                         UInt32 inNumberFrames,
                         AudioBufferList * ioData)
{

    MyAUGraphPlayer *player = (MyAUGraphPlayer*) inRefCon;

    // Have we ever logged output timing? (for offset calculation)
    if (player->firstOutputSampleTime < 0.0) {
        player->firstOutputSampleTime = inTimeStamp->mSampleTime;
        if ((player->firstInputSampleTime > 0.0) &&
            (player->inToOutSampleTimeOffset < 0.0)) {
            player->inToOutSampleTimeOffset =
                player->firstInputSampleTime - player->firstOutputSampleTime;
        }
    }
```

As before, this offset calculation needs to run only once, the first time in either callback that both `firstInputSampleTime` and `firstOutputSampleTime` have values other than the -1 flag value you initialized them with.

Aside from the possible offset calculation, the real work of this callback is to fetch samples from the ring buffer. This is a one-line call to the `CARingBuffer`'s `Fetch()` method, as shown in Listing 8.22.

> **Note**
>
> The three-argument version of `Fetch()` is the one provided by the corrected version of `CARingBuffer`, as explained in an earlier footnote. If you get a compile error and find that your version of `Fetch()` takes a `bool` as a fourth argument, then you're using the old, buggy `CARingBuffer` and you need to get the new version from Apple Technical Q&A 1665, on Apple's developer site.

Listing 8.22   **Fetching Samples from CARingBuffer**

```
// Copy samples out of ring buffer
OSStatus outputProcErr = noErr;
outputProcErr = player->ringBuffer->Fetch(ioData,
                                        inNumberFrames,
                                        inTimeStamp->mSampleTime +
                                            player->inToOutSampleTimeOffset);
}
```

Notice that this is where you use your calculated `inToOutSampleTimeOffset`, adjusting the time stamp you ask the buffer for.

You might be wondering what happens if the first output callback happens before the first input callback, in which case there would be nothing in the ring buffer to fetch. The `CARingBuffer` class falls back to filling the `ioData` buffer with zeros (silence in PCM) whenever not enough data is available.

Running the Play-Through Example

Wow, you did *a lot* in this example, all for the sake of getting audio from the default input device and playing it out to the default output. Let's review what you've written:

- You created an AUHAL audio unit to handle the input. You discovered the audio device that's currently set as the default input device, and you connected that to your AUHAL.

- You created a `CARingBuffer` to hold samples received from the input unit and wrote an input callback to store samples to this buffer.

- You built an `AUGraph` with a single node, the default output unit, and you gave it a render callback that reads from the ring buffer.

- You started the input unit and the graph, which causes both of them to connect to the audio hardware and start calling your callbacks.

At this point, you've accounted for everything and you can build the application. Take a look at your selected input and output devices in the Sound pane of the System Preferences application; these are the devices that the application will use. When you've got input on that device, such as an A/V device playing into a line-in connection or your own voice speaking into a microphone, run the application and listen for the result on the default output device (probably your speakers or headphones). Because you're not processing or resampling or doing anything else with the sound, it should sound pretty good. When you're done playing, you can click Stop in Xcode or press any key in the Console window to exit the application.

You did a lot of work to provide some pretty simple functionality in this example. You'd be right to think that this is a grueling amount of work for something as simple as play-through. If all you want is play-through, you could do this application with two audio queues (one each for input and output), and it would be a lot simpler. But by taking on all this responsibility, you give yourself the ability to do cool stuff. In the last section, you'll build on this to get a taste of what's possible down here in the dark depths of audio units.[2]

Mixing

In the current play-through application, your code actually sees the captured audio data twice: once in `InputRenderProc()` and again in `GraphRenderProc()`. If you wanted to perform some sort of DSP on the samples, you could do so in those functions (with the earlier proviso that you have to complete your work fast enough to not block the real-time callback thread).

Another option is to run those samples through some audio units. For example, you could put the `AUMatrixReverb` effect that you applied to the speech synthesizer earlier at the front of the graph, to echo the captured audio. You do this by connecting the output unit to the effect unit and then setting the render callback on the effect unit. When the graph runs, the render callback gets the captured audio from the ring buffer and supplies it to the reverb unit, which performs its reverb effect and sends the modified samples on to the output unit for play-out to the audio hardware. With an `AUGraph` at your disposal, it would be straightforward to apply any number of effects, from practical to silly, to the captured audio before its play-out through the output unit.

So far, the graphs have been straight-line affairs: All the audio takes the same path through a sequence of nodes until it gets to the output unit. But that's not the whole story of `AUGraph`s: One of the most powerful things you can do with them to have multiple paths for your audio. You do this with an important type of audio unit: mixer units. In the abstract, these units combine multiple input streams of audio in some way and produce one or more streams of audio. Often mixer units take multiple input buses and produce a single bus of output, or two for noninterleaved stereo. Mac OS X supplies three standard mixers:

- `AUMixer`: Mixes an arbitrary number of mono or stereo inputs and produces a single stereo output.

- `AUMatrixMixer`: Mixes an arbitrary number of inputs and produces an arbitrary number of outputs.

- `AUMixer3D`: Mixes an arbitrary number of sources and makes them sound as if they are positioned in a 3D sound field, relative to the listener. This unit is the basis of Core Audio's implementation of OpenAL, which you'll study in the next chapter.

---

[2] We tried to keep our example as simple as possible: Even with the next section's bells and whistles, it's about 500 lines of code. For a more thorough example of these techniques, take a look at Apple's `CAPlayThrough` example (in your documentation bundle or on the Apple website), which is more than twice as long.

> **Note**
>
> The `AUSplitter`, a subtype of converter units, does the opposite of mixing: It takes a single input stream and splits it into multiple, identical streams.

With mixer units, you can get to some of the real payoff of `AUGraphs`: the capability to have many streams of audio from many sources, performing effects on individual streams and mixing them together before sending them out to the audio hardware.

In this example, you'll add one other audio source and mix it with the captured audio. It would be pretty natural to use the file player unit and mix with the audio play-through code to create a karaoke-style sing-along application. But because setting up the file player was kind of a hassle, we leave that as an exercise for ambitious readers. Of the earlier examples, the easiest to set up was the speech synthesizer, so let's use that. To your existing play-through code, add another stream that comes from the speech synthesis unit and mix them together before they go into the output unit. Remember to `#import` and link the Application Services framework, which provides the speech synthesizer.

First, add the speech synthesis audio unit to the `MyAUGraphPlayer` struct at the top of the file where the struct is defined (see Listing 8.23).

Listing 8.23   **Adding a Speech Synthesis Audio Unit to the MyAUGraphPlayer Struct**

```
#ifdef PART_II
    AudioUnit speechUnit;
#endif
```

The bulk of the new work will be in `BuildMyAUGraph()`. Currently, this function creates an `AUNode` for the default output unit, gets the unit out of the node, and connects the render callback to it. In a more elaborate unit, you need a few more nodes and some connections. The new graph will have three nodes: the default output, a speech synthesis node, and a mixer node to mix the synthesized audio with the captured audio and send the mixed audio to the output unit.

Think about the `AUGraph` and its pull model. You'll still have the output node at the end, which you set up at the beginning of `CreateMyAUGraph()`. That doesn't need to change. Currently, it has a render callback that collects samples from the ring buffer. Connect the output node to a mixer node, which, in turn, has two inputs: the render callback that pulls from the ring buffer and a node connection to a new speech synthesizer node.

Start your new code, shown in Listing 8.24, inside the empty `#ifdef` that you set up earlier, in Listing 8.20.

Listing 8.24   **Creating a Stereo Mixer Unit in an AUGraph**

```
#ifdef PART_II

    // Add a mixer to the graph
    AudioComponentDescription mixercd = {0};
```

Listing 8.24   **Continued**

```
mixercd.componentType = kAudioUnitType_Mixer;
mixercd.componentSubType = kAudioUnitSubType_StereoMixer;
mixercd.componentManufacturer = kAudioUnitManufacturer_Apple;
AUNode mixerNode;
CheckError(AUGraphAddNode(player->graph,
                         &mixercd,
                         &mixerNode),
          "AUGraphAddNode[kAudioUnitSubType_StereoMixer] failed");


// Add the speech synthesizer to the graph
AudioComponentDescription speechcd = {0};
speechcd.componentType = kAudioUnitType_Generator;
speechcd.componentSubType = kAudioUnitSubType_SpeechSynthesis;
speechcd.componentManufacturer = kAudioUnitManufacturer_Apple;
AUNode speechNode;
CheckError(AUGraphAddNode(player->graph,
                         &speechcd,
                         &speechNode),
          "AUGraphAddNode[kAudioUnitSubType_AudioFilePlayer] failed");
```

This should be a common sight. Describe an audio unit with an `AudioComponent Description` and then use `AUGraphAddNode()` to create an audio unit that matches the description, wrapped in an `AUNode` and associated with the `AUGraph`. Do this twice, first for the mixer and then again for the speech synthesizer.

Next, you get the `AudioUnits` wrapped by the `AUNodes` in Listing 8.25; you probably want to set properties on them, such as the stream format.

Listing 8.25   **Getting Default Output, Speech Synthesis, and Mixer Audio Units from Enclosing AUNodes**

```
// Opening the graph opens all contained audio
// units but does not allocate any resources yet
CheckError(AUGraphOpen(player->graph),
          "AUGraphOpen failed");


// Get the reference to the AudioUnit objects for the
// various nodes
CheckError(AUGraphNodeInfo(player->graph,
                           outputNode,
                           NULL,
                           &player->outputUnit),
          "AUGraphNodeInfo failed");
CheckError(AUGraphNodeInfo(player->graph,
                           speechNode,
                           NULL,
```

Listing 8.25   **Continued**

```
                              &player->speechUnit),
              "AUGraphNodeInfo failed");
    AudioUnit mixerUnit;
    CheckError(AUGraphNodeInfo(player->graph,
                               mixerNode,
                               NULL,
                               &mixerUnit),
              "AUGraphNodeInfo failed");
```

Recall from when you set up the input unit that you reset the output unit's streamFormat to use the sample rate of the input hardware. You need to do the same thing inside your graph in Listing 8.26, setting it for the streams going into the output unit and into the mixer unit.

Listing 8.26   **Setting streamFormat of Output Unit and Mixer Unit**

```
// Set ASBDs here
UInt32 propertySize = sizeof (AudioStreamBasicDescription);
CheckError(AudioUnitSetProperty(player->outputUnit,
                                kAudioUnitProperty_StreamFormat,
                                kAudioUnitScope_Input,
                                0,
                                &player->streamFormat,
                                propertySize),
           "Couldn't set stream format on output unit");

CheckError(AudioUnitSetProperty(mixerUnit,
                                kAudioUnitProperty_StreamFormat,
                                kAudioUnitScope_Input,
                                0,
                                &player->streamFormat,
                                propertySize),
           "Couldn't set stream format on mixer unit bus 0");
CheckError(AudioUnitSetProperty(mixerUnit,
                                kAudioUnitProperty_StreamFormat,
                                kAudioUnitScope_Input,
                                1,
                                &player->streamFormat,
                                propertySize),
           "Couldn't set stream format on mixer unit bus 1");
```

Notice that you've set this property twice on the mixer unit. The difference between the two calls to AudioUnitSetProperty() is that you need to set the stream format on two input buses: bus 0 and bus 1. This gives you a clue to how the mixer works. You provide any number of inputs as buses 0 to *n*, and the result is a single mixed stream: bus 0 of the mixer's output scope.

Setting up those connections is the last thing you need to do. Make the following connections in Listing 8.27:

- Mixer output scope/bus 0 connects to the output unit's input scope/bus 0. This sends the mixed audio to the output unit for play-out to the audio hardware (as indicated by your using bus 0 with an I/O unit).

- Mixer input scope/bus 0 is a render callback (not a connection between nodes) to the `GraphOutputProc()` function that collects samples from the `CARingBuffer`, left for you by the input unit and its callback.

- Mixer input scope/bus 1 connects to the speech synthesis unit's output scope/bus 0, so the synthesized speech flows into the mixer as another input.

Listing 8.27   Connecting Speech Synthesis, Stereo Mixer, and Default Output Units

```
// Connections
// Mixer output scope / bus 0 to outputUnit input scope / bus 0
// Mixer input scope / bus 0 to render callback
//    (from ringbuffer, which in turn is from inputUnit)
// Mixer input scope / bus 1 to speech unit output scope / bus 0

CheckError(AUGraphConnectNodeInput(player->graph,
                                   mixerNode,
                                   0,
                                   outputNode,
                                   0),
           "Couldn't connect mixer output(0) to outputNode (0)");
CheckError(AUGraphConnectNodeInput(player->graph,
                                   speechNode,
                                   0,
                                   mixerNode,
                                   1),
       "Couldn't connect speech synth unit output (0) to mixer input (1)");
AURenderCallbackStruct callbackStruct;
callbackStruct.inputProc = GraphRenderProc;
callbackStruct.inputProcRefCon = player;
CheckError(AudioUnitSetProperty(mixerUnit,
                                kAudioUnitProperty_SetRenderCallback,
                                kAudioUnitScope_Global,
                                0,
                                &callbackStruct,
                                sizeof(callbackStruct)),
           "Couldn't set render callback on mixer unit");
#else
```

Figure 8.4 shows the connections created by this PART_II version of the program. At this point, it's a complicated graph, fed in part by the asynchronous interaction with the ring buffer.

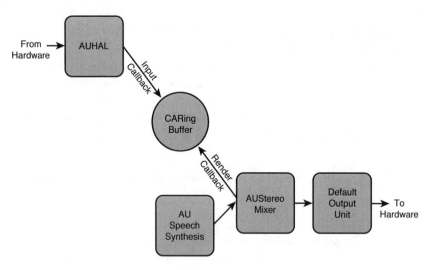

Figure 8.4   Audio flow of play-through example,
mixed with speech synthesis

What's left now is to configure the speech synthesis unit and get it started when you start the input unit and the graph. There's an #ifdef left in main() to let us do just that with Listing 8.28.

Listing 8.28   **Starting the Speech Synthesis Unit**

```
#ifdef PART_II
    // Configure the speech synthesizer
    PrepareSpeechAU(&player);
#endif
```

Of course, you need to provide that PrepareSpeechAU() function, which simply sets the kAudioUnitProperty_SpeechChannel property as before and uses SpeakCFString() to speak a short phrase. Feel free to replace the string in Listing 8.29 with one of your own choosing; just make it last long enough that you can hear what it sounds like when it's mixed with your voice (or whatever your input source is).

Listing 8.29   **Setting the Speech Unit's Speech Channel and Speaking a String**

```
#ifdef PART_II
void PrepareSpeechAU(MyAUGraphPlayer *player)
{
    SpeechChannel chan;

    UInt32 propsize = sizeof(SpeechChannel);
    CheckError(AudioUnitGetProperty(player->speechUnit,
                                    kAudioUnitProperty_SpeechChannel,
                                    kAudioUnitScope_Global,
                                    0,
                                    &chan,
                                    &propsize),
            "AudioFileGetProperty[kAudioUnitProperty_SpeechChannel] failed");

    SpeakCFString(chan,
                  CFSTR("Please purchase as many copies of our\
                      Core Audio book as you possibly can"),
                  NULL);
}
#endif
```

At this point, you can uncomment the #define PART_II and build and run the advanced version of the example program. The input device (likely a microphone) will start capturing at the same time the speech synthesizer begins speaking, and the mix of the two will play out to the speakers or headphones.

You might wonder whether you can adjust the respective volumes of the captured audio and the speech synthesis. As was the case with audio queues, audio units have parameters; they differ from properties, in that they're appropriate to expose to the user and can be reset on the fly. Some mixer units have a volume property that you can set on each of their input buses via AudioUnitSetParameter, to adjust their respective levels. This works for the AUMatrixMixer, but not for the simple AUStereoMixer in this example. If you want to see what parameters (if any) are exposed by system-supplied units, look up "Audio Unit Parameters References" in Xcode's documentation, or take a look through AudioUnitParameters.h.

Summary

The previous chapter used the analogy of a rock band's setup as an analogy to how Audio Units work. You imagined that you might have a guitar connected to an effects box, a synthesizer, a drum kit with a couple strategically placed mics, and more mics for the band's vocalists, along with mics for some backup singers.

Hopefully at this point, you can imagine this arrangement as a big `AUGraph`: The guitar goes into an input unit and is then run through one or more effect units, the synthesizer could be its own software instrument, the mics are all connected to input units, and all these units connect to a mixer, which then goes to an output unit to be played out to the speakers. Or maybe the backup singers' mics go into their own mix earlier, and that unit then connects as an input to the final mix. You can connect and configure it all in many ways. That kind of flexibility and power is what Core Audio was built for. In fact, its use in professional recording applications such as Logic Pro, Soundtrack, and Garage Band explicitly reflects this design and how well Core Audio is suited for it.

Now that you've had a deep immersion in this most challenging part of Core Audio, you might want a break! Who's up for some gaming? In the next chapter, you'll get into OpenAL, the audio API for 3D spatialized sound that was built for great game audio.

9

Positional Sound

"**A**nd now for something completely different …."

We're not kidding. The OpenAL library, which is included with both Mac OS X and iOS, is a completely different audio framework than Core Audio's pull-based world of audio units. It's different in part because it comes from a third party. It also solves completely different problems—namely, placing audio in a 3D sound field. Its primary purpose is to deliver audio for games, but you can use it as a general-purpose audio engine because of its interesting traits that you can bring to your own applications.

In this chapter, you dive into the design and architecture of OpenAL and look at how it represents positional sound as a C API. After you're introduced to its core concepts, you'll build two sample applications to get a feel for coding with OpenAL. First, you'll build a simple application to load a sound into memory and fly it around the listener. In the second example, you'll rework this program to work with files of any length, using OpenAL's streaming APIs. You'll also look at how to integrate Core Audio and OpenAL in the same program.

Sound in Space

OpenAL was originally developed by a company called Loki Software to help port Windows games to Linux. However, the company went bust and the open-source community tended to the project for a time until it was substantially taken over by sound card maker Creative Technologies, Ltd., a company that develops OpenAL with contribution from Apple and others. The specification, developer's guide, and other documentation are hosted on Creative's website: Visit http://openal.org/, and you'll be redirected (currently to http://connect.creativelabs.com/openal/default.aspx).

Because of its heritage as a technology for games, OpenAL has traits that are specifically useful for game development that sometimes differ from Core Audio's focus on audio professionals. In many ways, its API is deliberately similar to OpenGL, the popular 3D graphics library. The appeal is obvious: It's hugely advantageous to be able to think of your audio environment in the same terms as your visual one. Being game oriented, OpenAL also affords extremely low latency—you wouldn't want your action game's sounds to lag behind the onscreen action.

Note

When we talk about sound in a 3D space, you might wonder whether this is the same as "surround sound," which you'd get from Dolby Digital or DTS when you play a DVD or Blu-Ray disc. It isn't, really. First, in OpenAL, we're concerned with the *modeling* of a 3D sound-space, leaving it to the library and hardware to actually produce that sound. And when it comes to that step, there isn't a widely used standard for real-time 3D audio as there is for stereo PCM. Dolby Digital and DTS are compressed formats, which is easy enough to create in an A/V codec when you're mastering a disc but much less practical to do on-the-fly. So although OpenAL models sound in three dimensions, it ultimately renders it in one dimension: a left-to-right stereo mix. That said, if Macs ever do get sound cards that let you plug in more than two speakers, and if Apple supports them in their OpenAL drivers, your code wouldn't need any updates to support more dimensions.

OpenAL works with a 3D Cartesian coordinate space, which just means that positions within this space are indicated by x, y, and z coordinates. The axes of this space follow a "right hand rule," which you can imagine by holding up your right hand, making an "L" shape with your thumb and index finger, and bending your middle finger toward you, as shown in Figure 9.1. If you imagine that the approximate middle of your hand is the origin of this coordinate system, the direction your fingers point indicate which direction is positive for each axis, where your thumb is the x-axis, your index finger is the y-axis, and your middle finger is the z-axis. So, x values increase as they go right, y values increase as they go up, and z values increase as they go toward you.

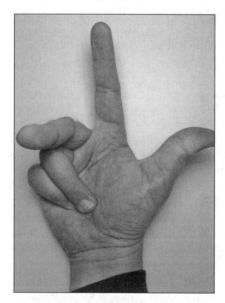

Figure 9.1   "Right hand rule" for visualizing 3D coordinate space

A *source* is an object in this space that produces sound. There can be, and usually are, many sources, and they can all produce either the same sound or different sounds. You attach *buffers* to sources. A buffer is just what it says: a memory buffer of audio data. A given buffer can be attached to one or many sources. In a game with a lot of objects that sound more or less the same (such as a racing game, in which each car's engine produces the same sound), you would just attach the same buffer to many sources. And in cases where each source has a distinct sound, you use different buffers for different sources. The third object in OpenAL is the *listener*, which represents the single listener in this space. OpenAL takes the sound data in the buffers; figures out how the listener would hear that sound, given the relative position and orientation of the listener and all the sources; and plays that resulting mix out to the audio hardware.

The OpenAL API

OpenAL represents sources, listeners, and buffers primarily through a property-style interface. After a listener, buffer, or source has been created, you work with it mainly by setting or getting its properties. In fact, the bulk of the OpenAL API consists of function calls that get or set various argument lists: `alSourcei()` sets a source property with one integer value, `alGetBuffer3f()` gets a property from a buffer as three floats, and so on. Getter functions all have `Get` in their name; functions without `Get` are setters.[1] Depending on the property you are working with, you either set or get a single int or float, set or get three discrete values (often for coordinates), or set or get a "vector," which is a C array usually containing three or six values, depending on the property.[2] When you get the hang of it, the naming is pretty predictable: getters for sources are `alGetSourcei()`, `alGetSource3i()`, `alGetSourcef()`, and so on; these functions then get one int, pointers to three ints, and a float, respectively. Meanwhile, setters for the listener include `alListeneri()`, `alListener3i()`, `alListenerf()`, and so on.

But what can you set? Tables 9.1, 9.2, and 9.3 provide a quick summary of the properties (and their types) that can be set on buffers, listeners, and sources, respectively. Don't worry if you don't understand them all; some of them are esoteric, most have sensible defaults, and you generally need to set or get only a handful of properties specific to your current needs. The OpenAL spec reveals the math behind the advanced sound-modeling features.

---

[1] This is the exact *opposite* of the Objective-C convention, in which you explicitly use the word "set" for setters but omit "get" in getters.

[2] Any OpenAL property that consists of a single value can be accessed with a one-member vector as well.

Table 9.1   **Property Constants for OpenAL Buffer Functions**

Property Constant	Description
AL_DATA	The original location in memory that the buffer's data was copied from. This is useless if the caller has subsequently `free()`'d that memory, but in some cases (like using the optional "static buffering" API), it's viable.
AL_FREQUENCY	Sample rate of the audio data (in Hz), as an int.
AL_BITS	Bit depth of the buffer (such as 8 or 16), as an int.
AL_CHANNELS	Number of channels in each sample, as an int. Must be 1 to get positional sound (stereo sounds play with their existing left–right mix).
AL_SIZE	Size of the buffer in bytes, as an int.

Table 9.2   **Property Constants for OpenAL Listener Functions**

Property Constant	Description
AL_GAIN	Master gain ("volume"), after all sources are mixed (a float).
AL_POSITION	Listener's position in space as three coordinates (x, y, z), either ints or floats.
AL_ORIENTATION	Direction the listener is facing, as a vector of six ints or floats (one vector expressing the direction of "forward" for the listener, and a second for "up").
AL_VELOCITY	Listener's velocity, as an int or float vector. This doesn't actually change the AL_POSITION; it just applies a Doppler effect, increasing the pitch if the source is moving toward the listener and decreasing it if moving away.

Table 9.3   **Property Constants for OpenAL Source Functions**

Property Constant	Description
AL_POSITION	Position of the source in space, as (x, y, z) floats.
AL_VELOCITY	Source's velocity, as an int or float vector. This doesn't actually change the AL_POSITION; it just applies a Doppler effect, increasing the pitch if the source is moving toward the listener and decreasing it if moving away.
AL_DIRECTION	A vector (of three ints or floats, or a vector of ints or floats) describing which direction the source is pointing.
AL_SOURCE_RELATIVE	Flag to indicate whether source positions are relative to the listener or absolute. The default for this int value is AL_FALSE.
AL_PITCH	A pitch multiplier, enabling you to change the pitch of a sound. Must be a positive float.
AL_GAIN	Gain (volume boost or attenuation) for the source (float).

Table 9.3 **Continued**

Property Constant	Description
AL_MAX_DISTANCE	Distance (int or float) at which the source becomes completely inaudible (used only with the Inverse Clamped Distance model).
AL_ROLLOFF_FACTOR	How quickly sound "rolls off" from the source (float or int).
AL_REFERENCE_DISTANCE	Distance (float or int) that source volume would normally fall by half (barring modifications from AL_REFERENCE_DISTANCE or AL_MAX_DISTANCE).
AL_MIN_GAIN	Minimum gain for this source (float).
AL_MAX_GAIN	Maximum gain for this source (float).
AL_CONE_OUTER_ANGLE	Outer angle of the sound cone, which affects how sound propagates out from the source, as int or float degrees. Default is 360.
AL_CONE_INNER_ANGLE	Inner angle of the sound cone, as int or float degrees. Default is 360.
AL_CONE_OUTER_GAIN	The gain factor for listeners outside the cone produced by the source, as a float. Inside the cone, the gain is AL_GAIN, and a linear interpolation is used for points in between.
AL_SOURCE_TYPE	An enumerated int to indicate the source type (either AL_UNDETERMINED, AL_STATIC, or AL_STREAMING), as determined by which functions you used to attach buffers.
AL_LOOPING	An int flag to either loop the current buffers (AL_TRUE) or not (AL_FALSE).
AL_BUFFER	An int representing the attached buffer.
AL_SOURCE_STATE	An enumerated int indicating the current state: AL_INITIAL, AL_PLAYING, AL_PAUSED, or AL_STOPPED.
AL_BUFFERS_QUEUED	For streaming, how many buffers are queued up on this source (read-only int).
AL_BUFFERS_PROCESSED	For streaming, how many queued buffers have been used up (read-only int).
AL_SEC_OFFSET	Playback in the current buffer in seconds, as int or float.
AL_SAMPLE_OFFSET	Playback in the current buffer in sample count, as int or float.
AL_BYTE_OFFSET	Playback in the current buffer in byte count, as int or float.

Beyond the property accessors, the remaining functions perform specific tasks. There are a few functions to identify your computer's available audio devices. With one of these, you can create an OpenAL context that will be the output device for all subsequent OpenAL calls. Functions exist to create and destroy buffers, sources, and listeners; to attach buffers to sources; and to start and stop playing sound from sources. Beyond the buffer, source, and listener functions, OpenAL's remaining functions deal with getting or setting global state, such as the speed of sound or the model by which sounds fade with distance, as well as some functions to check the error state of previous OpenAL calls.

All the OpenAL functions are documented in the *OpenAL Programmer's Guide* (available at the openal.org website), or you can just look in the al.h and alc.h header files. You'll generally #include or #import in both of these header files; alc.h defines functions and constants for working with the OpenAL context and devices, and al.h has the definitions related to sources, listeners, and containers, as well as typedefs, such as ALfloat and ALuint for floating-point and unsigned integer values, respectively.[3] The website also has an "OpenAL 1.1 Specification" that defines the semantics of the API, such as how sounds are interpolated and attenuated, given the various source and listener properties you set.

> **Beware Geeks Bearing OpenAL Gifts**
>
> Searching the Web for OpenAL sample code often leaves you disappointed on the Mac—and especially on iOS. A collection of utility functions, alut.h, are not part of the OpenAL spec, were effectively deprecated by 2005, and are therefore not included with Apple's implementations of OpenAL (for more information, see Apple's "Technical Q&A QA1504: The Header File 'alut.h' Is Missing from the OpenAL Framework").
>
> The big problem is that a lot of the sample code you find on the Web assumes that these utilities are available. Even the *OpenAL Programmer's Guide*[4] makes use of a loadWAVFile() function that is defined in alut.h and, therefore, doesn't exist on Mac or iOS. Later in this chapter, you'll see how you can use Core Audio, specifically ExtAudioFile, as a much more capable replacement for loadWAVFile().

Putting a Sound in Space

To exercise OpenAL, you'll develop a simple application to put a sound in space and move it around. You'll use all three dimensions, even though your speakers or headphones are one-dimensional, meaning the sound will ultimately be rendered as a left-to-right stereo mix.

How do you move a source in the OpenAL space? You repeatedly set its AL_POSITION. For the first example, we load a sound into a buffer, attach it to a source and set AL_LOOPING (so the buffer plays over and over), and then "orbit" the sound around the listener's default position of (0,0,0). Leaving the listener at the origin makes the

---

[3] OpenAL also defines a capture API, but this is not implemented on Mac OS X or iOS. To perform capture, use the Audio Queue (Chapter 4), the AUHAL unit (Chapter 8), or the RemoteIO unit (Chapter 10).

[4] Available from Creative Labs' website, at http://connect.creativelabs.com/openal/Documentation/OpenAL_Programmers_Guide.pdf.

math easier: You can create an orbit with simple trigonometry, using the following formulas to set the source's location:

$$x = 3 \cos (\theta);$$
$$y = \tfrac{1}{2} \sin (\theta);$$
$$z = \sin (\theta);$$

This creates a three-dimensional ellipse shown in Figure 9.2. (You can also easily graph this formula with `/Applications/Utilities/Grapher.app`, which we used to create the figure.) Notice that the biggest movement is along the *x*-axis (because you multiply the cosine by 3), so we expect to hear wide left-to-right swipes.

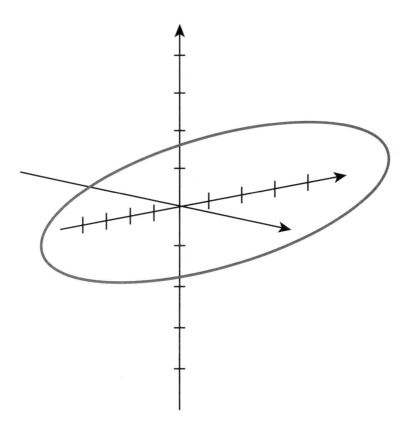

Figure 9.2   Orbit of example 3D sound source

Setting Up the Example

To begin the example, create an Xcode command-line project. Because you're using OpenAL, you need to add the `OpenAL.framework` to the application target. You will also be using `ExtAudioFile` to read the audio loop from disk, so also add `AudioToolbox.framework`, as usual.

Let's start with an overview of the program, shown in Listing 9.1. As in our Core Audio examples, this program has a struct to pass state information, some utility functions, and a `main()`.

Listing 9.1   Outline of an OpenAL Program to Orbit a Looping Source Around the Listener

```
#import <AudioToolbox/AudioToolbox.h>
#import <OpenAL/al.h>
#import <OpenAL/alc.h>

#pragma mark user-data struct
// Insert Listing 9.3 here

#pragma mark - utility functions -
// Insert Listing 4.2 here
// Insert Listing 9.2 here

void updateSourceLocation (MyLoopPlayer player)
// Insert Listing 9.17 here

OSStatus loadLoopIntoBuffer(MyLoopPlayer* player)
// Insert Listings 9.18 - 9.21 here

#pragma mark main
int main (int argc, const char * argv[]) {
// Convert to an OpenAL-friendly format and read into memory
// Insert Listings 9.4 - 9.5 here

// Set up OpenAL buffer
// Insert Listings 9.6 - 9.8 here

// Set up OpenAL source
// Insert Listings 9.9 - 9.11 here

// Connect buffer to source
// Insert Listing 9.12 here

// Set up listener
// Insert Listing 9.13 here
```

Listing 9.1   **Continued**

```
// Start playing
// Insert Listing 9.14 here

// Loop and wait
// Insert Listing 9.15 here

// Clean up
// Insert Listing 9.16 here
}
```

You should copy over the OSStatus error checker (see Listing 4.2) that you've been using for the last few chapters, but that brings up an interesting question: How does OpenAL handle errors? As a third-party library, it has its own conventions, different from Apple's. Instead of returning an OSStatus from every function call, OpenAL has a single error value that gets set on nearly every OpenAL call. You retrieve (and clear) this error value with the alGetError() function, which returns one of a small number of AL_ constants: AL_INVALID_NAME, AL_INVALID_NUMBER, AL_INVALID_ENUM, AL_INVALIDNAME_OPERATION, AL_OUT_OF_MEMORY, or AL_NO_ERROR.

Listing 9.2 shows a CheckALError() function in the spirit of the original CheckError() function. It checks the error with alGetError() and returns immediately if it is AL_NO_ERROR. Otherwise, it logs an appropriate error message (incorporating a string the caller provides) and exits the program abnormally.

Listing 9.2   **Convenience Function to Check and Report the OpenAL Error**

```
static void CheckALError (const char *operation) {
    ALenum alErr = alGetError();
    if (alErr == AL_NO_ERROR) return;
    char *errFormat = NULL;
    switch (alErr) {
        case AL_INVALID_NAME:
            errFormat = "OpenAL Error: %s (AL_INVALID_NAME)";
            break;
        case AL_INVALID_VALUE:
            errFormat = "OpenAL Error: %s (AL_INVALID_VALUE)";
            break;
        case AL_INVALID_ENUM:
            errFormat = "OpenAL Error: %s (AL_INVALID_ENUM)";
            break;
        case AL_INVALID_OPERATION:
            errFormat = "OpenAL Error: %s (AL_INVALID_OPERATION)";
            break;
        case AL_OUT_OF_MEMORY:
            errFormat = "OpenAL Error: %s (AL_OUT_OF_MEMORY)";
            break;
```

Listing 9.2   **Continued**

```
    }
    fprintf (stderr, errFormat, operation);
    exit(1);
}
```

The key difference between this function and the Core Audio `CheckError()` function is that the OpenAL version doesn't take an error code as a parameter because the most recent error is tracked as a sort of state variable within OpenAL and isn't explicitly returned to the caller like the `OSStatus` that nearly every Core Audio call returns.

As with other examples in this book, you use a struct to pass state information among the program's various functions. You'll need the AL source here so you can repeatedly set its position. It's also convenient to pass around the `AudioStreamBasicDescription` that you'll read from the file, as well as the memory buffer that you read samples into. Listing 9.3 shows the `MyLoopPlayer` struct.

Listing 9.3   **MyLoopPlayer Struct for State Variables**

```
typedef struct MyLoopPlayer {
    AudioStreamBasicDescription    dataFormat;
    UInt16                         *sampleBuffer;
    UInt32                         bufferSizeBytes;
    ALuint                         sources[1];
} MyLoopPlayer;
```

Using OpenAL Objects

Now that setup is done, let's figure out the responsibilities of the program's `main()` function. You want the program to do the following:

- Initialize OpenAL and create a buffer, a source, and a listener
- Read some audio into the buffer and attach it to the source
- Start playing the source
- Go into a loop and change the position of the source so that it sounds like it is orbiting the listener

To start, in Listing 9.4, create an instance of `MyLoopPlayer` and call a yet-to-be-written `loadLoopIntoBuffer()` helper function to fill `sampleBuffer` with the audio for the looping sound.

Listing 9.4   **Initial Main Setup for OpenAL Looping Program**

```
int main (int argc, const char * argv[]) {
    MyLoopPlayer player;
    // Convert to an OpenAL-friendly format and read into memory
    CheckError(loadLoopIntoBuffer(&player),
               "Couldn't load loop into buffer") ;
```

The first task for using OpenAL is to initialize the library and create a context. It's possible to discover multiple audio devices and choose from them, although it's simplest to just work with the default device, which you get by calling `alcOpenDevice(NULL)`. After you have opened the device, you create an OpenAL context from it by passing it to `alcCreateContext()`. If this succeeds, you can make your new context the current context, meaning that this device will play all subsequent OpenAL calls. These tasks are shown in Listing 9.5.

Listing 9.5   **Opening a Default OpenAL Device and Creating a Context**

```
    ALCdevice* alDevice = alcOpenDevice(NULL);
    CheckALError ("Couldn't open AL device");
    ALCcontext* alContext = alcCreateContext(alDevice, 0);
    CheckALError ("Couldn't open AL context");
    alcMakeContextCurrent (alContext);
    CheckALError ("Couldn't make AL context current");
```

Notice that every one of the OpenAL calls is followed by a call `CheckALError()`, which you wrote in Listing 9.2 to check the AL error with `alGetError()` and terminate if it has any value other than `AL_NO_ERROR`. Assuming that setting up the context worked, you can move on to your buffer, source, and listener. Start with the buffer, shown in Listing 9.6, created with `alGenBuffers()`.

Listing 9.6   **Creating OpenAL Buffers**

```
    ALuint buffers[1];
    alGenBuffers(1,
                 buffers);
    CheckALError ("Couldn't generate buffers");
```

Notice that even though you have only one buffer, you used an array simply because `alGenBuffers()` takes the number of buffers to create an array of ALuints to put them in. You could have used an `*ALuint` instead of the array, of course.

Next, you want to turn to the audio data that your `loadLoopIntoBuffer()` function will load into `player.sampleBuffer` and copy it to the OpenAL buffer. You do this in Listing 9.7 with a call to `alBufferData()`, which takes the pointer to the buffers array, a format constant, the buffer, the buffer size, and the sample rate.

Listing 9.7   Attaching a Buffer of Audio Samples to an OpenAL Buffer

```
alBufferData(*buffers,
             AL_FORMAT_MONO16,
             player.sampleBuffer,
             player.bufferSizeBytes,
             player.dataFormat.mSampleRate);
CheckALError ("Couldn't buffer data");
```

Notice the format constant `AL_FORMAT_MONO16`. OpenAL is far more picky than Core Audio about the PCM formats it supports; it gets by with just a few constants and a sample rate argument instead of the many options provided by the `AudioStreamBasicDescription`. The supported constants are `AL_FORMAT_MONO8`, `AL_FORMAT_MONO16`, `AL_FORMAT_STEREO8`, and `AL_FORMAT_STEREO16`. As mentioned earlier, only mono sound is rendered positionally by OpenAL; stereo sounds are played as is. Accordingly, you'll likely use only the two bit depths of mono:

- For 8-bit data, OpenAL uses unsigned integers in the 0–255 range, where 128 (the middle of the range) is silence.
- With 16-bit data, OpenAL uses signed integers from −32,768 to 32,767, where 0 is silence.

The 16-bit value is easy to provide with Core Audio and an ASBD, and it sounds better than 8-bit anyway; that's what you need to be sure to put into `sampleBuffer` after you write `loadLoopIntoBuffer()`, as in Listing 9.8. OpenAL copies the data from your buffer to its own, so it's okay to free the `sampleBuffer`. You'll be `malloc()`'ing this `sampleBuffer` later, when you write `loadLoopIntoBuffer()`.

Listing 9.8   Freeing a Sample Buffer After Its Contents Have Been Copied to OpenAL

```
free(player.sampleBuffer);
```

With the OpenAL buffer accounted for, let's move on to the source. You generate the source with a call to `alGenSources()` (shown in Listing 9.9), whose syntax is identical to the `alGenBuffers()` call in Listing 9.6, taking a count argument and an array of ALuints to identify the created sources.

Listing 9.9   Creating an OpenAL Source

```
alGenSources(1,
             player.sources);
CheckALError ("Couldn't generate sources");
```

As with the buffer, it's easy to use a single-member array for the source, but you could also use an `*ALuint` instead. After you've created the source, you call the setter methods `alSourcei()` and `alSourcef()` to set the source's integer and floating-point properties, respectively. For this example, you'll set the AL_LOOPING value to AL_TRUE to indicate that you want it to continue to loop its buffer over and over, and you set AL_GAIN to the maximum value AL_MAX_GAIN, as shown in Listing 9.10.

Listing 9.10   Setting AL_LOOPING and AL_GAIN Properties on an OpenAL Source

```
alSourcei(player.sources[0],
          AL_LOOPING,
          AL_TRUE);
CheckALError ("Couldn't set source looping property");
alSourcef(player.sources[0],
          AL_GAIN,
          AL_MAX_GAIN);
CheckALError("Couldn't set source gain");
```

You also need to set the source's initial AL_POSITION. However, you're going to be repeatedly doing this in the loop that orbits the source, so you can just insert an initial call to an updateSourceLocation() function, as shown in Listing 9.11, which you'll write later.

Listing 9.11   Setting Initial Source Position

```
updateSourceLocation(player);
CheckALError ("Couldn't set initial source position");
```

Now that you have initialized your buffer and source, you can attach the buffer to the source, thereby providing the source with the audio you want it to play. This is another property of the source, AL_BUFFER, which you set with the usual alSourcei(), like in Listing 9.12.

Listing 9.12   Attaching an OpenAL Buffer to a Source

```
alSourcei(player.sources[0],
          AL_BUFFER,
          buffers[0]);
CheckALError ("Couldn't connect buffer to source");
```

The buffer and source are done. You can now set up the listener. You don't need to generate an array of listeners, as you had to do with buffers and sources, because there is always only one listener. The only thing to worry about is whether you want to set any of the various listener properties. Listing 9.13 ensures that the listener is situated at the origin of the coordinate system, (0,0,0) because that makes your math easier.

Listing 9.13   **Setting the Initial Position of the OpenAL Listener**

```
// Set up listener
alListener3f (AL_POSITION,
                0.0,
                0.0,
                0.0);
CheckALError("Couldn't set listener position");
```

Notice that this property takes three values—x, y, and z—so it's set with the alListener3f() function, which takes three ALfloats. You could also have used alListenerfv, which would take a vector (an ALfloat*) as a three-member array.

With this, your setup work is done. You can start playing the source, which causes the audio to start looping from the source's current position in space. You play a source with alSourcePlay(), as shown in Listing 9.14.

Listing 9.14   **Playing an OpenAL Source**

```
alSourcePlay(player.sources[0]);
CheckALError ("Couldn't play");
```

If you had multiple members in player.sources, you could use alSourcePlayv(), which takes a vector (an array) as its argument and starts all the sources in the vector simultaneously.

Although you don't need them in this program, OpenAL provides a number of functions that might be useful after you play a source. alSourcePause() temporarily pauses a source but enables you to resume with a subsequent alSourcePlay(). alSourceStop() is a full stop, and alSourceRewind() returns playback to the beginning of the buffer. All these functions have equivalents that take vector arguments, indicated by function names that end with a *v*.

With the source playing its loop, the only task left for the program is to orbit the source around the listener for a while. In Listing 9.15, you enter a do-while loop and repeatedly call your yet-to-be-written updateSourceLocation() function, check the AL error, and then sleep for a tenth of a second with CFRunLoopInMode().

Listing 9.15   **Looping to Animate the Source Position**

```
// And wait
printf("Playing...\n");
  time_t startTime = time(NULL);
do
{
    // Get next theta
    updateSourceLocation(player);
    CheckALError ("Couldn't set looping source position");
```

Listing 9.15   **Continued**

```
        CFRunLoopRunInMode(kCFRunLoopDefaultMode,
                           0.1,
                           false);
    } while (difftime(time(NULL), startTime) < RUN_TIME);
}
```

You fall out of the loop when you have played for RUN_TIME seconds, so you'll need to define that value (this code uses 20 seconds) somewhere earlier in your source file:

```
#define RUN_TIME 20.0
```

When you break out of the do-while loop, you should clean up all the OpenAL resources you created. You explicitly created an AL device, context, source, and buffer, so you need to free up all of those now. Listing 9.16 shows how to do this.

Listing 9.16   **Cleaning Up OpenAL Resources**

```
    // cleanup:
    alSourceStop(player.sources[0]);
    alDeleteSources(1,
                    player.sources);
    alDeleteBuffers(1,
                    buffers);
    alcDestroyContext(alContext);
    alcCloseDevice(alDevice);
    printf ("Bottom of main\n");
}
```

Aside from stopping the source, your cleanup tasks are all destroy/delete/close-style functions that have a one-to-one correspondence to open/create/gen-style functions called earlier. So you use alDeleteSources() and alDeleteBuffers() to clean up buffers and sources (the listener is implicit and is neither generated nor deleted), alcDestroyContext() to unload the OpenAL context, and alcCloseDevice() to finish using the audio device.

Animating the Source's Position

Your code makes multiple calls to an updateSourceLocation() function in Listing 9.11 to set its initial location and in Listing 9.15 to repeatedly update its location. This function needs to update the AL_POSITION of the source for some arbitrary time so that, over time, the source's position is animated as an orbit around the listener.

Earlier, we proposed formulas for x, y, and z to create the orbit, illustrated in Figure 9.1. Here are those formulas again:

$$x = 3 \cos (\theta);$$
$$y = \tfrac{1}{2} \sin (\theta);$$
$$z = \sin (\theta);$$

In this function, you need to adapt a given wall clock time to a repeating series of theta values in the range of 0 to 2π, which is what C's `sin()` and `cos()` functions take. To keep it simple, just multiply the time by a speed constant, divide by 2π, and take the remainder. So at the top of the program, define an ORBIT_SPEED constant:

```
#define ORBIT_SPEED 1
```

If you define the ORBIT_SPEED as 1, each orbit will take 2π (6.28) seconds. Now let's calculate an angle, theta, and do some trigonometry in Listing 9.17.

Listing 9.17   **Function to Update the AL_POSITION of a Source as an "Orbit"**

```
void updateSourceLocation (MyLoopPlayer player) {
    double theta = fmod (CFAbsoluteTimeGetCurrent() * ORBIT_SPEED, M_PI * 2);
    ALfloat x = 3 * cos (theta);
    ALfloat y = 0.5 * sin (theta);
    ALfloat z = 1.0 * sin (theta);
    alSource3f(player.sources[0],
               AL_POSITION,
               x,
               y,
               z);
}
```

This function simply performs its trig functions to calculate the ALfloats x, y, and z, and sets the source's AL_POSITION with alSource3f. If it were convenient, you could replace x, y, and z with an ALfloat array and then set the AL_POSITION with alSourcev() instead of alSource3f(); the only difference is whether it's more convenient to provide an array of floats or three distinct values.

Loading Samples for an OpenAL Buffer

The only remaining bit of work to do is to load the samples that the source will play. You've already seen two constraints on how you're going to do this:

- In Listing 9.7, the alBufferData() call used the format constant AL_FORMAT_MONO16, so you need to be sure to produce that format: one channel of 16-bit signed integers.

- Because the Mac OS X and iOS implementations of OpenAL do not contain the utilities defined in alut.h, you cannot count on the AL function loadWAVFile() to get the samples for you.

So how do you get a pointer to some data that you can load into the AL buffer object? Hopefully, you remember the file I/O you did in earlier chapters. In particular, ExtAudioFile (covered in Chapter 6, "Conversion") is your friend here: It reads from a file and converts to or from a PCM format of your choice. Because you need PCM, you can use an ExtAudioFile to read any Core Audio–supported format. This means that you could read from the AAC and MP3 songs in your iTunes Library and feed those to OpenAL. But before you get your hopes up, consider that all this PCM data is going to be loaded into memory, so maybe you should use a smaller file. For example, chances are good that iLife came preinstalled on your Mac. If so, you have a *big* collection of perfectly good music and sound effect loops sitting on your hard drive. Let's #define a path to one of them:

```
#define LOOP_PATH CFSTR ("/Library/Audio/Apple Loops/Apple/iLife Sound
Effects/Transportation/Bicycle Coasting.caf")
```

The alBufferData() function takes a simple void* to the data that you want to provide to the AL buffer. So the purpose of the loadLoopIntoBuffer() function is to malloc() and fill such a pointer.

Working backward from that, you know that ExtAudioFileRead() works with AudioBufferLists, so how do you bridge the worlds? Actually, it's easier than it looks: Each AudioBufferList has an array of AudioBuffers, and each AudioBuffer has three fields. The last of these fields, mData, is a plain old pointer to some audio data. You'll create one AudioBufferList with one AudioBuffer and then fill this AudioBuffer's mData.

You've got enough of a plan to start the loadLoopIntoBuffer() function. First, you create the ExtAudioFileRef to read from, as shown in Listing 9.18.

Listing 9.18   Creating an ExtAudioFile for Reading into OpenAL

```
OSStatus loadLoopIntoBuffer(MyLoopPlayer* player) {
    CFURLRef loopFileURL = CFURLCreateWithFileSystemPath(kCFAllocatorDefault,
                           LOOP_PATH,
                           kCFURLPOSIXPathStyle,
                           false);
    ExtAudioFileRef extAudioFile;
    CheckError (ExtAudioFileOpenURL(loopFileURL,
                                    &extAudioFile),
                "Couldn't open ExtAudioFile for reading");
```

To fill the mData, ExtAudioFile needs you to provide the client format that you want to convert to. Recalling your ExtAudioFile adventures in Chapter 6, you perform conversion by setting the client data format you want to receive as a property on the ExtAudioFile, as shown in Listing 9.19. This format is an AudioStreamBasicDescription, and you already know from the OpenAL docs what the format needs to be: one-channel, signed 16-bit integers.

Listing 9.19   **Describing the AL_FORMAT_MONO16 Format as an
AudioStreamBasicDescription and Using It with an ExtAudioFile**

```
memset(&player->dataFormat, 0, sizeof(player->dataFormat));
player->dataFormat.mFormatID = kAudioFormatLinearPCM;
player->dataFormat.mFormatFlags = kAudioFormatFlagIsSignedInteger |
                                  kAudioFormatFlagIsPacked;
player->dataFormat.mSampleRate = 44100.0;
player->dataFormat.mChannelsPerFrame = 1;
player->dataFormat.mFramesPerPacket = 1;
player->dataFormat.mBitsPerChannel = 16;
player->dataFormat.mBytesPerFrame = 2;
player->dataFormat.mBytesPerPacket = 2;

// Tell extAudioFile about our format
CheckError(ExtAudioFileSetProperty(extAudioFile,
                                   kExtAudioFileProperty_ClientDataFormat,
                                   sizeof (AudioStreamBasicDescription),
                                   &player->dataFormat),
           "Couldn't set client format on ExtAudioFile");
```

This gives you an `ExtAudioFile` that's ready to convert, but there's nowhere to put
the data yet. You need to allocate a sufficiently large buffer to hold the data after it's been
converted to PCM. You do this by asking the `ExtAudioFile` for the file length in
frames; then you allocate an `AudioBufferList` and an `mData` buffer big enough to
hold this many samples (16 bits each and only one sample per frame because it's mono).
Listing 9.20 shows these steps.

Listing 9.20   **Allocating a Read Buffer for the ExtAudioFile-to-OpenAL Transfer**

```
SInt64 fileLengthFrames;
UInt32 propSize = sizeof (fileLengthFrames);
ExtAudioFileGetProperty(extAudioFile,
                        kExtAudioFileProperty_FileLengthFrames,
                        &propSize,
                        &fileLengthFrames);
player->bufferSizeBytes =
    fileLengthFrames * player->dataFormat.mBytesPerFrame;

AudioBufferList *buffers;
UInt32 ablSize = offsetof(AudioBufferList,
                          mBuffers[0]) + (sizeof(AudioBuffer) * 1);
buffers = malloc (ablSize);

player->sampleBuffer = malloc(sizeof(UInt16) * player->bufferSizeBytes);
```

Listing 9.20   **Continued**

```
buffers->mNumberBuffers = 1;
buffers->mBuffers[0].mNumberChannels = 1;
buffers->mBuffers[0].mDataByteSize = player->bufferSizeBytes;
buffers->mBuffers[0].mData = player->sampleBuffer;
```

With your one-member `AudioBufferList` set up, you are finally ready to read the file into memory (see Listing 9.21). You might get the entire buffer filled with one call to `ExtAudioFileRead()`, but be careful to check how many bytes were actually read and loop the reading until you know the buffer is full.

Listing 9.21   **Reading Data with an ExtAudioFile for Use in an OpenAL Buffer**

```
// Loop reading into the ABL until buffer is full
UInt32 totalFramesRead = 0;
do {
    UInt32 framesRead = fileLengthFrames - totalFramesRead;
    // While doing successive reads
    buffers->mBuffers[0].mData = player->sampleBuffer +
                            (totalFramesRead * (sizeof(UInt16)));
    CheckError(ExtAudioFileRead(extAudioFile,
                            &framesRead,
                            buffers),
                "ExtAudioFileRead failed");
    totalFramesRead += framesRead;
    printf ("read %d frames\n", framesRead);
} while (totalFramesRead < fileLengthFrames);
free(buffers);
return noErr;
}
```

Notice that you `free()` the `AudioBufferList` that you `malloc()`'d at the top of the function. The samples are in `player->sampleBuffer`, and the ABL is no longer needed, so you should now free the memory. You free the actual sample buffer after providing it to OpenAL, which you already wrote as part of `main()` in Listing 9.8.

Assuming that this works, your call to this function (back in Listing 9.4) fills `player.sampleBuffer` (which is the same pointer as `buffers->mBuffers[0].mData`) with the converted PCM data.

This loader function is a bit of a distraction from the chapter's focus on OpenAL, but hopefully it comforts you to know that Core Audio and OpenAL can and should play nicely together. And now that it's written, you can build and run the program. Assuming that all goes well, you will hear your loop go back and forth between your speakers or headphones on about a 6.2-second cycle.

That gives you a first taste of OpenAL. Time to recall what you've covered:

- You converted an audio file to a memory buffer of PCM samples.
- You created an OpenAL source and a buffer, loaded the sample data into the buffer, and set properties on the source, buffer, and listener.
- You started the source and updated its `AL_POSITION` to provide the illusion of a sound orbiting around the listener.

Now that you've covered these basics of OpenAL, you're going to change how you deliver samples to the source, to open up a lot of new possibilities.

Streaming Audio in OpenAL

Short sounds are fine for one-off sound effects or loops from sources that more or less indefinitely make the same sound. But that doesn't account for the variety of sounds you might need to produce in OpenAL. What do you do for a sound that constantly changes, such as a synthesized sound, a song playing from a file, or a voice chat being received over a network connection? And what do you do if you don't want to have to load the entire sound into memory and keep it there? OpenAL sounds have to be PCM, so they consume a lot of space, even though they're only mono.

Well, you have a way to deal with this. Instead of supplying one block of data to a buffer and forgetting about it, you can stream audio to a source. The arrangement is a lot like the Audio Queues you worked with in Chapters 4, "Recording," and 5, "Playback": You put data into OpenAL buffers and queue them up on a source. The source consumes the buffers, and when a buffer is used up, you retrieve it and fill it with more data.

OpenAL's streaming API isn't that different from what you're already used. Pretty much everything involving your source, listener, and buffer remains the same. The difference is that, instead of setting a source's `AL_BUFFER` property once and forgetting about it, you call `alSourceQueueBuffers()` to queue up one or more buffers on the source. The source plays these buffers in the order they were queued.

That description should sound a lot like "priming" the queue, as you did before with Audio Toolbox. The difference is in the refill cycle. OpenAL streaming is push driven rather than pull driven. In OpenAL, you don't register for callbacks with empty buffers to refill, as with Apple's API. Instead, you have to poll the source for consumed buffers, retrieve them yourself, and requeue them on the source. You might complain that the timing of queue retrieval is not optimized; either you poll too frequently and waste cycles, or you poll not frequently enough and get dropouts. Still, you are free to push in at any time whatever size data buffer suits you instead of having to fill an exact number of samples for a callback.

Setting Up the OpenAL Streaming Example

Let's walk through this with another example. You'll do the same thing as in the first example (orbit a sound around the listener), except that this time you'll play a source file in its entirety and stream it to the source instead of just loading the whole thing into RAM.

The overall structure of the program is also similar to the previous case, except that when you loop to update the source's position, you'll also want to check whether you have exhausted buffers to refill. Listing 9.22 shows our outline of the streaming program.

Listing 9.22   **Outline of an OpenAL Program to Orbit a Streaming Source Around the Listener**

```
#import <AudioToolbox/AudioToolbox.h>
#import <OpenAL/al.h>
#import <OpenAL/alc.h>

#pragma mark user-data struct
typedef struct MyStreamPlayer
// Insert Listing 9.23 here

#pragma mark - utility functions -
// Insert Listing 4.2 here
// Insert Listing 9.2 here

void updateSourceLocation (MyStreamPlayer player)
// Insert Listing 9.17 here

OSStatus setUpExtAudioFile (MyStreamPlayer* player)
// Insert Listing 9.30 here

void fillALBuffer (MyStreamPlayer* player, ALuint alBuffer)
// Insert Listings 9.31 - 9.33 here

void refillALBuffers (MyStreamPlayer* player)
// Insert Listings 9.34 - 9.35 here

#pragma mark main
int main (int argc, const char * argv[]) {
// Prepare the ExtAudioFile for reading
// Set up OpenAL buffers
// Insert Listings 9.24 - 9.25 here

// Set up streaming source
// Insert Listing 9.26 here

// Queue up the buffers on the source
// Insert Listing 9.27 here
```

Listing 9.22   **Continued**

```
// Set up listener
// Start playing
// Insert Listing 9.28 here

// Loop and wait
// Insert Listing 9.29 here

// Clean up
// Insert Listing 9.29 here
}
```

You can reuse several previous functions as is. You need the Core Audio CheckError() function from Listing 4.2 and the CheckALError() function that you wrote earlier in Listing 9.2.

The struct you use to pass variables between the various functions needs a few more things in this program. Because you'll be keeping the ExtAudioFile open all the time to progressively read deeper and deeper into the file, you need to hold on to the ExtAudioFileRef, the file length in frames, the total frames read so far, and the size of the memory buffer you can read into, as Listing 9.23 shows.

Listing 9.23   **Structure for Passing Program State Around Streaming OpenAL Example**

```
#define BUFFER_COUNT 3
typedef struct MyStreamPlayer {
    AudioStreamBasicDescription     dataFormat;
    UInt32                          bufferSizeBytes;
    SInt64                          fileLengthFrames;
    SInt64                          totalFramesRead;
    ALuint                          sources[1];
    ExtAudioFileRef                 extAudioFile;
} MyStreamPlayer;
```

The main() remains responsible for creating the OpenAL context. It should also call a function to set up the ExtAudioFile for later reading (as shown in Listing 9.24), which you previously did in loadLoopIntoBuffer(). You'll write this setUpExtAudioFile() function later.

Listing 9.24   **Setting up ExtAudioFile and Creating an OpenAL Context for Streaming**

```
int main (int argc, const char * argv[]) {
    MyStreamPlayer player;
    CheckError(setUpExtAudioFile(&player),
               "Couldn't open ExtAudioFile") ;
    ALCdevice* alDevice = alcOpenDevice(NULL);
```

Listing 9.24   **Continued**

```
CheckALError ("Couldn't open AL device"); // default device
ALCcontext* alContext = alcCreateContext(alDevice, 0);
CheckALError ("Couldn't open AL context");
alcMakeContextCurrent (alContext);
CheckALError ("Couldn't make AL context current");
```

Next, you need to generate and prime the buffers (see Listing 9.25), as you did with the audio queue in Chapter 5. As with that chapter, it's handy to have a convenience function that fills a buffer with the next bunch of data from the file; this function can be called to prime the stream and can be repeatedly called later to continue the streaming by refilling the buffer. You'll write this fillALBuffer() function later.

Listing 9.25   **Creating and Filling OpenAL Buffers for Streaming**

```
ALuint buffers[BUFFER_COUNT];
alGenBuffers(BUFFER_COUNT,
             buffers);
CheckALError ("Couldn't generate buffers");
for (int i=0; i<BUFFER_COUNT; i++) {
    fillALBuffer(&player, buffers[i]);
}
```

With the buffers prepared, set up the OpenAL source exactly as before, with the exception of the AL_LOOPING property, which, of course, is incompatible with streaming, as Listing 9.26 shows.

Listing 9.26   **Creating an OpenAL Source for Streaming**

```
alGenSources(1,
             player.sources);
CheckALError ("Couldn't generate sources");
alSourcef(player.sources[0],
          AL_GAIN,
          AL_MAX_GAIN);
CheckALError("Couldn't set source gain");
updateSourceLocation(player);
CheckALError ("Couldn't set initial source position");
```

In the first example program, in Listing 9.12, you connected the buffer to the source by setting an AL_BUFFER property on the source. For streaming, you provide an array of buffers to the stream with the alSourceQueueBuffers() function. Listing 9.27 shows this call.

Listing 9.27   Queuing Buffers on an OpenAL Source for Streaming

```
alSourceQueueBuffers(player.sources[0],
                     BUFFER_COUNT,
                     buffers);
CheckALError("Couldn't queue buffers on source");
```

With the buffers queued up on the source, you just need to set up the source and start playing. Listing 9.28 works just like in the looping example (see Listings 9.13 and 9.14).

Listing 9.28   Creating a Listener and Starting a Stream-Orbiting Source

```
// Set up listener
alListener3f (AL_POSITION,
             0.0,
             0.0,
             0.0);
CheckALError("Couldn't set listener position");

// Start playing
alSourcePlayv (1,
               player.sources);
CheckALError ("Couldn't play");
```

At the bottom of main(),you loop for RUN_TIME seconds (remember to #define this elsewhere). However, this time, you call both the updateSourceLocation() function and a yet-to-be-written refillALBuffers() function that polls the source for exhausted buffers and refills them with your fillALBuffer(). Listing 9.29 shows all these steps.

Listing 9.29   Infinite Loop to Update the OpenAL Source Position and Refill Exhausted Buffers, and Post-Loop AL Cleanup

```
// And wait
printf("Playing...\n");
  time_t startTime = time(NULL);
do
{
    // Get next theta
    updateSourceLocation(player);
    CheckALError ("Couldn't set looping source position");

    // Refill buffers if needed
    refillALBuffers (&player);

    CFRunLoopRunInMode(kCFRunLoopDefaultMode, 0.1, false);
} while (difftime(time(NULL), startTime) < RUN_TIME);
```

Listing 9.29   **Continued**

```
    // Cleanup:
    alSourceStop(player.sources[0]);
    alDeleteSources(1,
                    player.sources);
    alDeleteBuffers(BUFFER_COUNT,
                    buffers);
    alcDestroyContext(alContext);
    alcCloseDevice(alDevice);
    printf ("Bottom of main\n");
}
```

The `updateSourceLocation()` function that you call in this loop is exactly the same as what you wrote in Listing 9.17, so copy that over now.

Notice that the post-loop cleanup code—which disposes of the source, buffers, context, and device—is nearly identical to Listing 9.16 from the previous example, except that you now have `BUFFER_COUNT` buffers to delete. Still, only one call to `alDeleteBuffers()` is needed to free up all the buffers in the array.

The program has now accounted for the source, buffers, and listener, so next you need to fill out the three convenience functions that will read data from the `ExtAudioFile` and refresh the `AL` buffers as needed.

Setting Up an ExtAudioFile for Streaming

The `setUpExtAudioFile()` function that you call at the top of `main()` to create an `ExtAudioFile()` is actually a little simpler than the first example's `loadLoopIntoBuffer()`. It only needs to create the `ExtAudioFile` and get a few properties from it, including the information you need to create memory buffers for reading from the file and the length of the file in frames. Be sure to `#define` a `BUFFER_DURATION_SECONDS` value, which you'll multiply by the sample rate and bytes per frame to figure out how large each read buffer needs to be.

So that you don't spend too much breath on Audio Toolbox stuff, Listing 9.30 presents the entire function. Refers you back to the first example, or Chapter 6, if the setup or use of the `ExtAudioFile` throws you. You can `#define STREAM_PATH` to be any file playable by Core Audio; the online sample code uses a long jingle track from the iLife collection:

```
#define STREAM_PATH CFSTR ("/Library/Audio/Apple Loops/Apple/iLife Sound
Effects/Jingles/Kickflip Long.caf")
```

But we're not above a funny musical reference every now and then, either; for example, see Listing 9.30.

Listing 9.30   **Setting up an ExtAudioFile for Reading into a Stream**

```
#define  STREAM_PATH CFSTR ("/Users/cadamson/Music/iTunes/iTunes Music/Yes/Fragile
(Remastered)/Long Distance Runaround.m4a")

OSStatus setUpExtAudioFile (MyStreamPlayer* player) {
    CFURLRef streamFileURL = CFURLCreateWithFileSystemPath(kCFAllocatorDefault,
                            STREAM_PATH,
                            kCFURLPOSIXPathStyle,
                            false);

    // Describe the client format - AL needs mono
    memset(&player->dataFormat, 0, sizeof(player->dataFormat));
    player->dataFormat.mFormatID = kAudioFormatLinearPCM;
    player->dataFormat.mFormatFlags =
        kAudioFormatFlagIsSignedInteger | kAudioFormatFlagIsPacked;
    player->dataFormat.mSampleRate = 44100.0;
    player->dataFormat.mChannelsPerFrame = 1;
    player->dataFormat.mFramesPerPacket = 1;
    player->dataFormat.mBitsPerChannel = 16;
    player->dataFormat.mBytesPerFrame = 2;
    player->dataFormat.mBytesPerPacket = 2;

    CheckError (ExtAudioFileOpenURL(streamFileURL,
                                    &player->extAudioFile),
                "Couldn't open ExtAudioFile for reading");

    // Tell extAudioFile about our format
    CheckError(ExtAudioFileSetProperty(player->extAudioFile,
                                    kExtAudioFileProperty_ClientDataFormat,
                                    sizeof (AudioStreamBasicDescription),
                                    &player->dataFormat),
                "Couldn't set client format on ExtAudioFile");

    // Figure out how big file is
    UInt32 propSize = sizeof (player->fileLengthFrames);
    ExtAudioFileGetProperty(player->extAudioFile,
                            kExtAudioFileProperty_FileLengthFrames,
                            &propSize,
                            &player->fileLengthFrames);

    printf ("fileLengthFrames = %lld frames\n", player->fileLengthFrames);

    player->bufferSizeBytes = BUFFER_DURATION_SECONDS *
                            player->dataFormat.mSampleRate *
                            player->dataFormat.mBytesPerFrame;
```

Listing 9.30   **Continued**

```
    printf ("bufferSizeBytes = %d\n", player->bufferSizeBytes);

    printf ("Bottom of setUpExtAudioFile\n");
    return noErr;
}
```

Refilling the OpenAL Buffers

The real work of the `ExtAudioFile` needs to happen in two functions, shown in
Listing 9.31. `fillALBuffer()` fills an OpenAL buffer with the next bunch of converted
PCM samples from the file. The first half of this function needs to allocate an
`AudioBufferList` and a `void*` sample buffer, just as you did with your one-time read
in the first example.

Listing 9.31   **Setting up an AudioBufferList and Its Single AudioBuffer for Reading
from ExtAudioFile**

```
void fillALBuffer (MyStreamPlayer* player, ALuint alBuffer) {
    AudioBufferList *bufferList;
    UInt32 ablSize = offsetof(AudioBufferList, mBuffers[0]) +
                            (sizeof(AudioBuffer) * 1); // 1 channel
    bufferList = malloc (ablSize);

    // Allocate sample buffer
    UInt16 *sampleBuffer = malloc(sizeof(UInt16) * player->bufferSizeBytes);

    bufferList->mNumberBuffers = 1;
    bufferList->mBuffers[0].mNumberChannels = 1;
    bufferList->mBuffers[0].mDataByteSize = player->bufferSizeBytes;
    bufferList->mBuffers[0].mData = sampleBuffer;
    printf ("allocated %d byte buffer for ABL\n",
            player->bufferSizeBytes);
```

Then, as before, you read bytes with `ExtAudioFileRead()` until you've filled the
buffer, advancing your `totalFramesRead` count as you go (see Listing 9.32).

Listing 9.32   **Reading from ExtAudioFile**

```
    UInt32 framesReadIntoBuffer = 0;
    do {
        UInt32 framesRead = player->fileLengthFrames - framesReadIntoBuffer;
        bufferList->mBuffers[0].mData = sampleBuffer +
                                        (framesReadIntoBuffer * (sizeof(UInt16)));
        CheckError(ExtAudioFileRead(player->extAudioFile,
                            &framesRead,
```

Listing 9.32   **Continued**

```
                            bufferList),
            "ExtAudioFileRead failed");
    framesReadIntoBuffer += framesRead;
    player->totalFramesRead += framesRead;
    printf ("read %d frames\n", framesRead);
} while (framesReadIntoBuffer < (player->bufferSizeBytes / sizeof(UInt16)));
```

When this while loop exits, the sampleBuffer is filled with converted PCM samples.[5] Now you need to get those samples into an OpenAL buffer; for this, use Listing 9.33. This works just like it did in the looping case: Call alBufferData() to copy from the memory buffer into the AL buffer.

Listing 9.33   **Copying Samples from Memory Buffer to OpenAL Buffer**

```
    // Copy from sampleBuffer to AL buffer
    alBufferData(alBuffer,
                 AL_FORMAT_MONO16,
                 sampleBuffer,
                 player->bufferSizeBytes,
                 player->dataFormat.mSampleRate);

    free (bufferList);
    free (sampleBuffer);
}
```

Notice in Listing 9.33 that you free() the AudioBufferList and the sampleBuffer, which you created at the top of the function. alBufferData() copies the data into OpenAL's own space, so you can (and should) free the memory you malloc()'d now.[6]

This function is all you need to prime the buffers when the program starts up. The remaining task is to check the source periodically and see if any buffers are exhausted and need to be refilled. In main(), you looped over a refillALBuffers() function to do this, so let's write that in Listing 9.34. First you ask the source how many exhausted buffers it has, which is the read-only property AL_BUFFERS_PROCESSED.

---

[5] For simplicity, you haven't handled the case of reaching the end of the file, which would require noticing whether ExtAudioFileRead() set framesRead to 0 and, if so, reopening the file with ExtAudioFileOpenURL(). You'd think that you could return to frame 0 via ExtAudioFileSeek() when you hit the EOF, but that doesn't work; reaching EOF effectively closes the file for further reading.

[6] As an aside, if you object to all this repeated malloc()'ing and free()'ing, you might be interested in the oalStaticBufferExtension.h header, which defines a "static buffer" API in which your code maintains ownership of the data buffers, passing just a pointer to OpenAL instead of repeatedly copying samples. For streaming OpenAL, it can be a desirable optimization.

Listing 9.34   **Checking an OpenAL Source for Exhausted Streaming Buffers**

```
void refillALBuffers (MyStreamPlayer* player) {
    ALint processed;
    alGetSourcei (player->sources[0],
                    AL_BUFFERS_PROCESSED,
                    &processed);
    CheckALError ("couldn't get al_buffers_processed");
```

If any buffers have been fully drained, you get them back from the source with the
alSourceUnqueueBuffers() function, which takes a source, a maximum number of
buffers to return, and an ALuint array to receive those buffers. Because you wrote your
fillALBuffer() function to work on only one buffer at a time (that makes the code
easier to follow), you'll loop and repeatedly dequeue and refill a single buffer in
Listing 9.35.

Listing 9.35   **Unqueueing and Refilling OpenAL Buffers**

```
    while (processed > 0) {
        ALuint freeBuffer;
        alSourceUnqueueBuffers(player->sources[0],
                                1,
                                &freeBuffer);
        CheckALError("Couldn't unqueue buffer");
        printf ("Refilling buffer %d\n", freeBuffer);
        fillALBuffer(player, freeBuffer);
        alSourceQueueBuffers(player->sources[0],
                                1,
                                &freeBuffer);
        CheckALError ("Couldn't queue refilled buffer");
        printf ("Re-queued buffer %d\n", freeBuffer);
        processed--;
    }
}
```

In this loop, any time you unqueue and refill a buffer, you immediately requeue it on
the source with alSourceQueueBuffers(), the same function you called in Listing
9.27 to prime the source with buffers.

That's all you need to do. Build and run this program, and you should hear your
source stream orbiting around you—well, oscillating between speakers, anyway—for as
long as you choose to let it play.

Summary

The streaming example used a flat file as its source, but you can use any technique to provide data to the buffers, such as synthesized sounds, in which you write samples on the fly, or network sources, in which you get data over the network. In the latter case, imagine a virtual world where the radios play streaming web radio but have distinct positions in space so that you hear them differently as your onscreen avatar moves around them.

OpenAL also has the distinction of being very low latency. It has to be, after all, to be of any use for gaming. In fact, OpenAL is implemented atop a 3D mixer audio unit, meaning that you're picking up the low latency of audio units with a programming model that's a little easier to work with; you don't have to deal with threading, callback timeouts, or ring buffers as you did in Chapters 7, "Audio Units: Generators, Effects, and Rendering," and 8, "Audio Units: Input and Mixing." It wouldn't be completely unreasonable to use OpenAL for general-purpose streaming audio in your application; it's both performant and easy to port to and from other platforms.

IV

Additional Topics

10

Core Audio on iOS

Although it started on Mac OS X, Core Audio is at least as important—and maybe more so—on iOS, where its low latency and extreme efficiency are a phenomenally good fit for the limited environment that exists on mobile devices such as the iPhone, iPod touch, and iPad. It was the first media API available when Apple opened the iPhone's SDK, and for a lot of apps, it's still the right choice.

This chapter looks at how you can immediately put to use on iOS everything you've already learned. Then it moves to the traits that are specific to iOS, including its simplified hardware abstraction, its strengths and limits, and how you collaborate with other apps to share the device's audio system.

Is That Core Audio in Your Pocket?

If you think of yourself primarily as an iOS developer, you might feel as if you've been toughing it out for the first nine chapters of this book, enduring all this "Mac stuff" as you worked through command-line based examples. The iPhone doesn't even have a command-line, *fercryinoutloud*!

We'd like to thank you for your patience. You've finally arrived at the iOS chapter. We'd also like to congratulate you. If you worked through the first nine chapters, you now know most of Core Audio on iOS already.

Core Audio on iOS is really similar to its original form on OS X—really, really similar. Consider the following APIs:

- Audio File Services
- Audio Conversion
- Extended Audio File Services
- Audio Queue Services
- Audio Units
- Audio Unit Graphs
- OpenAL

All these APIs exist more or less unchanged on iOS. Where differences exist, they're generally in the small details, not in the functions themselves or the big picture of how to use them. The differences generally come from what can reasonably be expected from small devices and what's appropriate for the more tightly controlled environment of third-party app development for iOS.

This chapter looks at the diffs, to focus on what's unique to Core Audio on iOS. Fundamentally, two underlying differences make things different on iOS:

- **Applications run in a managed environment.** On Mac OS X, applications (or other processes, such as daemons) have substantial access to system resources and operate with a high degree of independence. On iOS, third-party applications run in a rigidly defined and controlled context. Apps can only be apps—they cannot be daemons, agents, drivers, command-line executables, and so on—and running as a UIApplication imposes rules on apps in terms of how they share system resources, including access to the audio system. This also means there is no sharing of resources between applications, which has profound implications for Audio Units: You can't make a third-party plug-in that other apps can see, so there isn't a aftermarket for Audio Units as there is on OSX.

- **The audio hardware is simpler.** Your Mac could potentially have many audio devices, such as audio cards and I/O devices, all of which have different timing and performance characteristics. An iOS has exactly *one* audio device. This greatly simplifies some of the APIs and eliminates others: It's easier to get an I/O audio unit when you don't have to specify a device. As a result, the Audio Hardware Services functions (which Chapter 4, "Recording," touched on) are completely absent.

The differences in iOS manifest themselves primarily in two ways:

- A new set of functions, Audio Session Services, manages your app's use of audio system resources and provides access to information about the audio hardware.

- Audio Units are more limited in what they can do. Part because of the simplicity of the hardware and the need to conserve resources, iOS provides a much smaller collection of Audio Units, and the nature of "sandboxed" applications doesn't allow for third-party AU development. On the other hand, having only a single audio device means that doing audio input and output with audio units and AUGraphs is actually a lot easier.

This chapter looks at these traits separately. You'll develop two sample apps to exercise both the Audio Session API and Audio Units as they exist on iOS.

Playing Nicely with Others: Audio Session Services

Let's start by looking at the Audio Session Services. This set of APIs in the Audio Toolbox provides just a handful of services that relate to an audio session, which represents the app's access to and use of the device's audio system. The functions enable you to do the following:

- Initialize the audio session
- Set whether the session is active (producing and/or receiving audio)
- Get and set property values

That's pretty much it, but as with the other Core Audio APIs, the getting and setting of properties provides a great deal of functionality. These are some of the most important properties:

- `kAudioSessionProperty_AudioInputAvailable`

  Specifies whether the device is capable of audio capture. Many iOS devices come with built-in microphones (including all iPhones and iPads), but on early iPod touch models, audio input is available only if you attach a headset with a microphone or some other external device.

- `kAudioSessionProperty_CurrentHardwareSampleRate`

  `kAudioSessionProperty_CurrentHardwareInputNumberChannels`

  `kAudioSessionProperty_CurrentHardwareOutputNumberChannels`

  `kAudioSessionProperty_CurrentHardwareOutputVolume`

  `kAudioSessionProperty_CurrentHardwareInputLatency`

  `kAudioSessionProperty_CurrentHardwareOutputLatency`

  `kAudioSessionProperty_CurrentHardwareIOBufferDuration`

  Read-only properties that report various details about the audio hardware.[1]

- `kAudioSessionProperty_PreferredHardwareSampleRate`

  `kAudioSessionProperty_PreferredHardwareIOBufferDuration`

  Settable properties for adjusting audio hardware properties.

- `kAudioSessionProperty_AudioRoute`

  The current output (and possibly input) route as a read-only `CFString` (`"Headphone"`, `"Speaker"`, `"HeadsetInOut"`)

- `kAudioSessionProperty_OverrideAudioRoute`

  A write-only property that enables you to change the audio route to either `kAudioSessionOverrideAudioRoute_Speaker` or `kAudioSessionOverrideAudioRoute_None` (which means using the normal audio route for the current hardware).

---

[1] In Chapter 4, the hardware sampling rate property came from the Audio Object API, and we noted that iOS had an alternative approach for that. These properties are that alternative.

- **kAudioSessionProperty_AudioCategory**

  Defines how the app interacts with the rest of the audio system on the device.

The audio category has a set of semantic values that describe how you want your app to behave in terms of sharing access to the rest of the audio system: whether it mixes with other audio (such as from the Music app) or it wants to own the output, whether it wants to capture audio, whether it should honor the iPhone's ring/silent switch, and so on. The possible values are defined semantically, meaning in terms of your intent instead of as a set of specific behaviors. For iOS 4.0, the following values are provided:[2]

- **kAudioSessionCategory_AmbientSound**

  Background audio that is not necessarily critical to the application's activity. It mixes with the Music app and can be silenced with ring/silent switch. It does not allow capture and cannot play when the app is in the background.

- **kAudioSessionCategory_SoloAmbientSound**

  Background audio that does not mix with audio from other apps. It honors the ring/silent switch and does not allow capture or playing in the background. This is the default category if you neglect to set one.

- **kAudioSessionCategory_MediaPlayback**

  Foreground audio (that is, audio is the point of the application) that cannot be turned off by the ring/silent switch. It allows your app to keep playing when in the background. It does not mix with other apps' audio, although you can override this by setting the property kAudioSessionProperty_OverrideCategoryMix WithOthers. It does not allow recording.

- **kAudioSessionCategory_RecordAudio**

  Allows audio capture for apps that perform only capture and do not produce or play audio (which makes mixing and ring/silent considerations moot). It can continue recording when the app is in the background, although this turns the status bar red and shows the name of the application, to warn the user that he or she is being recorded.

- **kAudioSessionCategory_PlayAndRecord**

  Apps that both capture and produce audio, possibly simultaneously. It does not honor the ring/silent switch and typically does not mix with other apps (although you can override this with a property, as noted earlier). It can record and play in the background, as with the previous two categories.

---

[2] We have omitted deprecated values.

- `kAudioSessionCategory_AudioProcessing`

  Used for apps that process audio (say, through an `AUGraph`) without actually recording or playing. It can continue processing in the background.

An Audio Session Example

A lot of what makes iOS Core Audio programming unique is how you coordinate with the rest of the system. A simple example exercises these traits. In fact, it's so simple that it just generates a sine wave, drawing on the Audio Queue player from Chapter 5, "Playback," and the sine generator from Chapter 7, "Audio Units: Generators, Effects, and Rendering." But what's different is that the app changes tone it when is sent to the background. This means you do several things that are unique to iOS:

- You need to negotiate with Audio Session Services for access to the audio hardware.
- You need to adjust your app's settings to inform iOS that you need to keep running in the background.
- You need to react to delegate messages that tell you the app has been foregrounded or backgrounded.
- You need to react to interruptions that take the audio system away from you, such as incoming calls.

Setting Up the App

There's no such thing as a command-line executable on iOS. To do the next best thing and keep the example as simple as possible, you'll use what Xcode 4.2 calls an "Empty Application," which contains just an `UIApplicationDelegate` and a `UIWindow`.[3] In the sample code, this is called `CH10_iOSBackgroundingTone`, which means that Xcode created the Objective-C class `CH10_iOSBackgroundingToneAppDelegate` for you, with a header (`.h`) and implementation file (`.m`).

You have a full-blown object, so you use that instead of a struct to pass state around: You can pass the app delegate object as the `userInfo` pointer to anything that's going to drive callbacks; in the callback, you cast the pointer back to the app delegate and get its members as properties. Edit the header file (`.h`) as shown in Listing 10.1.

---

[3] We assume that you have a passing knowledge of iOS programming to even read this chapter. If you need to get up to speed, we recommend *iOS Programming: The Big Nerd Ranch Guide, Second Edition*, from the good folks at, well, The Big Nerd Ranch (www.bignerdranch.com).

Listing 10.1   **Header File for iOS Tone-Player App**

```
#import <UIKit/UIKit.h>
#import <AudioToolbox/AudioToolbox.h>


@interface CH10_iOSBackgroundingToneAppDelegate : NSObject <UIApplicationDelegate>


@property (nonatomic, retain) IBOutlet UIWindow *window;


@property (nonatomic, assign) AudioQueueRef audioQueue;
@property (nonatomic, assign) AudioStreamBasicDescription streamFormat;
@property (nonatomic, assign) UInt32 bufferSize;
@property (nonatomic, assign) double currentFrequency;
@property (nonatomic, assign) double startingFrameCount;


-(OSStatus) fillBuffer: (AudioQueueBufferRef) buffer;


@end
```

You'll use an Audio Queue to play your samples. As you saw in Chapter 5, this means you need a function or method to fill an `AudioQueueBufferRef`, both at startup when you "prime" the queue and when the queue consumes a buffer and needs more data. This is the `fillBuffer` method. That method needs to know the `audioQueue` to fill. As we developed it for this example, we found that we needed state variables you've seen in earlier sine-wave examples: the stream format, how big the buffers are, the desired frequency to generate, and where we are in the current wave.

Now let's start on the app delegate implementation file. The Xcode template already defines several methods for managing application state: You will be adding to the implementations of `applicationDidFinishLaunching:withOptions:`, `applicationDidEnterBackground`, and `applicationWillEnterForeground:`. You'll also be adding some C functions of your own and an implementation of the `fillBuffer:` method declared in the header. Listing 10.2 offers a roadmap of the file, adding to what Xcode originally provided.

Listing 10.2   **Outline of Implementation File for iOS Tone-Player App**

```
#import "CH10_iOSBackgroundingToneAppDelegate.h"

#pragma mark - #defines

// Insert Listing 10.4 here

@implementation CH10_iOSBackgroundingToneAppDelegate

#pragma mark - @synthesizes
```

Listing 10.2   **Continued**

```objc
@synthesize window=_window;
// Insert Listing 10.3 here

#pragma mark helpers
// Insert Listing 4.2 here

#pragma mark callbacks
// Insert Listings 10.11, 10.12, and 10.13 here

#pragma mark app lifecycle

- (BOOL)application:(UIApplication *)application
  didFinishLaunchingWithOptions:(NSDictionary *)launchOptions
{
    // Set up the audio session
    // Insert Listings 10.5 and 10.6 here

    // Set the stream format
    // Insert Listing 10.7 here

    // Set up the audio queue
    // Insert Listings 10.8 and 10.9 here

    // Start the audio queue
    // Replace to the bottom of the method with Listing 10.10

    // Override point for customization after the application launches.
    [self.window makeKeyAndVisible];
    return YES;
}

- (void)applicationWillResignActive:(UIApplication *)application
{}

- (void)applicationDidEnterBackground:(UIApplication *)application
{
    // Insert Listing 10.14 here
}

- (void)applicationWillEnterForeground:(UIApplication *)application
{
    // Insert Listing 10.15 here
}
```

Listing 10.2   **Continued**

```
- (void)applicationDidBecomeActive:(UIApplication *)application
{}

- (void)applicationWillTerminate:(UIApplication *)application
{}

- (void)dealloc
{
    [_window release];
    [super dealloc];
}

@end
```

You can fill in a few of the blanks right away. First, you know that you have to @synthesize (or provide setters and getters) for all your properties, so let's do that in Listing 10.3.

Listing 10.3   **Synthesizing Properties for iOS Tone Generator**

```
@synthesize streamFormat=_streamFormat;
@synthesize bufferSize;
@synthesize currentFrequency;
@synthesize startingFrameCount;
@synthesize audioQueue;
```

You can back all the properties with specific instance variables, if you want. The reason for spelling out a specific instance variable for the streamFormat property will become clear after Listing 10.7.

Some #defines appear at the top of the file. Thinking back to the audio queues in Chapters 4 and 5, remember that you need to specify how many buffers you're using, and having a constant for the duration of each buffer is also handy for the math. You also want to #define the frequencies you want to play in foreground and background modes. Listing 10.4 shows the #defines.

Listing 10.4   **Defining Frequencies and Audio Queue Constants for the iOS Tone Generator**

```
#define FOREGROUND_FREQUENCY    880.0
#define BACKGROUND_FREQUENCY    523.25
#define BUFFER_COUNT            3
#define BUFFER_DURATION         0.5
```

You'll use the handy `CheckError()` function that has served you well since Chapter 4. The same Mac OS X code in Listing 4.2 works exactly as is on iOS, so paste it in.

Initializing the Audio Session and Audio Queue

When the app comes up, the `application:didFinishLaunchingWithOptions:` method is called, so for the purposes of this example, that's where you'll get to work. Of course, you can put your Core Audio code elsewhere—in view controllers or custom classes, for example—but you should do your Audio Session setup early and, certainly, before any other audio calls you will be making. And because the app delegate is your app's point of contact with the rest of the system, it's a pretty good place for Audio Session management code. Let's begin in Listing 10.5 by setting up the app's audio session with `AudioSessionInitialize()`.

Listing 10.5   **Establishing an Audio Session with AudioSessionInitialize()**

```
- (BOOL)application:(UIApplication *)application
  didFinishLaunchingWithOptions:(NSDictionary *)launchOptions
{
    CheckError(AudioSessionInitialize(NULL,
                                      kCFRunLoopDefaultMode,
                                      MyInterruptionListener,
                                      self),
               "Couldn't initialize the audio session");
```

`AudioSessionInitialize` takes four parameters, all of which have to do with a call to an interruption handler function that will be called when the system needs to alert you to changes in your access to system audio:

- The first two parameters are the run loop and run loop mode on which you want to receive the interruption callback: `NULL` for the first parameter specifies the main run loop and is the most typical choice.
- The third parameter is a function pointer to an interruption listener function that you will write later.
- The fourth parameter is the user info object (called client data here) that provides a single pointer for the callback function to use.

> **Note**
>
> In previous examples, you've always passed around a struct, but because the app delegate is a full-blown Objective-C object, which itself is just a pointer, you can use `self`.

Next, you need to declare the audio category, as described earlier. Because you want the audio to keep playing in the background, and because it doesn't need to record, the

sensible choice is kAudioSessionCategory_MediaPlayback. This has the side effect of
ignoring the ring/silent switch and shutting down another apps' audio. Listing 10.6
shows how to set the audio category.

Listing 10.6   **Setting the Audio Category for an iOS Application**

```
UInt32 category = kAudioSessionCategory_MediaPlayback;
CheckError(AudioSessionSetProperty(kAudioSessionProperty_AudioCategory,
                          sizeof(category),
                          &category),
          "Couldn't set category on audio session");
```

You're going to set up an audio queue, which means you need to pick a stream format (as an AudioStreamBasicDescription) to provide to the queue. When you created a playback queue in Chapter 5, you got the format from the file you were reading.
Because this example generates its own samples, you can define your own format, as we
did in Chapter 8, " Audio Units: Input and Mixing," when you wrote a sine wave to an
I/O audio unit. Listing 10.7 sets up the stream format.

Listing 10.7   **Creating AudioStreamBasicDescription for a Programmatically Generated
Sine Wave**

```
self.currentFrequency = FOREGROUND_FREQUENCY;
_streamFormat.mSampleRate = 44100.0;
_streamFormat.mFormatID = kAudioFormatLinearPCM;
_streamFormat.mFormatFlags = kAudioFormatFlagsCanonical;
_streamFormat.mChannelsPerFrame = 1;
_streamFormat.mFramesPerPacket = 1;
_streamFormat.mBitsPerChannel = 16;
_streamFormat.mBytesPerFrame = 2;
_streamFormat.mBytesPerPacket = 2;
```

You're accessing the streamFormat property by its instance variable because the com-
piler won't let you do an assignment of the form self.streamFormat.mSampleRate.
What's more important in this example is the mFormatFlags. Chapter 3, "Audio
Processing with Core Audio," described how the canonical formats are those that the
system is best suited to use and that Core Audio automatically converts to for its own
internal use. On Mac OS X, kAudioFormatFlagsCanonical and kAudioFormat
FlagsAudioUnitCanonical both use floating point samples, but floating point is a significant expense on the low-power chips of ARM devices. So on iOS, kAudioFormat
FlagsCanonical uses signed integer samples, and kAudioFormatFlagsAudioUnit
Canonical uses 8.24 fixed point. This means that the high 8 bits are the value to the
left of the decimal, and the other 24 bits are the fractional part. Without convenience
functions to perform the needed math on the fixed-point samples, we prefer the simple
integer math of kAudioFormatFlagsCanonical whenever we can use it.

With the stream format defined, you can call `AudioQueueNewOutput()` to create the audio queue that will play your tone, as in Listing 10.8.

Listing 10.8   Creating an Audio Queue on iOS

```
// Create the audio queue
CheckError( AudioQueueNewOutput(&_streamFormat,
                                MyAQOutputCallback,
                                self,
                                NULL,
                                kCFRunLoopCommonModes,
                                0,
                                &audioQueue),
            "Couldn't create the output AudioQueue");
```

> **Note**
>
> Sorry if we're hammering the point repeatedly, but this is the exact same function used to create an Audio Queue for OS X in Chapter 5. It takes the stream format, a buffer-refiller function and user-info pointer, a callback run loop and run loop mode, an unused flags argument, and a pointer to receive the created `AudioQueueRef`.

If you remember the playback audio queue from five chapters back, maybe you remember what you have to do after creating the queue: You have to prime the queue with some buffers, filled with the first samples to be played. You do this in Listing 10.9.

Listing 10.9   **Priming an Audio Queue on iOS**

```
// Create and enqueue buffers
AudioQueueBufferRef buffers [BUFFER_COUNT];
bufferSize = BUFFER_DURATION * self.streamFormat.mSampleRate *
self.streamFormat.mBytesPerFrame;
NSLog (@"bufferSize is %ld", bufferSize);
for (int i=0; i<BUFFER_COUNT; i++) {
    CheckError (AudioQueueAllocateBuffer(audioQueue,
                                         bufferSize,
                                         &buffers[i]),
                "Couldn't allocate the Audio Queue buffer");
    CheckError([self fillBuffer:buffers[i]],
                "Couldn't fill buffer (priming)");
    CheckError(AudioQueueEnqueueBuffer(audioQueue,
                                       buffers[i],
                                       0,
                                       NULL),
                "Couldn't enqueue buffer (priming)");
}
```

Start with a little math to figure out how big the buffers should be. Because you're using constant bit rate PCM, this is easier than the Chapter 5 example that had to deal with VBR and packet descriptions. Here, you just know that each buffer is *buffer duration* × *sample rate* × *bytes per frame*.

After that, you loop through BUFFER_COUNT times to create buffers with AudioQueueAllocateBuffer(), fill them with the fillBuffer: method that you declared in the header (and need to write later), and put them in the queue with AudioQueueEnqueueBuffer().

All that's left for main()—oops, we mean application:didFinishLaunchingWithOptions:—is to start the audio queue. Listing 10.10 shows that one-line call.

Listing 10.10   **Starting an Audio Queue on iOS**

```
CheckError(AudioQueueStart(audioQueue,
                           NULL),
           "Couldn't start the AudioQueue");
// Override point for customization after application launch.
[self.window makeKeyAndVisible];
return YES;
}
```

Earlier examples sometimes had to put in a call such as CFRunLoopRunInMode() to keep the main run loop going and thus prevent the command-line program from terminating. That's not necessary on iOS, where the UIApplication structure keeps the app around. iOS apps aren't even *allowed* to terminate. So aside from letting application: didFinishLaunchingWithOptions: do its default job of calling [self.window makeKeyAndVisible] and returning YES, you are finished setting up the tone-generating audio queue. You're not done with the example—you have some callbacks and other stuff to write—but outside of the Audio Session material, this should seem very similar to the kinds of Core Audio calls you've been working with all along.

The Tone Generator Method

Let's keep with the tried-and-true for a moment and deal with the fillBuffer: method that you called when you seeded the queue and that you'll need again in your callbacks from the queue. You wrote a sine wave generator back in Chapter 7 to feed an Audio Unit render callback, so all that's different in Listing 10.11 is that you're filling an AudioQueueBufferRef instead of an AudioBufferList.

Listing 10.11   **Method to Refill Buffers with Sine Wave Samples**

```
-(OSStatus) fillBuffer: (AudioQueueBufferRef) buffer {
     double j = self.startingFrameCount;
     double cycleLength = 44100. / self.currentFrequency;
     int frame = 0;
```

Listing 10.11   **Continued**

```
    double frameCount = bufferSize / self.streamFormat.mBytesPerFrame;
    for (frame = 0; frame < frameCount; ++frame)
    {
        SInt16 *data = (SInt16*)buffer->mAudioData;
        (data)[frame] = (SInt16) (sin (2 * M_PI * (j / cycleLength)) *
                                  0x8000);
        j += 1.0;
        if (j > cycleLength)
            j -= cycleLength;
    }
    self.startingFrameCount = j;
    buffer->mAudioDataByteSize = bufferSize;
    return noErr;
}
```

As in Chapter 7, you need to keep track of where you are in the wave each time you leave and re-enter the method; starting every buffer from `theta=0` would create a discontinuity in the wave and, therefore, cause a repeating click or pop. Start with a little math to figure out where to begin the cycle, along with figuring the wavelength in frames. But aside from that, you're doing fundamentally the same thing: looping over theta values, calculating a sine, and multiplying that value (which will be between `-1.0` and `1.0`) by the maximum 16-bit signed integer value of `0x8000`. The result is a signed 16-bit integer sample, exactly as promised by `streamFormat`.

The `fillBuffer:` method is called to prime the queue, but you also need to call it when the audio queue needs a buffer refilled. `AudioQueueNewOutput()` provided a function pointer to a `MyAQOutputCallback` function that could do this, so let's write that now (see Listing 10.12).

Listing 10.12   **Callback Function to Refill an AudioQueueBufferRef on iOS**

```
static void MyAQOutputCallback(void *inUserData,
                               AudioQueueRef inAQ,
                               AudioQueueBufferRef inCompleteAQBuffer)
{
    CH10_iOSBackgroundingToneAppDelegate *appDelegate =
        (CH10_iOSBackgroundingToneAppDelegate*)inUserData;
    CheckError([appDelegate fillBuffer: inCompleteAQBuffer],
               "can't refill buffer");
    CheckError(AudioQueueEnqueueBuffer(inAQ,
                                       inCompleteAQBuffer,
                                       0,
                                       NULL),
               "Couldn't enqueue the buffer (refill)");
}
```

Because you used the app delegate itself as the user-info object, this callback ends up being trivial: You cast `inUserData` to a local variable called `appDelegate` and call its `fillBuffer` method, which you just wrote back in Listing 10.10. With the buffer filled, you give it back to the queue with `AudioQueueEnqueueBuffer()`.

So far, this app could run as is back on Mac OS X, as long as you started with a Cocoa application template, skipped the iOS-specific Audio Session stuff, and dealt with the difference in sample formats (for instance, you declared an `AudioStreamBasic Description` that used signed `int`s, or you rewrote `fillBuffer` to use floats). The higher-level APIs such as Audio Queue really are the same on both platforms.

Now let's get into some iOS nitty-gritty.

Handling iOS Interruptions

When we created the audio session, we provided a function pointer to `MyInterruption Listener()`. This function is `typedef`'d as `AudioSessionInterruptionListener`; it takes a user-info pointer and a `UInt32 inInterruptionState` and returns void. The interruption state indicates whether an interruption is beginning or ending. The idea is that an event such as an incoming phone call might cause your app to lose access to the audio system, so it plays the ring tone and doesn't worry about what your app wants. However, it doesn't kill the app outright, because the user might choose to decline the call. In this case, the interruption ends and you get a second callback.

The start of an interruption automatically stops playback engines such as OpenAL or your Audio Queue, so you don't have to do anything special in that case. More elaborate audio apps might have some teardown or state maintenance to perform, however. If and when the interruption ends, you need to restart the audio queue. Listing 10.13 shows simple handling of these cases.

Listing 10.13   **Handling Audio Interruptions**

```
void MyInterruptionListener (void *inUserData,
                             UInt32 inInterruptionState) {

    printf ("Interrupted! inInterruptionState=%ld\n", inInterruptionState);
    CH10_iOSBackgroundingToneAppDelegate *appDelegate =
        (CH10_iOSBackgroundingToneAppDelegate*)inUserData;
    switch (inInterruptionState) {
        case kAudioSessionBeginInterruption:
            break;
        case kAudioSessionEndInterruption:
            CheckError(AudioQueueStart(appDelegate.audioQueue, 0),
                       "Couldn't restart the audio queue");
            break;
        default:
            break;
    };
}
```

An incoming call isn't the only event that causes an interruption: Notifications, alarms, and other asynchronous events are delivered to the app as interruptions.

We also said the app was going to change the tone frequency when it goes between background and foreground. You need to do a few things to make that work. First, you have to use a special flag introduced in iOS 4.0 to tell the system that the app needs to keep running in the background and state why. In the app's `Info.plist` file, create a new key with the provided name "Required background modes" (if you look at the `.plist` file with an XML editor, this key is really called `UIBackgroundModes`). This key takes an array as its `value:` add one item, with the canned value "App plays audio" (which is a synonym for the value `"audio"`). Setting this in the `Info.plist` allows the app to keep the tone going when you send it to the background with the Home button.[4]

When the app moves between foreground and background, the app delegate gets notified via its usual callback methods: `applicationWillEnterForeground:` and `applicationDidEnterBackground:`. When you background, all you need to do is change the frequency value, as in Listing 10.14.

Listing 10.14   **Handling Backgrounding on iOS**

```
- (void)applicationDidEnterBackground:(UIApplication *)application
{
    self.currentFrequency = BACKGROUND_FREQUENCY;
}
```

Because the audio queue keeps going in the background, the next call to `fillBuffer` picks up this new value. Of course, with three buffers of 0.5 seconds each, there will be an audible lag in doing so.

The foregrounding case is similar but involves a little more work, as Listing 10.15 shows.

Listing 10.15   **Handling Foregrounding on iOS**

```
- (void)applicationWillEnterForeground:(UIApplication *)application
{
    CheckError(AudioSessionSetActive(true),
               "Couldn't re-set audio session active");
    CheckError(AudioQueueStart(self.audioQueue, 0),
               "Couldn't restart audio queue");
    self.currentFrequency = FOREGROUND_FREQUENCY;
}
```

---

[4] The Xcode 4.1 iOS Simulator doesn't keep the audio going in the background; it works only on the device.

If the user leaves the app to take a call, the interruption results in a stopped audio queue; its access to the audio session is cut off. To get the tone going again when you come to the foreground, you need to reassert yourself to the audio session. Instead of initializing the audio session again, it's enough to just say "I'm active" via the `AudioSessionSet Active()` call. Then you can use `AudioQueueStart()` to get the queue going again and reset the frequency. Calling `AudioSessionSetActive()` and `AudioQueueStart()` if you weren't stopped by an interruption is harmless, so you can call these anytime you enter the foreground, even if the user has just been switching apps and never actually interrupted you.

With these methods written, the example is ready to go. Run it on your device with Xcode, and try backgrounding and foregrounding the app to hear the tone change. If you're on an iPhone, you can try the interruption by calling yourself from another phone. Another way to get an interruption is to run another app whose audio session category wants exclusive access to audio output—games are often a good example of this.

Audio Units on iOS

Aside from working with Audio Sessions, the other big change on iOS is how Audio Units work. Not that the API is any different—it's exactly the same as you studied in Chapters 7 and 8—but what you can do with audio units is significantly different.

First, the bad news: iOS has far fewer system-provided audio units. Several of the major types of units, such as generators, are completely absent; others have only a few units available. For example, whereas Mac OS X offered a large set of effects units (including the reverb unit that you played in Chapter 7), iOS 4 has only one.[5]

Here's a list of the seven—yes, just seven—audio units you get on iOS 4:

- I/O
  - **Remote I/O:** The iOS equivalent of AUHAL, providing capture and play-out; with only one audio device, however, it doesn't need the HAL abstraction. You'll be using this later in the chapter.
  - **Voice Processing I/O:** Similar to Remote I/O, with the addition of echo-cancellation filters that make it ideal for voice-over-IP applications.
  - **Generic I/O:** Just as on OS X, this is an output unit that's not connected to hardware. You can put it at the end of an `AUGraph` and pull samples through the graph with `AudioUnitRender()`.
- Effects
  - **iPodEQ:** Performs the same audio equalization as the built-in Music or iPod app, enabling the user to choose from a set of canned equalizer settings, such as Bass Booster and Spoken Word.

---

[5] The situation is significantly better in iOS 5, as you'll see in the final chapter.

- Mixers
    - **Multichannel Mixer:** A mixer that takes an arbitrary number of input buses and mixes them down to a stereo output.
    - **3D Mixer:** A mixer that can render sounds based on their properties in a 3D space. It's used by the OpenAL implementation but can be used in your own AUGraphs (although this is rare).
- Converter
    - **Format converter:** Same as on OS X; converts between different flavors of PCM.

So that's the bad news. The worse news is that it's not even possible to extend the collection of audio units. Whereas OS X has an entire industry of third-party audio units, this kind of plug-in isn't possible with the "sandbox" model of iOS applications.

Note

In fact, iPhone OS 3 added the capability to build your own audio units to be used only in your own app, based on the CFPlugin API. However, we have it on good authority that this capability never actually worked, and it was removed in iOS 4.

Now that you've lowered your expectations, here's some good news: Working with the I/O units is vastly easier in iOS. Think back to Chapter 8, where you grabbed input from the microphone and ran it through an AUGraph. You had to use separate AUHAL units for the input and the output because they were potentially different devices serviced by different I/O threads. That meant you had to use a ring buffer to transfer samples between the two units. On iOS, this never happens: There's only one audio device, providing both input and output, as shown in Figure 10.1. With this arrangement, the awful threading headaches go away: You use a single RemoteIO unit for input or output, and if you're doing both, you use the one unit for both.

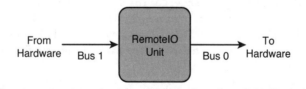

Figure 10.1   Input to and output from RemoteIO Audio Unit on iOS

Building an Audio Pass-Through App with the iOS RemoteIO Unit

Here you exercise iOS audio units by building another pass-through app, which shows off both the good and the bad of audio units on iOS. And just to show that you can still have some fun at the unit level, you'll perform our own audio effect on the captured audio, even though you don't have effect units to rely on.

So how do you perform an effect? Let's step back a minute and think about how a pass-through app works with just one I/O unit doing both input and output. As you learned in Chapter 8, you collect captured samples from bus 1 of an I/O unit's output scope and provide samples to be played to bus 0 of an I/O unit's input scope. If the same unit will provide both input and output, the trick is connect bus 1's output to bus 2's input, as in Figure 10.2.

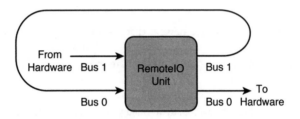

Figure 10.2   Connecting RemoteIO Audio Unit
capture to its own play-out

You do this in a few straightforward ways:

- Set the kAudioUnitProperty_MakeConnection property on bus 0/input scope, providing an AudioUnitConnection struct that refers to the unit's bus 1/output scope.

- Create an AUGraph with a node for the RemoteIO unit as its only member. Then call AUGraphConnectNodeInput() to connect bus 1/output scope to bus 0/input scope.

- Create a render callback function and set it as the kAudioUnitProperty_SetRenderCallback property on bus 0/input scope. In the callback function, call AudioUnitRender() on bus 1 of the RemoteIO unit to manually pull the most recent set of captured samples. This works only because input and output are coming from the same hardware and are thus wrapped by the same I/O unit.

You'll use the third option here, even though it means writing more code, because it offers a nice opportunity to mess with the samples as they pass through the callback function. Figure 10.3 shows this arrangement.

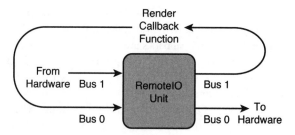

Figure 10.3   Connecting RemoteIO Audio Unit capture
to its own play-out with render callback

Setting Up the Pass-Through Example

Once again, you need to create an Empty Application in Xcode 4; in the sample code,
it's called CH10_iOSPlayThrough. This gives you an app delegate class that has just a
UIWindow. You'll add some properties and a struct to that. Rewrite the app delegate
header file, as shown in Listing 10.16.

Listing 10.16   **Header File for iOS Audio Unit Pass-Through App**

```
#import <UIKit/UIKit.h>
#import <AudioToolbox/AudioToolbox.h>

typedef struct {
    AudioUnit rioUnit;
    AudioStreamBasicDescription asbd;
    float sineFrequency;
    float sinePhase;
} EffectState;

@interface CH10_iOSPlayThroughAppDelegate : UIResponder <UIApplicationDelegate>

@property (nonatomic, retain) UIWindow *window;
@property (assign) EffectState effectState;

@end
```

This defines a struct that you will use to pass state to the render callback function. You
might ask, wouldn't it be easier to just pass the app delegate object, as you did with the
interruption handler in the previous example? And you'd be right to say that it's easier to
work with objects than pointers. However, Objective-C messaging is more expensive

than C function calls and struct member access. Worse, the expense is unpredictable. That was okay for the interruption handler, which is called only in exceptional circumstances and only once per event. But render callbacks are called many times each second, and as Chapter 7 stated, you need to keep the work you do in a render callback fast and predictable, which Obj-C messaging is not. If you can possibly work with simple pointers instead of Objective-C objects, you should.

The struct has the Remote I/O audio unit itself (so you know where to pull captured samples from), the stream format as an `AudioStreamBasicDescription` (so you know how to do your DSP math on samples in the callback), and two sine-related floats that we're saving as a surprise for later. As far as properties go, you simply need one for this `EffectState` struct and the window that the Xcode template provides.

In the implementation file, Xcode has already set up the usual app delegate lifecycle methods. You will be building out `applicationDidFinishLaunching:withOptions:`, as well as adding callback and helper functions of our own. Listing 10.17 shows the outline of the .m file.

Listing 10.17   Outline of App Delegate Implementation File for iOS Play-Through

```objc
#import "CH10_iOSPlayThroughAppDelegate.h"

@implementation CH10_iOSPlayThroughAppDelegate

#pragma mark - @synthesizes
// Insert Listing 10.18 here

#pragma mark helpers
// Insert Listing 4.2 here
// Insert Listings 10.28 - 10.30 here

#pragma mark callbacks
// Insert Listing 10.27 here

#pragma mark app lifecycle

- (BOOL)application:(UIApplication *)application
didFinishLaunchingWithOptions:(NSDictionary *)launchOptions
{
    // Set up audio session
    // Insert Listing 10.19 here

    // Is audio input available?
    // Insert Listing 10.20 here

    // Get hardware sample rate
    // Insert Listing 10.21 here
```

Listing 10.17   **Continued**

```
    // Get Rio unit from audio component manager
    // Insert Listing 10.22 here

    // Configure Rio unit
    // Insert Listings 10.23 - 10.24 here

    // Set callback method
    // Insert Listing 10.25 here

    // Start Rio unit
    // Replace to bottom of method with Listing 10.26

    // Override point for customization after application launch.
    [self.window makeKeyAndVisible];
    return YES;
}


- (void)applicationWillResignActive:(UIApplication *)application
{}


- (void)applicationDidEnterBackground:(UIApplication *)application
{}


- (void)applicationWillEnterForeground:(UIApplication *)application
{}


- (void)applicationDidBecomeActive:(UIApplication *)application
{}


- (void)applicationWillTerminate:(UIApplication *)application
{}


@end
```

You can start filling out this implementation with the easy stuff. Copy over your CheckError() function from Listing 4.2 and then fill in the obvious synthesize statements, as in Listing 10.18.

Listing 10.18   **Synthesizing Properties for iOS Play-Through Example**

```
@synthesize window = _window;
@synthesize effectState = _effectState;
```

Setting Up the RemoteIO Audio Unit for Capture and Play-Out

Now let's write an `applicationDidFinishLaunching:withOptions:` method that sets up the audio unit at startup, setting aside for now any of the callback methods you need. As with the previous example, you begin by initializing the audio session, in Listing 10.19.

Listing 10.19   **Setting Up Audio Session for iOS Play-Through**

```
- (BOOL)application:(UIApplication *)application
  didFinishLaunchingWithOptions:(NSDictionary *)launchOptions
{
    // Set up the audio session
    CheckError(AudioSessionInitialize(NULL,
                                      kCFRunLoopDefaultMode,
                                      MyInterruptionListener,
                                      self),
             "Couldn't initialize the audio session");

    UInt32 category = kAudioSessionCategory_PlayAndRecord;
    CheckError(AudioSessionSetProperty(kAudioSessionProperty_AudioCategory,
                                       sizeof(category),
                                       &category),
             "Couldn't set the category on the audio session");
```

Notice that, this time, you set `kAudioSessionCategory_PlayAndRecord` as the category for the audio session. This is crucial because you don't get access to capture hardware unless you specifically ask for with a suitable category.

You're not done with the audio session. You also need to check to see whether audio input is available. All iPhones and iPads have microphones, but early iPod touches did not, and if Apple ever releases an SDK for the Apple TV, that will probably be another no-mic device. You can query the audio session for the property `kAudioSessionProperty_AudioInputAvailable`. The value of the property is nonzero if input is available. If it's not, the app shows a failure alert and bails. Listing 10.20 shows this logic.

Listing 10.20   **Checking for Audio Input Availability on iOS**

```
UInt32 ui32PropertySize = sizeof (UInt32);
UInt32 inputAvailable;
CheckError(AudioSessionGetProperty(kAudioSessionProperty_AudioInputAvailable,
                                   &ui32PropertySize,
                                   &inputAvailable),
          "Couldn't get current audio input available prop");
if (! inputAvailable) {
    UIAlertView *noInputAlert =
```

Listing 10.20   **Continued**

```
    [[UIAlertView alloc] initWithTitle:@"No audio input"
                    message:@"No audio input device is currently attached"
                    delegate:nil
        cancelButtonTitle:@"OK"
        otherButtonTitles:nil];
    [noInputAlert show];
    [noInputAlert release];
    return YES;
}
```

Granted, your own apps should be more robust than just giving up if there's no input hardware at startup. One way to do this is to use AudioSessionAddProperty Listener() to provide a function that can be called when the kAudioSession Property_AudioInputAvailable property changes (when a microphone is attached or removed). That function could re-enable the recording-specific parts of your UI, start recording automatically, and so on.

Another interesting property to inspect is the hardware sampling rate. Later in this example, you'll be setting up an AudioStreamBasicDescription to declare the format you want to work with. Instead of assuming that an arbitrary value (say, 44100.0) is suitable, you can scale up or down to whatever the hardware is using and maybe save Core Audio the expense of resampling to a rate you've declared. Listing 10.21 shows how to get the sampling rate property.

Listing 10.21   **Getting the Hardware Sampling Rate on an iOS Device**

```
Float64 hardwareSampleRate;
UInt32 propSize = sizeof (hardwareSampleRate);
CheckError(AudioSessionGetProperty(
                    kAudioSessionProperty_CurrentHardwareSampleRate,
                    &propSize,
                    &hardwareSampleRate),
            "Couldn't get hardwareSampleRate");
NSLog (@"hardwareSampleRate = %f", hardwareSampleRate);
```

As with pretty much every other property-based API in Core Audio, you need to look in the docs to get the property value's type and be prepared to receive that as a pointer. In the case of kAudioSessionProperty_CurrentHardwareSampleRate, it's a Float64, which makes sense because that's also the type the mSampleRate uses in AudioStreamBasicDescription.

Now you need an instance of the I/O unit. iOS uses the Audio Component Manager API, described in Chapter 7, and has never included the legacy Component Manager; you need to worry about only the modern versions of these calls. Listing 10.22 shows how we get the Remote IO unit.

Listing 10.22   Getting RemoteIO AudioUnit from Audio Component Manager

```
// Describe the unit
AudioComponentDescription audioCompDesc;
audioCompDesc.componentType = kAudioUnitType_Output;
audioCompDesc.componentSubType = kAudioUnitSubType_RemoteIO;
audioCompDesc.componentManufacturer = kAudioUnitManufacturer_Apple;
audioCompDesc.componentFlags = 0;
audioCompDesc.componentFlagsMask = 0;

// Get the RIO unit from the audio component manager
AudioComponent rioComponent = AudioComponentFindNext(NULL,
                                                    &audioCompDesc);
CheckError(AudioComponentInstanceNew(rioComponent,
                                    &_effectState.rioUnit),
          "Couldn't get RIO unit instance");
```

As when specifying and finding Audio Units on OS X, you use a struct to describe what you're looking for, in terms of component type, subtype, and manufacturer. Then you iterate over matches with `AudioComponentFindNext()`. The description itself is a lot like the earlier `AudioComponentDescriptions`, except that instead of using `kAudioUnitSubType_DefaultOutput` or `kAudioUnitSubType_HALOutput`, iOS uses the subtype `kAudioUnitSubType_RemoteIO`. This matches only one component on iOS, so you don't have to bother iterating over `AudioComponentFindNext()`. Instead, you grab the first `AudioComponent` returned by this call. You can then use that with `AudioComponentInstanceNew()` to populate an `AudioUnit` pointer.

When you have this audio unit, you need to enable IO on the scope/bus combinations that you will use, as you did in Chapter 8's pass-through example: by setting the `kAudioOutputUnitProperty_EnableIO` property to 1 (see Listing 10.23).

Listing 10.23   Enabling IO on RemoteIO Audio Unit

```
// Set up the RIO unit for playback
UInt32 oneFlag = 1;
AudioUnitElement bus0 = 0;
CheckError(AudioUnitSetProperty (_effectState.rioUnit,
                                kAudioOutputUnitProperty_EnableIO,
                                kAudioUnitScope_Output,
                                bus0,
                                &oneFlag,
                                sizeof(oneFlag)),
          "Couldn't enable RIO output");

// Enable RIO input
AudioUnitElement bus1 = 1;
CheckError(AudioUnitSetProperty(_effectState.rioUnit,
                                kAudioOutputUnitProperty_EnableIO,
```

Listing 10.23 **Continued**

```
                                kAudioUnitScope_Input,
                                bus1,
                                &oneFlag,
                                sizeof(oneFlag)),
          "Couldn't enable RIO input");
```

With IO enabled, you should also set the format you want to receive from capture (bus 1/output scope) and provide to play-out (bus 0/input scope). If you weren't going to mess with the samples in the render callback, you could skip this step; however, you do want to do that here, so you might as well make sure that the sample format is something that you can easily work with. For example, if it defaulted to 8.24 fixed point, it would be a lot harder to do interesting math. Listing 10.24 sets up a 16-bit, stereo, signed integer PCM format that will be easier to work with.

Listing 10.24 **Setting Stream Format on RemoteIO Audio Unit**

```
// Setup an ASBD in the iPhone canonical format
AudioStreamBasicDescription myASBD;
memset (&myASBD, 0, sizeof (myASBD));
myASBD.mSampleRate = hardwareSampleRate;
myASBD.mFormatID = kAudioFormatLinearPCM;
myASBD.mFormatFlags = kAudioFormatFlagsCanonical;
myASBD.mBytesPerPacket = 4;
myASBD.mFramesPerPacket = 1;
myASBD.mBytesPerFrame = 4;
myASBD.mChannelsPerFrame = 2;
myASBD.mBitsPerChannel = 16;

// Set format for output (bus 0) on the RIO's input scope
CheckError(AudioUnitSetProperty (_effectState.rioUnit,
                                kAudioUnitProperty_StreamFormat,
                                kAudioUnitScope_Input,
                                bus0,
                                &myASBD,
                                sizeof (myASBD)),
          "Couldn't set the ASBD for RIO on input scope/bus 0");

// Set ASBD for mic input (bus 1) on RIO's output scope
CheckError(AudioUnitSetProperty (_effectState.rioUnit,
                                kAudioUnitProperty_StreamFormat,
                                kAudioUnitScope_Output,
                                bus1,
                                &myASBD,
                                sizeof (myASBD)),
          "Couldn't set the ASBD for RIO on output scope/bus 1");
```

As you fill in the `AudioStreamBasicDescription`, you use the `hardwareSampleRate` that you looked up in Listing 10.21. Beyond that, you specify `kAudioFormatFlags Canonical` (which means you'll be working with signed integer samples) and two channels, in case the user has a stereo mic connected.

Next, you set up your render callback. Recall from Chapters 7 and 8 that this function is called every time the `RemoteIO` unit needs to pull a buffer full of samples. As you set the callback in Listing 10.25, you provide a single user data pointer to this function, and that's what the `EffectState` struct is for.

Listing 10.25   Setting Up Render Callback for RemoteIO Audio Unit

```
_effectState.asbd = myASBD;
_effectState.sineFrequency = 30;
_effectState.sinePhase = 0;

// Set the callback method
AURenderCallbackStruct callbackStruct;
callbackStruct.inputProc = InputModulatingRenderCallback;
callbackStruct.inputProcRefCon = &_effectState;

CheckError(AudioUnitSetProperty(_effectState.rioUnit,
                                kAudioUnitProperty_SetRenderCallback,
                                kAudioUnitScope_Global,
                                bus0,
                                &callbackStruct,
                                sizeof (callbackStruct)),
           "Couldn't set RIO's render callback on bus 0");
```

The callback function, which you'll write later, needs the `AudioStreamBasicDescription` to make sense of the samples, as well as these `sineFrequency` and `sinePhase` variables that we're still keeping secret. We'll unveil their purpose when we cover the `InputModulatingRenderCallback()` function. That's all the setup needed. Listing 10.26 starts the `RemoteIO` unit and lets `applicationDidFinishLaunching:withOptions:` finish its usual setup.

Listing 10.26   Starting the RemoteIO Unit

```
    // Initialize and start the RIO unit
    CheckError(AudioUnitInitialize(_effectState.rioUnit),
            "Couldn't initialize the RIO unit");
    CheckError (AudioOutputUnitStart (_effectState.rioUnit),
             "Couldn't start the RIO unit");
    printf("RIO started!\n");

    // Override point for customization after application launch.
    [self.window makeKeyAndVisible];
    return YES;
}
```

When the application startup reaches the bottom of this method, the RemoteIO unit starts making callbacks to a function called InputModulatingRenderCallback(), which you still need to write. It continues to do this until you leave the application (because you don't have the audio-in-background mode to the Info.plist) or until it's interrupted.

When you initialized the audio session, you provided an interruption callback function, so let's add that now (see Listing 10.27).

Listing 10.27   **Handling RemoteIO Unit Interruptions on iOS**

```
static void MyInterruptionListener (void *inUserData,
                        UInt32 inInterruptionState) {
    printf ("Interrupted! inInterruptionState=%ld\n",
            inInterruptionState);
    CH10_iOSPlayThroughAppDelegate *appDelegate =
        (CH10_iOSPlayThroughAppDelegate*)inUserData;
    switch (inInterruptionState) {
        case kAudioSessionBeginInterruption:
            break;
        case kAudioSessionEndInterruption:
            CheckError(AudioSessionSetActive(true),
                        "Couldn't set audio session active");
            CheckError(AudioUnitInitialize(appDelegate.effectState.rioUnit),
                        "Couldn't initialize RIO unit");
            CheckError (AudioOutputUnitStart (appDelegate.effectState.rioUnit),
                         "Couldn't start RIO unit");
            break;
        default:
            break;
    };
}
```

As in the previous example, the case you care about is the end of an interruption, which happens, for example, when the user declines an incoming phone call. When this happens, try to reset the audio session active and restart the RemoteIO unit.

Still, all the real work of the app happens in the render callback. It's the one thing left to do, so let's do it...

The RemoteIO Render Callback

The render callback gets called whenever RemoteIO needs samples to play. This is similar to Chapter 8's example, where the player AUHAL called you for samples, which you fetched from a CARingBuffer that was being filled by an input AUHAL. That sort of complexity isn't needed on iOS, where the input and output devices are both represented by a single audio unit. When `RemoteIO` needs to play samples, you can just pull from `RemoteIO`'s own bus 1 capture buffers.

Of course, the only reason you're using a render callback is to perform some processing on the samples. So just what are you going to do with them? For kicks, you'll implement a simple and very popular audio filter called a ring modulator. This effect consists of multiplying two signals: a source signal and a modulator signal. Mathematically, this means that for a given time, t:

$$R(t) = C(t) \times M(t)$$

Here, C is the source signal, M is the modulator function, and R is the resulting signal.

It might sound obscure, but this is an effect that you've probably heard before; it was one of the first really interesting effects that could be created with analog signal processing. In fact, the name ring modulator comes from the ring of diodes originally used to produce the effect on analog equipment. One of its most common uses is in creating "robotic" voices; the BBC Radiophonic Workshop famously used it in the early 1960s to create the voices of the Daleks on TV's *Doctor Who*.[6]

You can create a ring modulator by calculating your own sine wave, as you have done in several examples, but instead of playing a sine wave, you will multiply the captured samples by the current sine value. The best robotic voices come from a sine wave in the range of 20–30 Hz, so that's why you set `_effectState.sineFrequency = 30` back in Listing 10.25.

The first thing to do in the render callback, as shown in Listing 10.28, is to cast the user data pointer back to an `EffectState` pointer so that you can get to the fields you'll need.

Listing 10.28   **Initial Setup of Render Callback from RemoteIO**

```
static OSStatus InputModulatingRenderCallback (
                         void *                        inRefCon,
                         AudioUnitRenderActionFlags *  ioActionFlags,
                         const AudioTimeStamp *        inTimeStamp,
                         UInt32                        inBusNumber,
                         UInt32                        inNumberFrames,
                         AudioBufferList *             ioData) {
    EffectState *effectState = (EffectState*) inRefCon;
```

Next, in Listing 10.29, you pull captured samples from the `RemoteIO` unit's bus 1 output and put them into the `ioData` parameter that the `RemoteIO` unit passed in and expects you to fill.

---

[6] Owen Spratley's "Dalek Vocal FX Creation: A Short Primer" (http://homepage.powerup.com.au/~spratleo/Tech/Dalek_Voice_Primer.html) covers how the BBC used ring modulators to voice the Daleks and how the effect has been tweaked over the years.

Listing 10.29   Copying Captured Samples to Play-Out Buffer in RemoteIO Render Callback

```
// Just copy samples
UInt32 bus1 = 1;
CheckError(AudioUnitRender(effectState->rioUnit,
                           ioActionFlags,
                           inTimeStamp,
                           bus1,
                           inNumberFrames,
                           ioData),
           "Couldn't render from RemoteIO unit");
```

If you were interested in only audio pass-through, you would be done: Captured samples would be in the ioData buffer, ready to play out. That's a lot easier than working with the CARingBuffer on OS X, right? But of course, the idea in this example is to perform an effect by processing the samples. Listing 10.30 shows the loop that does this.

Listing 10.30   Performing Ring Modulation Effect on a Buffer of Samples

```
// Walk the samples
AudioSampleType sample = 0;
UInt32 bytesPerChannel = effectState->asbd.mBytesPerFrame /
                         effectState->asbd.mChannelsPerFrame;
for (int bufCount=0; bufCount<ioData->mNumberBuffers; bufCount++) {
    AudioBuffer buf = ioData->mBuffers[bufCount];
    int currentFrame = 0;
    while ( currentFrame < inNumberFrames ) {
        // Copy sample to buffer, across all channels
        for (int currentChannel=0;
             currentChannel<buf.mNumberChannels;
             currentChannel++) {
            memcpy(&sample,
                   buf.mData +
                     (currentFrame * effectState->asbd.mBytesPerFrame) +
                     (currentChannel * bytesPerChannel),
                   sizeof(AudioSampleType));

            float theta = effectState->sinePhase * M_PI * 2;

            sample = (sin(theta) * sample);

            memcpy(buf.mData +
                     (currentFrame * effectState->asbd.mBytesPerFrame) +
                     (currentChannel * bytesPerChannel),
                   &sample,
                   sizeof(AudioSampleType));
```

Listing 10.30   **Continued**

```
                effectState->sinePhase += 1.0 /
                                    (effectState->asbd.mSampleRate /
                                    effectState->sineFrequency);
            if (effectState->sinePhase > 1.0) {
                effectState->sinePhase -= 1.0;
            }
        }
        currentFrame++;
    }
}
    return noErr;
}
```

This is a triply nested loop, so here's what's going on:

1. Loop over all the buffers in the `AudioBufferList` (which you've already filled with the capture data) and get each as an `AudioBuffer`.

2. For each buffer, loop over the number of frames that the callback asks for.

3. For each frame, loop over the number of channels, which you set as 2 in the `AudioStreamBasicDescription`.

4. You `memcpy` out one sample (of type `AudioSampleType`) by calculating its address.

5. Multiply the sample by the value of the sine function, which varies from `-1.0` to `1.0`.

6. You `memcpy` the modified sample back to its original address.

7. Update the `sinePhase`, which is simply a value that increases from `0.0` to `1.0` and gets reset if it ever exceeds `1.0`. Then you multiply this phase by 2π to get the theta for the sine function in the earlier step.

So outside of a little trigonometry, this is mostly about looking up samples in a buffer and playing with them. (Well, that and sounding like a Dalek.) This function is the last thing you need to do, so you can start up the app on the Simulator or on a device (be sure you have a mic set up) and start speaking into it. You should hear your own voice with a nice robotic effect added to it.

The ring modulator is a simple function, but the steps here are the key to doing any kind of digital signal processing on iOS: Run the audio through a render callback and operate directly on the samples there. If you wanted to use some other arbitrary DSP function on your audio, such as an "auto tune" type of effect, you would use pretty much these same steps: The difference would be only in the specifics of the sample processing.

Other iOS Audio Tricks

Knowing your way around Audio Session and the specific behavior of the `RemoteIO` unit represents most of what is unique to the iOS platform. However, you need to be aware of a few other interesting features—and a few hazards.

Remote Control on iOS

iOS devices have optional hardware accessories that are meant to control audio playback applications. Examples include the default headset, which you can click to produce play, pause, next track, and previous track events. Bluetooth and dock keyboards also have play/pause, next, and previous buttons. Even without these accessories, you can generate these events by double-clicking the home button and swiping right on the dock, which exposes soft play/pause, next, and previous buttons, as well as the icon of the active audio app.

All these inputs create `UIEvents` of type `UIEventTypeRemoteControl`, with a variety of subtypes that include `UIEventSubtypeRemoteControlPlay`, `UIEventSubtypeRemoteControlNextTrack`, and so on.

To opt in to handling these events, you need some member of your responder chain—view, view controller, or even a custom subclass of `UIApplication`—to be able to become the first responder by overriding `canBecomeFirstResponder` to return `YES`. Before actually becoming the first responder, your event-handling class needs to call `-[UIApplication beginReceivingRemoteControlEvents]` to start receiving these events. The events are received in the callback method `-[UIResponder remoteControlReceivedWithEvent:]`, which passes in a `UIEvent` that you can then inspect and respond to. For example, if you had an Audio Queue–based player app, you might respond to `UIEventSubtypeRemoteControlPause` by calling `AudioQueuePause()`.

Most of these devices also have the capability to control volume, via volume up and down buttons or a slider in the dock controls. The master gain volume of the device is not delivered to your app as an event, nor are you able to change it programmatically. The Media Player framework does provide an `MPVolumeView` that you can add to a UIKit GUI and that is bound to the system volume: Adjusting its slider raises or lowers the system volume, and changing the volume via remote controls is reflected in the slider. If one or more Apple TV or other AirPlay device is in range of the device, this view also shows a route button that enables the user to send audio (and video) to a selected device.

Bluetooth creates another complication. Ordinarily, Bluetooth headsets are not used for audio input. However, if you've set your Audio Session category to allow recording, you can use a paired Bluetooth headset by calling `AudioSessionSetProperty()` to set the `kAudioSessionProperty_OverrideCategoryEnableBluetoothInput` property with a value of `1`.

iOS Hardware Hazards

A few low-level hazards might catch you by surprise, depending on how demanding your app is.

Compressed formats can use hardware-accelerated encoding and decoding, which saves CPU and battery life, but whether you get it depends on a number of factors. Chief among these is that only one instance of a given codec can be decoded in hardware at a given time. If the Music application is playing an AAC file from your iTunes collection, and your app starts playing an AAC file with an Audio Queue, your app will perform its decoding in software instead. You can inspect the availability of hardware decoding using `AudioFormatGetProperty()`; the Apple document "Technical Q&A QA1663: Determining the Availability of the AAC Hardware Encoder at Runtime," has details on how to get the needed properties and interpret the results.[7]

Not every codec on iOS is supported in hardware. AAC, Apple Lossless (ALAC), and MP3 are the only formats decoded by both hardware and software. Formats such as PCM, IMA4, μ-law, and α-law are uncompressed and don't benefit from hardware decoding. iLBC (Internet Low Bitrate Codec), a useful codec for VoIP apps, is also software-only. On the other hand, High-Efficiency AAC (HE-AAC) does not have a software decoder in iOS 4 and, therefore, can be decoded only in hardware; this means that an iOS device can play only one HE-AAC stream at a time.

Audio apps that use an `AUGraph` and keep running in the background have a different hardware hazard to worry about. When the screen locks, the size of the data being rendered changes from 1,024 samples (22 milliseconds at 44.1 KHz) to 4,096 samples (88 milliseconds). This is a power-saving optimization because the system doesn't need to run at a screen-based refresh rate when the screen is off. An output-only `AUGraph` can glitch, in this case, because units are not typically prepared to produce this much audio. The fix, as explained in Apple Q&A 1606, is to set the `kAudioUnitProperty_MaximumFramesPerSlice` property to 4,096 on every node in your graph. Again, this affects only apps that use output-only `AUGraphs` and expect to keep running after the screen locks.

Summary

This chapter covered a lot of material—but really, you brought a lot of it with you. The use of Audio Queues and Audio Units here is not much different from the material on Mac OS X in earlier chapters, and most of the code in these examples just reuses and combines earlier examples. The syntax of these APIs is identical to what you covered before: What's different is the semantics because the ideas of application "backgrounding" and the single I/O device are unique to iOS. Even where this chapter dealt with new

---

[7] Apple Technical Q&A QA1663: http://developer.apple.com/library/ios/#qa/qa1663/_index.html.

APIs, such as the Audio Session, they're clearly in the style and spirit of the OS X APIs that preceded them.

Some other issues are specific to iOS Core Audio programming, to say nothing of other media frameworks on iOS (such as Media Player and AVFoundation), and are easier for new programmers and more appropriate to some tasks than Core Audio. Check out Apple's *Multimedia Programming Guide* for a comparison of these frameworks and their appropriate uses.[8] You'll also find a few points of overlap in their respective docs. For example, Core Media, which underlies AVFoundation, offers functions to convert between its `CMSampleBuffer` type and Core Audio's `AudioBufferList`.

The next chapter switches gears from sound processing to event processing and looks at how MIDI represents musical events and how you can tie this into the audio systems of Mac OS X and iOS with Core MIDI.

---

[8] Apple's Multimedia Programming Guide: http://developer.apple.com/library/ios/documentation/AudioVideo/Conceptual/MultimediaPG/.

Core MIDI

Music is one of the primary reasons to even have audio frameworks on Mac and iOS. Many APIs will be of great use to musicians. Audio Units and AUGraphs enable you to mix audio and add effects, Audio Conversion lets you export your sound to formats end users can enjoy on their devices, and Open AL can even put you in a virtual concert environment.

That said, one thing musicians really want from an audio platform is the capability to connect their instruments to the system so that their keyboards, drum kits, and other devices can play into or even be played by the computer. For decades, the way to do this has been through MIDI, a widely adopted standard for adapting musical performance as digital events. MIDI doesn't record or play sounds; it signals events that represent the music itself. And it's really good at what it does.

OS X and iOS both implement Core MIDI, which enables your software to interact with MIDI devices. This chapter looks as how Core MIDI works and how it ties into the rest of Core Audio to create a complete software platform for music apps.

MIDI Concepts

MIDI (pronounced "mid-e") is an acronym for Musical Instrument Digital Interface. It is an industry-standard digital communications protocol that enables musical instruments (synthesizers, drum machines, control surfaces, and so on), computers, and software to exchange information and control signals.

It's important to understand that MIDI isn't music and does not contain any actual sounds. It's nothing more than a set of events, or instructions, that tell a device how to perform an action. For example, a Note On message indicates that a note from an instrument has been played. Likewise, the corresponding Note Off message indicates that the note is done playing.

To start, you need to be familiar with the common terms of MIDI. Here are the main ones:

- **Synthesizers and controllers:** These are the two basic types of devices that generate MIDI data. The primary difference between them is that synthesizers generate both MIDI data and audible sound, whereas controllers generate only

MIDI data. An electronic piano keyboard is a good example of a synthesizer. An example of a controller might be a foot pedal or control surface, a device that does not emit any sound.

- **Sequencer:** A sequencer performs playback (and recording) of MIDI events. Sequencers can be software (GarageBand) or dedicated hardware devices.

- **Events:** A MIDI event, sometimes referred to as a message, is a variable-length collection of bytes that compose a MIDI command. Each event correlates to a specific musical action and can have additional attributes. Typical MIDI events are Note On, Note Off, Pitch Bend, and Aftertouch.

- **Channel:** MIDI contains a total of 16 discrete channels that events can travel through. For example, channel 2 could carry information about a piano keyboard to receive on channel 2 in the sequencer, and channel 5 could carry information about a different instrument. Playing more than 16 simultaneous instruments requires the use of banks (multiple MIDI interfaces).

Core MIDI

The Core MIDI framework provides a single set of MIDI system services. It offers high-performance access to MIDI hardware devices from your application and provides abstractions for interacting with MIDI devices on a MIDI network.

Core MIDI utilizes a central MIDI server that handles all the MIDI communications and allows for all MIDI devices and endpoints to be shared system wide simultaneously among all applications. However, you do not automatically start receiving and transmitting by default; your application must first opt in to the services you want from the MIDI server.

Core MIDI Architecture

At the kernel level of the Core MIDI implementation is IOKit, where all the actual I/O happens over the transport in use (USB, FireWire, Serial, and so on). Above the kernel in user space is the Core MIDI server subprocess that loads any MIDI drivers and processes MIDI requests. At the topmost level is the Core MIDI framework that your application links against. This arrangement is shown in Figure 11.1. MIDI services for your applications are communicated with the Core MIDI Server via Mach IPC.

Core MIDI Terminology

In Core MIDI, a device is represented by three basic objects: `MIDIDeviceRef`, `MIDIEntityRef`, and `MIDIEndpointRef`. All are `typedef`'d to a parent, `MIDIObjectRef`. These objects are layered together in a hierarchy so that devices contain entities, and entities contain endpoints. Figure 11.2 illustrates this hierarchy.

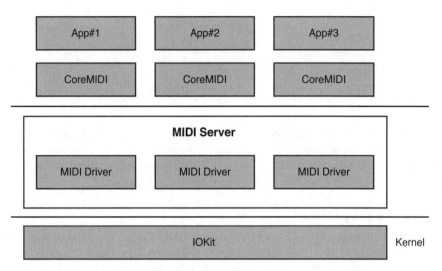

Figure 11.1   Core MIDI architecture

The bottom-level object is a `MIDIEndpointRef`, which is a simple MIDI source or destination, meaning a single 16-channel MIDI stream. The actual MIDI events are transmitted/received over an endpoint.

The next-higher-level object is the `MIDIEntityRef`. It is simply groups related and logical endpoints together. For example, if your program wants to communicate bidirectionally with a device, you know which endpoints represent a pair, as a way of associating the sources and destinations.

Finally, at the top is a `MIDIDeviceRef`. This object represents a physical device.

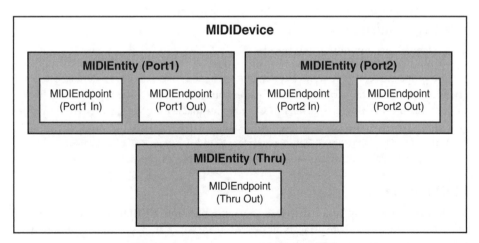

Figure 11.2   MIDI device hierarchy overview

Figure 11.3   MIDI device from Audio MIDI setup

The MIDI device is represented by the icon shown in Figure 1.3. The little "nubs" underneath the icon represent entities, which are a grouping of source and destination endpoints. In this example, the device has two entities, each with a source and destination endpoint, and a third entity with a single destination endpoint.

Core MIDI Properties

Similar to Core Audio and Audio Units, all Core MIDI devices, entities, and endpoints have properties. Typically, the Core MIDI server and driver layer create properties; however, the Core MIDI property system is also extensible. Applications can add their own custom properties to objects.

The Core MIDI property system also offers the feature of inheritance. Properties are inherited following the abstraction rule of devices, entity, endpoint. For example, a discrete endpoint would not necessarily contain a property with the manufacturer name. The manufacturer name would typically be a property assigned to the device. In that example, Core MIDI would still enable you to query the endpoint for the manufacturer name; if it was not found, it would ask its parent entity and finally would return the property found in the device.

You might expect to find these common properties assigned to Core MIDI objects:

- Devices, entities, and endpoints, with user-definable names
- Device's manufacturer and model name assigned by the driver
- Device's MIDI system-exclusive ID
- Device's maximum transmit speed

The properties come in various types: `CFStringRef`, `CFDataRef`, or `CFNumbers`. The documentation for the various property name constants indicates the type you get back. In contrast to other property getters in Core Audio that set a `void*`, Core MIDI's properties have type-specific getter and setter functions: `MIDIObjectGetString` `Property()`, `MIDIObjectSetDataProperty()`, and so on. A `MIDIObjectGet` `Properties()` call returns a `CFArrayRef` of all the object's properties.

MIDI Messages

MIDI messages are tiny. When delivered to your application, a MIDIPacket consists of a time stamp and a small byte array. Typically, MIDI messages are just 3 bytes, commonly referred to as `status`, `data1`, and `data2`.

The status byte indicates the command, and `data1` and `data2` deliver data specific to the semantics of the command. The simplest and most common events, the channel voice messages, use the high nybble of the status to indicate a command and use the low nybble to specify which of the 16 MIDI channels is affected by the event. Assuming *n* to represent the channel (0–F), these are some of the most common messages:

- `0x8n` - NOTE OFF: Stops playing a note
- `0x9n` - NOTE ON: Starts playing a note
- `0xBn` - POLYPHONIC AFTERTOUCH: Applies additional pressure to a note previously pressed
- `0xCn` - PROGRAM CHANGE: Changes the patch number
- `0xDn` - CHANNEL AFTERTOUCH: Indicates which of several previously pressed keys has the greatest pressure
- `0xEn` - PITCH WHEEL CHANGE: Applies variable pitch change

The `data1` and `data2` for these events depends on the particular status message. For the NOTE ON and NOTE OFF messages, the bottom 7 bits of `data1` are the specific note (where decimal 60 is middle C), and the bottom 7 bits of `data2` are a velocity that indicates how quickly the key was struck or released (the high bit of both `data1` and `data2` is always 1 for these messages).

Many more messages exist, including more elaborate commands that can be sent with multiple messages. You can look them up at www.midi.org/techspecs/midimessages.php and through other formal and informal references.

Instrument Units

It's great to get and send events via MIDI, but the initial purpose of the standard was to communicate musical data. So when do you get to the music part? Core MIDI handles only the signaling; to make sound, you need to look elsewhere.

You might recall that Chapter 7, "Audio Units: Generators, Effects, and Rendering," covered instrument units, a kind of audio unit that could produce sound (similar to generator units such as the `AUFilePlayer`). The key to instrument units is that they respond to MIDI commands, so you can take incoming MIDI events and use instrument units to create sounds in response to those commands. This is another place where the advantages of audio units come into play. Audio Units are low latency, and it's crucial in musical performance to generate sound more or less immediately in response to an event that represents a musician's press of a digital piano key or hit on a drum head.

The glue that connects MIDI to instrument units is the Music Device API, which consists of just four functions in the `MusicDevice.h` header file (and, as of Xcode 4.2, is not part of the OS X or iOS documentation bundle). The `MusicDeviceMIDIEvent()` function takes an instrument unit and the 3 bytes of a MIDI message, and makes the instrument act on the command: If its status is NOTE ON, the unit starts playing the note specified by `data1` with the velocity in `data2`; if it's NOTE OFF, it stops.

Building a Simple MIDI Synthesizer

Let's put this to work with a straightforward example. You'll create an AUGraph with an instrument and I/O unit, connect to any attached MIDI devices, and use Music Device to deliver the MIDI events to the instrument unit.

Create a new command-line Core Foundation project (ours is called CH11_MIDIToAUGraph) and link in the Audio Toolbox and Core MIDI frameworks.

Listing 11.1 shows the skeleton for the main.c program.

Listing 11.1   Outline of Core MIDI–Based Synthesizer Program

```
#include <CoreFoundation/CoreFoundation.h>
#import <CoreMIDI/CoreMIDI.h>
#import <AudioToolbox/AudioToolbox.h>

#pragma mark - state struct
// Insert Listing 11.2 here

#pragma mark utility functions
// Insert Listing 4.2 here

#pragma mark - callbacks
// Insert 11.8 - 11.12 here

#pragma mark - augraph
// Insert Listing 11.4 here

#pragma mark - midi
// Insert Listings 11.5 - 11.7 here

#pragma mark - main
int main (int argc, const char * argv[])
// Insert Listing 11.3
```

Start by copying over the CheckError() function from Listing 4.2. Next, you need a state struct to pass around your various functions. You need to hang on to your AUGraph, and the instrument unit within it, so that the MIDI event callbacks can send their commands to the instrument unit at the front of the graph. Listing 11.2 shows this MyMIDIPlayer struct.

Listing 11.2   State Struct for Core MIDI Synthesizer Program

```
typedef struct MyMIDIPlayer {
    AUGraph      graph;
    AudioUnit    instrumentUnit;
} MyMIDIPlayer;
```

The main() function defers all its functionality to convenience functions that set up the AUGraph and connect to the MIDI devices. After these are set up, all it needs to do is start the graph and keep the program from terminating. Listing 11.3 shows the complete main() function.

Listing 11.3   main() Function for Core MIDI Synthesizer Program

```
int main (int argc, const char * argv[]) {
    MyMIDIPlayer player;

    setupAUGraph(&player);
    setupMIDI(&player);

    CheckError (AUGraphStart(player.graph),
                "Couldn't start graph");

    CFRunLoopRun();
    // Run until aborted with Control-C

    return 0;
}
```

So much for the easy parts. Now let's do some real work. You set up the AUGraph first, so let's write that function first. Listing 11.4 shows setupAUGraph() in its entirety.

Listing 11.4   Setting Up an AUGraph with a MIDI-Controllable Instrument Unit

```
void setupAUGraph(MyMIDIPlayer *player) {

    CheckError(NewAUGraph(&player->graph),
                "Couldn't open AU Graph");

    // Generate description that will match our output
    // device (speakers)
    AudioComponentDescription outputcd = {0};
    outputcd.componentType = kAudioUnitType_Output;
    outputcd.componentSubType = kAudioUnitSubType_DefaultOutput;
    outputcd.componentManufacturer = kAudioUnitManufacturer_Apple;

    // Adds a node with above description to the graph
    AUNode outputNode;
    CheckError(AUGraphAddNode(player->graph,
                            &outputcd,
                            &outputNode),
        "AUGraphAddNode[kAudioUnitSubType_DefaultOutput] failed");
```

Listing 11.4   **Continued**

```
    AudioComponentDescription instrumentcd = {0};
    instrumentcd.componentManufacturer = kAudioUnitManufacturer_Apple;
    instrumentcd.componentType = kAudioUnitType_MusicDevice;
    instrumentcd.componentSubType = kAudioUnitSubType_DLSSynth;

    AUNode instrumentNode;
    CheckError(AUGraphAddNode(player->graph,
                              &instrumentcd,
                              &instrumentNode),
        "AUGraphAddNode[kAudioUnitSubType_DLSSynth] failed");

    // Opening the graph opens all contained audio units but
    // does not allocate any resources yet
    CheckError(AUGraphOpen(player->graph),
            "AUGraphOpen failed");

    // Get the reference to the AudioUnit object for the
    // instrument graph node
    CheckError(AUGraphNodeInfo(player->graph,
                               instrumentNode,
                               NULL,
                               &player->instrumentUnit),
            "AUGraphNodeInfo failed");

    // Connect the output source of the speech synthesis
    // AU to the input source of the output node
    CheckError(AUGraphConnectNodeInput(player->graph,
                                       instrumentNode,
                                       0,
                                       outputNode,
                                       0),
            "AUGraphConnectNodeInput failed");
    // Now initialize the graph (causes resources to be allocated)
    CheckError(AUGraphInitialize(player->graph),
            "AUGraphInitialize failed");
}
```

This is a fairly long listing, but it's all things you did repeatedly in Chapters 7 and 8. You create an AUGraph and set up the default output unit to connect to the audio output hardware. Then you use type kAudioUnitType_MusicDevice and subtype kAudioUnitSubType_DLSSynth to create a synthesizer instrument unit. You need to get the actual instrument unit from the AUNode so that you can send it your MIDI events. Aside from that, everything else here is the usual care and feeding of an AUGraph: Open it, connect nodes, and initialize.

Connecting to MIDI

Now let's get to figuring out what MIDI devices are available and make some connections. First, you start in Listing 11.5 by creating a `MIDIClientRef`, which is a "session" object that represents your application's participation in MIDI.

Listing 11.5   **Creating a MIDIClientRef**

```
void setupMIDI(MyMIDIPlayer *player) {

    MIDIClientRef client;
    CheckError (MIDIClientCreate(CFSTR("Core MIDI to System Sounds Demo"),
                                 MyMIDINotifyProc,
                                 player,
                                 &client),
                "Couldn't create MIDI client");
```

The `MIDIClientRef` takes a string to identify the client, a callback function, and a context/user info pointer to send to the callback, as well as an I/O pointer in which it returns the created `MIDIClientRef`. The callback, of type `MIDINotifyProc`, gets called when devices are added or removed, or when a device needs to signal a property change. You'll write a trivial `MyMIDINotifyProc()` later.

Now that you have a client, you can create an input port to receive incoming MIDI messages, as in Listing 11.6.

Listing 11.6   **Creating a MIDIPortRef**

```
MIDIPortRef inPort;
CheckError (MIDIInputPortCreate(client,
                                CFSTR("Input port"),
                                MyMIDIReadProc,
                                player,
                                &inPort),
            "Couldn't create MIDI input port");
```

The `MIDIInputPortCreate()` function takes the client object, a name string, a callback function pointer and its context object, and a pointer in which it returns the created `MIDIPortRef`. The input port receives incoming MIDI messages in the callback function, specified by the `MIDIReadProc` type. This is where you'll be writing your message-handling code.

You have an input port, but you haven't yet connected anything to it. To do that, you need to iterate over the available MIDI sources and get their endpoints. You do this in Listing 11.7.

Listing 11.7   **Connecting a MIDI Port to Available Sources**

```
unsigned long sourceCount = MIDIGetNumberOfSources();
printf ("%ld sources\n", sourceCount);
for (int i = 0; i < sourceCount; ++i) {
    MIDIEndpointRef src = MIDIGetSource(i);
    CFStringRef endpointName = NULL;
    CheckError(MIDIObjectGetStringProperty(src,
                                           kMIDIPropertyName,
                                           &endpointName),
            "Couldn't get endpoint name");
    char endpointNameC[255];
    CFStringGetCString(endpointName,
                       endpointNameC,
                       255,
                       kCFStringEncodingUTF8);
    printf(" source %d: %s\n", i, endpointNameC);
    CheckError (MIDIPortConnectSource(inPort,
                                      src,
                                      NULL),
            "Couldn't connect MIDI port");
}
```

You need to start with `MIDIGetNumberOfSources()` because `MIDIGetSource()` takes an index as its parameter. By getting the number of available sources, you can iterate over all of them and get `MIDIEndpointRefs` for each one. This example connects to every discovered source, meaning that if you plug in two MIDI devices, you will be playing notes when either sends an event. You could be more deliberate by inspecting each source and deciding, or letting the user decide whether to connect to a given source. The properties of each source might help you decide. In this example, you get just one property, the `kMIDIPropertyName`, and log it with `printf()`. Several dozen property constants are defined, so you might want to see whether a given device is from a certain manufacturer (`kMIDIPropertyManufacturer`), what kind of device it is (`kMIDIPropertyIsDrumMachine`, `kMIDIPropertyIsSampler`, and so on), what features it supports (`kMIDIPropertyReceivesNotes`, `kMIDIPropertyTransmitsClock`, and so on), or other criteria.

You connect to the source with `MIDIPortConnectSource()`, which takes your input `MIDIPortRef`, a source `MIDIEndpointRef`, and a second context object to send to the input port's callback that you declared in Listing 11.6. This enables you to set an object to associate a callback with a specific source that is sending the event. You don't need it if you're blindly accepting notes from all devices, so `NULL` is set here.

That's all you need to connect an input port in your code to all the MIDI sources discovered when the program comes up. The remaining task is to implement the two callback procs declared in this setup function.

Handling MIDI Notifications and Events

You've declared two callback functions: `MyMIDINotifyProc()`, to handle notifications about the MIDI environment as a whole, and `MyMIDIReadProc()`, to process events. Implementing those is your last step.

To keep things simple, you're going to log any messages you get in `MyMIDINotifyProc()`, as shown in Listing 11.8.

Listing 11.8   Simple Implementation of MIDINotifyProc Callback

```
void MyMIDINotifyProc (const MIDINotification  *message, void *refCon) {
    printf("MIDI Notify, messageId=%d,", message->messageID);
}
```

Aside from `refCon`, which is the context object you set up in `MIDIClientCreate`, the callback provides a `MIDINotification`, which contains details about the change to the MIDI environment. The `MIDINotification` type contains a message Id and a message size; depending on the message Id, the notification might have additional data. For example, if the message Id is `kMIDIMsgObjectAdded`, the notification includes a `MIDIObjectAddRemoveNotification`, a structure that describes the added object. Clearly, a robust music app would want to handle messages about MIDI devices being added and either automatically add them as sources or give the user a chance to do so.

For this example, the most interesting action happens in `MyMIDIReadProc()`, the callback declared in `MIDIInputPortCreate()`. Listing 11.9 shows the beginning of this callback function.

Listing 11.9   Getting a Context Object in MIDIReadProc

```
static void MyMIDIReadProc(const MIDIPacketList *pktlist,
                           void *refCon,
                           void *connRefCon) {
    MyMIDIPlayer *player = (MyMIDIPlayer*) refCon;
```

You start this function by retrieving the `MyMIDIPlayer` object that you declared as the context object in `MIDIInputPortCreate()`. It's the first of two context objects in this function. The `connRefCon` is the object declared in `MIDIPortConnectSource()`, which could be used to identify a specific source but that is set to `NULL`.

The other parameter provided to the callback is a `MIDIPacketList`, which has a `numPackets` and looks like an array of `MIDIPackets`. However, because the packets can be variable length, you can't get the packets with C's array accessor. You can get the first one from index 0, but after that, you need to use the macro `MIDINextPacket()`, passing in the current packet from the list.

Each MIDI packet has a time stamp, a length, and a byte array. Typically, the length is 2 or 3 and the array consists of the `status`, `data1`, and `data2` bytes. So in Listing 11.10, you start iterating over the packets.

Listing 11.10   **Iterating over a MIDIPacketList**

```
MIDIPacket *packet = (MIDIPacket *)pktlist->packet;
for (int i=0; i < pktlist->numPackets; i++) {
    Byte midiStatus = packet->data[0];
    Byte midiCommand = midiStatus >> 4;
```

The first member of data, which you assign to the variable midiStatus, is the status byte of the MIDI message. The high nybble of midiStatus is the command, and for the events that you care about here, the low nybble is the channel (0–15).

For simple play-through, the only commands to care about here are NOTE ON (0x9) and NOTE OFF (0x8), so we shift the status 4 bits right to get the command in its own byte and then see if it's one of these two commands. Listing 11.11 shows these steps.

Listing 11.11   **Parsing NOTE OFF and NOTE ON Events**

```
if ((midiCommand == 0x08) ||
    (midiCommand == 0x09)) {
    Byte note = packet->data[1] & 0x7F;
    Byte velocity = packet->data[2] & 0x7F;
```

The meanings of data1 and data2 depend on the command. For NOTE ON and NOTE OFF, the bottom 7 bits of data1 are the note to play, where the scale is calibrated to make decimal 60 (0x3c) a middle C. Each whole number up is a half-step, meaning that 61 is C#, 62 is D, and so on. Meanwhile, the bottom 7 bits of data2 are the velocity, the speed at which a key was struck or released (1–127).

These three values are all you need to send to your instrument unit to play the corresponding note in your AUGraph. MusicDeviceMIDIEvent() takes the receiving instrument unit; the status, data1, and data2 bytes; and an offset used for certain timing scenarios that don't concern you. Listing 11.12 shows these steps and brings us to the end of the MyMIDIReadProc() callback function.

Listing 11.12   **Sending a MIDI Event to an Instrument Unit**

```
    CheckError(MusicDeviceMIDIEvent (player->instrumentUnit,
                                     midiStatus,
                                     note,
                                     velocity,
                                     0),
               "Couldn't send MIDI event");

    }
packet = MIDIPacketNext(packet);
}
}
```

This call causes the NOTE ON or NOTE OFF event (and its channel, represented by the bottom 4 bits of midiStatus) to be processed by the instrument unit, which means that a note either starts or stops playing. Having processed this packet, you move on to the next one with MIDIPacketNext(), possibly falling out of the for loop if you have processed all the packets.

Playing Your AUGraph

At this point, the example is done. All you need to do now is hook up instruments and play them. That assumes you have suitable instruments. By far the most popular way to connect MIDI devices to Macs is with MIDI-to-USB adapters. They're commonly found in electronics and music stores, with prices ranging from less than US$10 to over US$100, depending on features, number of ports, and so on.

And if you don't have and don't want a MIDI keyboard ... well, we may have an alternative for you in the next section.

For now, let's take stock of what you've learned. You used Core MIDI to discover the various MIDI devices connected to your Mac, opened an input port and connected to their sources, and processed incoming MIDI messages from those sources. When the MIDI messages were NOTE ON or NOTE OFF, you used MusicDeviceMIDIEvent to send the event to an instrument unit in an AUGraph, which immediately plays the note or notes on a synthesized piano. Keep in mind that because the last step of this process takes you back to the Audio Units you're already familiar with, you could perform downstream effects on the synthesized sound via effect units or combine multiple synthesizers and other units (such as an I/O unit for captured audio from a mic) in a mixer unit, and thereby get a whole band going. The musical possibilities are compelling.

Creating MIDI Events

Aside from being a MIDI destination, Core MIDI enables you to be a MIDI source. For the second example, you'll use Core MIDI on iOS to turn your iPhone, iPod Touch, or iPad into an instrument that can act as a Wi-Fi-connected MIDI device.

Core MIDI defines several Objective-C objects (not C types, as you've seen thus far) from which you can get MIDIClientRefs, MIDIEndpointRefs and MIDIPortRefs, and the other kinds of objects used for strictly local MIDI message handling. By using these classes in an iOS app, you can create a virtual MIDI instrument that can play your previous example code over Wi-Fi.

Setting Up the MIDIWifiSource Example

To get started, create an iPhone single-view application project in Xcode (we called ours CH11_MIDIWifiSource) and link in the CoreMIDI.framework. Because this is a UI app and not a command-line program, you need to build a user interface. All this involves is telling the code what MIDI note to send in a message. A simple way to do that is to use UIButtons and to use the tag attribute (in the Attribute Inspector,

Command+Option+4) of each button to hold the note value you want to play. In
CH11_MIDIWifiSourceViewController.xib, shown in Figure 11.4, you have set up
buttons with all the notes in one octave of the keyboard. The C button has tag 60, C#
has 61, and so on, up to tag 71 for B.

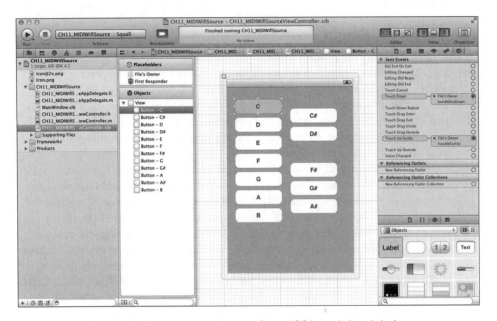

Figure 11.4　　Setting up buttons for an iOS-based virtual device

The view controller class needs to handle the button taps, sending NOTE ON when a
touch begins and NOTE OFF when it ends. So stub out the view controller, as shown in
Listing 11.13.

Listing 11.13　　IBActions Defined in CH11_MIDIWifiSourceViewController.h

```
#import <UIKit/UIKit.h>

@interface CH11_MIDIWifiSourceViewController : UIViewController

-(IBAction) handleKeyDown:(id)sender;
-(IBAction) handleKeyUp:(id)sender;

@end
```

In the NIB file, switch to the connections inspector (Option-⌘-6). Connect every
button's Touch Down event to File's Owner's handleKeyDown:, and connect Touch Up

Inside to handleKeyUp:. Figure 11.4 shows these connections as they've been set for the C button. You might find it easier to select the File's Owner, look at the Received Actions connections, and repeatedly make connections from this list to the separate buttons, selecting the appropriate event (Touch Down or Touch Up Inside) in the gray heads-up list each time it appears at the end of your connection.

In the view controller's implementation file, the Xcode template stubs out a few VC-related methods for you—but, of course, it knows nothing about MIDI. You use a class extension to define the helper methods you're going to write, along with properties (rather than simple instance variables) for the MIDI objects you'll need. These are in Listing 11.14 and must precede the @implementation statement.

Listing 11.14   Class Extension for CH11_MIDIWifiSourceViewController Helper Methods and Properties

```
@interface CH11_MIDIWifiSourceViewController()
- (void) connectToHost;
- (void) sendStatus:(Byte)status data1:(Byte)data1 data2:(Byte)data2;
- (void) sendNoteOnEvent:(Byte) note velocity:(Byte)velocity;
- (void) sendNoteOffEvent:(Byte)key velocity:(Byte)velocity;
@property (assign) MIDINetworkSession *midiSession;
@property (assign) MIDIEndpointRef destinationEndpoint;
@property (assign) MIDIPortRef outputPort;
@end
```

Don't forget to @synthesize midiSession, destinationEndpoint, and outputPort. Also, copy over the CheckError() function from Listing 4.2 and put it before any of the instance methods (which might need to call it).

Setting Up MIDI over Wi-Fi

Let's start by setting up your connection to the Wi-Fi host, which is the computer that will be running one or more MIDI-compatible apps. You stubbed this out in the class extension as the connectToHost method. You'll need it as soon as the view comes up, so override the viewDidLoad: method to call it, as shown in Listing 11.15.

Listing 11.15   Calling connectToHost When iPhone View Loads

```
- (void)viewDidLoad
{
    [super viewDidLoad];
    [self connectToHost];
}
```

The host you're connecting to is represented as the Objective-C class MIDINetworkHost. This object can be created either with an address and a port or with a resolved Bonjour NSNetService. The Bonjour approach is more robust, but this

example uses the address/port approach here to keep your focus on MIDI. Put a
#define for your Mac at the top of the file, as in Listing 11.16. Of course, the contents
of the string should be your Mac's IP address.

Listing 11.16   **#define for MIDI Host Address**

```
#define DESTINATION_ADDRESS @"192.168.2.108"
```

Now you can begin your connectToHost method, by creating the host object with
-[MIDINetworkHost hostWithName:address:port:], as shown in Listing 11.17.

Listing 11.17   **Creating a MIDINetworkHost**

```
-(void) connectToHost {
    MIDINetworkHost *host = [MIDINetworkHost hostWithName:@"MyMIDIWifi"
                                          address:DESTINATION_ADDRESS
                                          port:5004];

    if(!host)
        return;
```

The name parameter is only for the app's local use; it doesn't have to match any particular value on the other end.

With a host object created, you use the MIDINetworkConnection class to actually
connect to it, as shown in Listing 11.18.

Listing 11.18   **Creating a MIDINetworkConnection**

```
MIDINetworkConnection *connection =
    [MIDINetworkConnection connectionWithHost:host];
if(!connection)
    return;
```

When you've made the connection, you can get a MIDINetworkSession, a
MIDI entity with one source endpoint and one destination endpoint. These are
MIDIEndpointRefs, the same C type you worked with earlier, and are available via the
sourceEndpoint and destinationEndpoint instance methods. To know where the
destinationEndpoint actually is on the network, you need to add the connection you
created in Listing 11.18 to the session. You also need to enable the session before you try
to send or receive any data with it. Listing 11.19 shows these session setup steps.

Listing 11.19   **Setting Up MIDINetworkSession to Send MIDI Data**

```
self.midiSession = [MIDINetworkSession defaultSession];
if (self.midiSession) {
    NSLog (@"Got MIDI session");
    [self.midiSession addConnection:connection];
    self.midiSession.enabled = YES;
    self.destinationEndpoint = [self.midiSession destinationEndpoint];
```

With the `MIDIEndpointRef`, you can make MIDI calls to set up a port. However, this time you're creating an output port, so you can send MIDI messages rather than receive them. Again, create a `MIDIClientRef`. From this, create the output port with `MIDIOutputPortCreate()`. Listing 11.20 shows these final steps of the `connectToHost` method.

Listing 11.20   **Setting Up a MIDI Output Port**

```
        MIDIClientRef client = NULL;
        MIDIPortRef outport = NULL;
        CheckError (MIDIClientCreate(CFSTR("MyMIDIWifi Client"),
                                    NULL,
                                    NULL,
                                    &client),
                    "Couldn't create MIDI client");
        CheckError (MIDIOutputPortCreate(client,
                                    CFSTR("MyMIDIWifi Output port"),
                                    &outport),
                    "Couldn't create output port");
        self.outputPort = outport;
        NSLog (@"Got output port");
    }
}
```

Sending MIDI Messages

Assuming that `connectToHost` succeeded, the `outputPort` property has a `MIDIPortRef` that's ready for you to send it MIDI data. You send data with `MIDISend()`, which takes an output port, the destination endpoint, and a `MIDIPacketList`. For MIDI messages that take 2 data bytes, such as the NOTE ON and NOTE OFF messages, you can write a generic `sendStatus:data1:data2:` method like the one shown in Listing 11.21.

Listing 11.21   **Method to Create and Send a MIDIPacketList**

```
-(void) sendStatus:(Byte)status data1:(Byte)data1 data2:(Byte)data2 {
    MIDIPacketList packetList;

    packetList.numPackets = 1;
    packetList.packet[0].length = 3;
    packetList.packet[0].data[0] = status;
    packetList.packet[0].data[1] = data1;
    packetList.packet[0].data[2] = data2;
    packetList.packet[0].timeStamp = 0;
```

Listing 11.21   **Continued**

```
        CheckError (MIDISend(self.outputPort,
                            self.destinationEndpoint,
                            &packetList),
                    "Couldn't send MIDI packet list");
}
```

This method simply creates a MIDIPacketList, sets its length to 3 (1 status and 2 data bytes), and then fills in the data array with the parameter values. It then sends the packet list over the output port to the destination endpoint, by way of the MIDISend() function.

With your send method ready, you can call it with the specific NOTE ON (status 0x9n, where n is a channel, which will be 0 for this app) and NOTE OFF (status 0x8n) messages. For these messages, the high bits of data1 and data2 are always 0, so you need to mask those off. Listing 11.22 shows your implementations of sendNoteOnEvent:key: velocity: and sendNoteOffEvent:key:velocity:.

Listing 11.22   **Sending NOTE ON and NOTE OFF Events**

```
-(void) sendNoteOnEvent:(Byte)key velocity:(Byte)velocity {
    [self sendStatus:0x90 data1:key & 0x7F data2:velocity & 0x7F];

}

-(void) sendNoteOffEvent:(Byte)key velocity:(Byte)velocity {
    [self sendStatus:0x80 data1:key & 0x7F data2:velocity & 0x7F];
}
```

With the note event methods ready, you can finally add the tap-handling methods, which get the tag (and, therefore, the MIDI note to play) from the button that was tapped, and send it to these methods. Listing 11.23 shows this final step.

Listing 11.23   **Handling User Taps on Keys**

```
-(IBAction) handleKeyDown:(id)sender {
    NSInteger note = [sender tag];
    [self sendNoteOnEvent:(Byte) note velocity:127];
}

-(IBAction) handleKeyUp:(id)sender {
    NSInteger note = [sender tag];
    [self sendNoteOffEvent:(Byte) note velocity:127];
}
```

This is all it takes to send MIDI events via Wi-Fi. Actually, this illustrates what it takes to send MIDI events over a wired connection as well: Listing 11.20's steps for creating a `MIDIClientRef` and output port would be the same for a wired connection, as would sending the data with `MIDISend()`.

Setting Up Your Mac to Receive Wi-Fi MIDI Data

Now that you've set up an iOS app to generate network MIDI events, you need something to receive the events and do something with them, such as play notes. You configure this with the Audio MIDI Setup application located in Applications/Utilities. This utility configures MIDI connections to and from your computer, both hard-wired and wireless.

The main window (shown in Figure 11.5) shows your existing connections. By default, these include an IAC Driver for (interapplication communication) and Network; if you have any hard-wired MIDI devices plugged in, they're shown here as well. Because you're sending data wirelessly from the iPhone or iPad, you need to set up the Network connection, so double-click that icon.

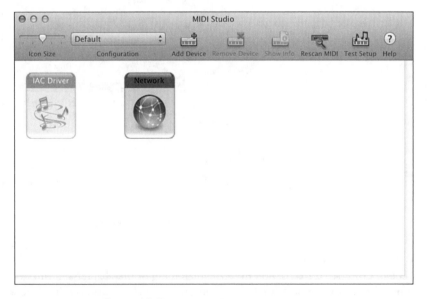

Figure 11.5   Audio MIDI Setup main window

The Network window shows a list of Sessions and a directory of available devices on the left. By default, the details of Session 1 are shown in the right pane. You can see the session name, the Bonjour name that clients can connect to, a list of participants, a Latency graph, and the IP address and port that clients should connect to. This is your

last chance to get the IP address and port right. In Xcode, check the DESTINATION_
ADDRESS you defined and make sure you're using the same host and port shown in
Audio MIDI Setup. If it's wrong, rebuild and reinstall to your device.

When the app is ready, run it on your device. You should see it appear in the MIDI
Network Setup window (see Figure 11.6), where the iPhone Squall automatically
appears in the directory and as one of Session 1's participants. If it doesn't work, force-
quit CH11_MIDIWifiSource and make sure you start it *after* you've started Audio MIDI
Setup. When you see your device in the MIDI Network Setup window, you're connected; you can tap on the squares on the device to send MIDI events over the network.
As you do, vertical red lines appear in the Latency graph to indicate the lag between creating the MIDI event on the device and its arrival on the Mac.

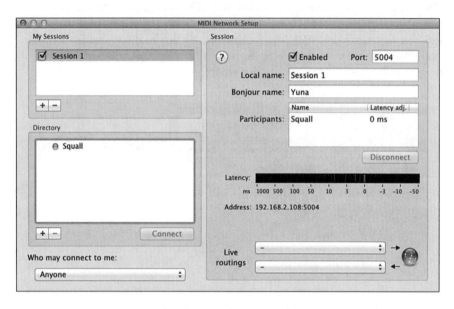

Figure 11.6   Audio MIDI Setup network window

Are you hearing any sound? If not, it might be because you're not running a MIDI
app. Reopen CH11_MIDIToAUGraph from the beginning of the chapter and run it. You
should now be able to tap notes on your iPhone, iPod Touch, or iPad and hear them
over your speakers or headphones. You'll also see the same logging messages in the
CH11_MIDIToAUGraph log, but this time the events are coming not from a wired MIDI
device, but over the air from a wireless device. Granted, it's not perfect: There can be a
lot of latency, especially if you pause briefly and thereby let the connection drop. But
you'll probably still find it pretty cool. After all, between these two apps, what starts as a
touch gesture on iOS goes out over Wi-Fi as a MIDI event, gets processed by a Mac

program, is rendered as synthesized PCM audio inside an AUGraph, and comes out your speakers as audible sound.

That's a lot of technology behind your hand-held rendition of "Chopsticks," isn't it?

Summary: MIDI Mastery ... but Mobility?

Obviously, you can do a lot more with MIDI: A look at the list of MIDI messages shows a lot of different events you can work with and support for different kinds of musical messages. With instrument units and the Music Device API bridging the world of MIDI and Core Audio, you can bring support for all these devices—including virtual MIDI devices that you create yourself on Mac or iOS—into Core Audio and literally mix it with the other audio frameworks on the platform.

One dangling issue we haven't addressed is processing MIDI event input into iOS devices. This was enabled in iOS 4.2, which brought Core MIDI to Apple's mobile devices. You can use the same techniques as in the first half of this chapter to handle events from MIDI devices connected to an iOS device. However, there are a few catches. The first is that an iPad obviously doesn't have a MIDI port or even a USB port. One answer to this objection is that third parties can develop MIDI-compliant devices that connect via the dock port.

The other option is to use the iPad Camera Connection Kit, which offers a USB port. Apple generally warns that this is neither intended nor supported as a generic USB connection, but it is known to work with many MIDI-to-USB adapters; Apple even discussed and demonstrated this in a WWDC 2011 session. The trick is that the iOS devices deliver a tiny amount of power over the dock connector, not enough to power many adapters. Another problem is that some adapters need drivers to work, and iOS doesn't support third-party drivers. However, the USB spec defines standards for MIDI devices, so a "class-compliant" or "driverless" device that doesn't draw much power (or is itself plugged in) can work on an iOS device. The "iOS MIDI" site has a page at http://iosmidi.com/devices/ that lists devices known to work (and others known *not* to work) with the iPad. It also offers a MIDI Monitor app that uses Core MIDI to log incoming MIDI events from a connected device.

The other problem with handling MIDI events in iOS is what to do with them after they arrive. iOS 4 doesn't provide the DLS Synthesizer or any other instrument units for the platform, so a straight port of CH11_MIDIToAUGraph from OS X to iOS doesn't work. You could handle the incoming events by synthesizing your own sound in a render callback or playing files via APIs Audio Queue or OpenAL. In the final chapter, as part of a look to the future, you'll see what iOS 5 offers to make MIDI on the mobile device more practical.

12

Coda

You've reached the end of the book, but hopefully your journey with Core Audio is just beginning. You have lots more to learn, lots more to play with, and lots more to do with Core Audio than will fit in this book—or any other book. Furthermore, the field of digital audio is much larger than any programming framework. The more you learn about how to work with audio, the more value you'll get out of Core Audio.

This chapter discusses what else might interest you in the OS X and iOS audio APIs and where you might want to go from here.

Still More Core Audio

All authors have to make hard decisions about what to include and what to leave out in a book. Although we've done much more than just scratch the surface of Core Audio, skimming the documentation reveals that there's much more to work with: more system-provided audio units, dozens of OpenAL properties, and more.

Within Core Audio, this book leaves out one major API: Audio File Stream Services. This set of functions, defined in `AudioFileStream.h`, enables you to create apps such as Web radio clients for the stream formats that OS X and iOS support. They enable you to send in buffers of raw data—which you've presumably read from the network, although it also works for reading files—and receive callbacks with packets of audio parsed from the stream. You can then decompress these packets can with the Audio Converter functions, send them to an Audio Queue, and so on. The catch is that you're limited to both the codecs and the stream formats that Core Audio supports, so although this helps you parse MP3 from an HTTP stream (Shoutcast-style web radio), it doesn't necessarily handle a lot of other stream formats. Still, because it follows the conventions of the other Core Audio APIs—heavy on the properties and callbacks—this shouldn't be difficult if you've made it all the way to this point.

Another topic that this book doesn't cover is the capability to create your own audio units. In Chapters 7, "Audio Units: Generators, Effects, and Rendering," and 8, "Audio Units: Input and Mixing," you saw how to add your own processing by way of render callbacks, which you could encapsulate inside a reusable audio unit. You can also create a

Cocoa-based UI for your unit so that users can configure them directly. This is mostly of interest if you're in the business of selling your audio unit as a third-party add-on, where it can be called from AUGraph-based applications such as GarageBand, Logic, and Final Cut Pro. The process of rolling your own audio unit involves a little programming and a lot of testing and packaging. If you're one of the few people who needs to do this (and isn't doing so already), you can find a full walkthrough in Apple's *Audio Unit Programming Guide.*

Third-party audio units are available only on Mac OS X. They don't make sense on iOS, where third parties can't deliver code to be shared between applications. Actually, Phone OS 3 added an API for encapsulating audio units for your own app's use, `AUPlugIn.h`, which supposedly enabled you to register a new audio unit and then create and add it to AUGraphs such as the system units. However, we have it on high authority that this never actually worked, and `AUPlugIn.h` was removed in iOS 4.0.

Next Steps

Now that you know all these APIs, what are you going to do with them? In many ways, the greatest power of Core Audio lies not in the APIs themselves, but in what you bring to the table in terms of working with the audio as it passes through the system. This book has talked a lot about "doing stuff" with samples in render callbacks or before passing buffers to OpenAL, but what does that really involve?

Digital Signal Processing

A whole science is involved in working with audio signals in a computer, or digital signal processing. Let's return to the science of sound and the waves of pressure moving through the air. In analog systems, you commonly use the amplitude of an electrical signal to represent sound. In digital, you sample this signal thousands of times a second, to get a numeric representation of the signal that's practical to store on disk, transmit over networks, and process in a CPU.

You can process that signal with various mathematical techniques. For example, the famous Fourier Transform enables you to convert a time-based function—that's all the audio signal really is, a function of amplitude at a given time—to a frequency-based function. This capability to find frequencies in time-based signals facilitates all kinds of useful applications, from effects that speed up playback without changing pitch, to frequency detectors that can determine what note is being sung or played. You've probably used both of these: The former is the double-speed playback available in the iOS Music app to get you through spoken podcasts and audiobooks faster, and the latter is used by apps that identify songs and by music-performance games such as *Karaoke Revolution* and *Rock Band.*

The topic of digital signal processing merits its own book. In fact, Pearson (who publishes this book) has a number of titles on the topic, including *Digital Signal Processing, 4th Edition,* by John G. Proakis and Dimitris K Manolakis; *Discrete-Time Signal Processing,* by

Alan V. Oppenheim and Ronald W. Schafer; and *Notes on Digital Signal Processing: Practical Recipes for Design, Analysis and Implementation,* by C. Britton Rorabaugh.

You can also find some great free resources on the Web for learning about DSP. "The DSP Dimension" has a series of tutorials at www.dspdimension.com that cover topics such as the Fourier transform and time-stretching/pitch-shifting effects. The Music-DSP Source Code Archive, at www.musicdsp.org, offers a grab bag of DSP analysis, effect, filter, and synthesis recipes in a number of languages (some C and C++, others MAT-LAB). A handful of iTunes U-courses offer a college-level introduction to DSP. If you can handle the math, Stanford's "The Fourier Transform and Its Applications" offers a deep dive into the theory behind this most useful technique.

Speaking of the Fourier transform, you should be aware of one more Apple framework. The Accelerate framework in OS X and iOS provides highly optimized and sometimes hardware-accelerated mathematical functions. The vDSP portion of Accelerate is particularly applicable to digital signal processing code, providing functions for vector and matrix arithmetic as well as the fast Fourier transform (FFT).

Lion and iOS 5

Mac OS X 10.7 (Lion) and iOS 5 are new as this book is being released, and both add APIs to Core Audio and the related media frameworks.

Among Lion's highlights, you now can inspect and use hardware encoding and decoding via the `AudioFormat.h` property `kAudioFormatProperty_HardwareCodec Capabilities` and a set of "prefer" and "use only" properties in `AudioQueue.h`. Among other changes, AudioFile introduces a new property for album art. Some new audio units also are available, some brought to the Mac from iOS, including `AUVoiceProcessingIO` (for echo cancellation in voice-over-IP apps) and `AUiPodEQ` (an equalizer that uses presets such as Bass Booster and Spoken Word).

AUSampler

Probably the most interesting of the new audio units in Lion is the AUSampler, `kAudioUnitSubType_Sampler`, an instrument unit that enables you to pitch-shift an arbitrary waveform sample to turn it into a musical instrument. It works like any other instrument unit, as with the `kAudioUnitSubType_DLSSynth` in Chapter 11, "Core MIDI," and can be controlled via `MusicDeviceMIDIEvent()`. The difference is that, by providing your own waveforms, you can make any kind of real-world instrument, or even sample a voice and pitch-shift it into a sort of virtual singing.

For the final example project, copy the `MIDIToAUGraph` example from Chapter 11 into a new command-line project. Because this feature is new for Lion, you should make Mac OS X 10.7 the Base SDK in the project settings. Link in the Audio Toolbox, Audio Unit, and Core MIDI frameworks as before.

The first change is trivial. In `setupAUGraph()`, replace the line that sets up the instrument audio unit, as shown in Listing 12.1.

Listing 12.1   **Declaring Subtype for AUSampler Unit**

```
instrumentcd.componentSubType = kAudioUnitSubType_Sampler;
```

That sets up an appropriate audio unit, but of course, you have some work to do to configure the unit.

You can set up the AUSampler in three ways, all of which are detailed in Apple Technical Note TN2283, "AUSampler—Loading Instruments." This chapter uses the first method, using the AUSampler preset file. This approach enables you to map sampled sounds to the notes they represent and bundle all that metadata into an `.aupreset` file.

To do this, you need the AULab[1] application, located in `/Developer/Applications/Audio`. This application provides a GUI for building and configuring AUGraphs and saving the results. When you launch it, you're asked what kind of graph you want to set up. From the list Factory Configurations, choose Stereo Out, meaning you care about only output and don't need capture. Click Create Document. This brings up a window with a long strip labeled Output 1, representing the output unit.

Here you want to add MIDI input to this document, so use the menu item Add Audio Unit Instrument. In the sheet that slides in, set the input source to Any MIDI Controller and set the instrument to AUSampler. This adds a second strip called Instrument and brings up a new window with a musical keyboard (if the window doesn't appear, click the tiny keyboard button under Instrument).

This keyboard is playable with your mouse or MIDI device, but by default, it plays only sine waves. To bring in a sampled sound, click the Show Editor button at bottom right. This shows the user interface in Figure 12.1.

The left side of the editor shows the list Layers and Zones. The idea here is that a sampled sound can be mapped to one zone of keys and that you can use a different sample for different zones. This is helpful because the AUSampler's pitch shifting can sound cheesy the farther you get from its original pitch. By default, the only sound is called Sine 440 built-in.

To add your own sound, first record a sound and save it uncompressed anywhere on your filesystem—we used Chris singing the words "Core Audio" while listening to C on a piano and saved it as `chris-coreaudio-c2.caf`. On the right side of the editor, click the Choose File button and locate the file. After it loads, look at the Key Range (which defines the zone of notes this sample will be used for, defaulting to the entire range of C-1 to G9) and the Root next to it. Assign a MIDI note number here, such as C2 for middle C. Play the piano keys to see what the pitch-shift sounds like.

When you're satisfied with the sample and the root note you've assigned it to, go to the third pull-down menu at the top of the window (currently untitled) and select Save Preset As to give the preset a name; leave the Type button set to Local. Show Presets, in the same menu, then slides out a drawer of all the user-created presets. This drawer also has a Show in Finder button. Click it to see that the preset has been saved to your home directory, as `~/Library/Audio/Presets/Apple/AUSampler/your-preset-name.aupreset`.

---

[1] As of Xcode 4.3, AULab is not provided by default, and is instead in the optional "Audio Tools for Xcode" download package.

Figure 12.1   Configuring AUSampler preset with AULab

This .aupreset file contains the path to the original sound you recorded, plus the metadata of which note it represents. That's all you need to configure the AUSampler unit in your application. Back in Xcode, scroll to the bottom of the setupAUGraph() function. This is where you load the preset file after the AUGraph has been set up and initialized.

Setting up the AUSampler unit requires setting a single kAudioUnitProperty_ClassInfo property with the contents of the .aupreset file. Unfortunately, that requires three sizable steps: loading the contents of the file into a CFDataRef, turning it into a CFPropertyListRef, and setting that as the property value. Listing 12.2 starts by getting a CFURLRef to the .aupreset file.

Listing 12.2   **Getting CFURLRef for .aupreset File**

```
CFURLRef presetURL = CFURLCreateFromFileSystemRepresentation(
                    kCFAllocatorDefault,
                    "/Users/cadamson/Library/Audio/Presets/Apple\
                    /AUSampler/ch12-aupreset.aupreset",
                    77,
                    false);
```

The second argument should be a full path as a C string; of course, your path will differ from what the listing shows. The third argument is the length of the second, and the fourth is a flag to indicate that the path is not a directory.

With presetURL created, you can now load the contents of the .aupreset file into a CFDataRef, as in Listing 12.3.

Listing 12.3   **Loading .aupreset File into a CFDataRef**

```
CFDataRef presetData = NULL;
SInt32 errorCode = noErr;
Boolean gotPresetData =
CFURLCreateDataAndPropertiesFromResource(kCFAllocatorSystemDefault,
                                         presetURL,
                                         &presetData,
                                         NULL,
                                         NULL,
                                         &errorCode);
CheckError(errorCode, "couldn't load .aupreset data");
CheckError(!gotPresetData, "couldn't load .aupreset data");
```

The CFURLCreateDataAndPropertiesFromResource() function creates a CFDataRef and/or a CFDictionaryRef from the contents of a URL. Because you want only the data, you can NULL out the dictionary-related parameters.

You're really after a CFPropertyListRef object, which you can now create from the data you just loaded. Listing 12.4 shows how to do this.

Listing 12.4   **Converting AU Preset CFDataRef into CFPropertyListRef**

```
CFPropertyListFormat presetPlistFormat = {0};
CFErrorRef presetPlistError = NULL;
CFPropertyListRef presetPlist =
    CFPropertyListCreateWithData(kCFAllocatorSystemDefault,
                                 presetData,
                                 kCFPropertyListImmutable,
                                 &presetPlistFormat,
                                 &presetPlistError);
if (presetPlistError) {
    printf ("Couldn't create plist object for .aupreset");
    return;
}
```

Now that you have an object of the correct type, you can set it as the value of the kAudioUnitProperty_ClassInfo property on the AUSampler unit in Listing 12.5.

Listing 12.5   **Setting ClassInfo Property on AUSampler Unit**

```
if (presetPlist) {
    CheckError(AudioUnitSetProperty(player->instrumentUnit,
                            kAudioUnitProperty_ClassInfo,
                            kAudioUnitScope_Global,
                            0,
                            &presetPlist,
                            sizeof(presetPlist)),
                "Couldn't set aupreset plist as sampler's class info");
}
```

Setting this property delivers all the metadata from the .aupreset file to the AUSampler unit. The unit can now load the .caf file with the audio. It knows from the metadata what note it represents and, therefore, what it needs to do to pitch-shift to play notes other than the root.

Run the application and start playing. If you play your declared root note, it should sound more or less like your original sample (subject to some attenuation, depending on how hard you strike the key and, thus, what the MIDI velocity is). Playing progressively higher or lower keys pitch-shifts the sample up or down accordingly.

It's just one new unit, but the potential of the AUSampler is significant: With carefully recorded samples and thoughtful adjustment of the .aupreset zones, you can offer deep support for realistic-sounding virtual instruments.

Core Audio on iOS 5

iOS 5 represents a major advance in the usefulness of Audio Units on iOS. It includes effects units to the mobile platform that previously had only the single AUiPodEQ effect. iOS 5 adds distortion, high- and low-pass filters, high- and low-shelf filters, and a parametric EQ that enables you to perform EQ in specific frequency bands instead of offering just the canned values of the AUiPodEQ. The effect units tend to default to floating-point stream formats (another first on iOS); you often need to adjust the rest of your AUGraphs to use the formats the effect units need or to add AUConverter units inline to convert integer PCM to float.

iOS 5 also adds the AUFilePlayer, which you used in Chapter 7, "Audio Units: Generators, Effects, and Rendering," to greatly simplify the process of getting file-based audio into an AUGraph.

As in Lion, iOS 5 adds AUSampler, which is the first instrument unit available on the iOS platform. This means that MIDI apps can play notes via the AUSampler. For this, the Music Device API also comes to iOS in version 5, so you can play the MIDI events into the AUSampler with MusicDeviceMIDIEvent().

In the AUSampler section, you might have wondered about the use of hard-coded paths. Of course, you could have stored the .ausampler file in the application bundle and read it from there, but the preset file itself refers to another file on the development filesystem; that reference breaks when running in iOS (as it does on Mac OS X, barring some installation-time wizardry to put the audio files in their expected locations).

The way around this is to edit the `.aupreset` file manually—it's just a property list, so you can edit it in Xcode or your favorite text editor. The key named `file-reference` has a dictionary as its value that itself has as its values the absolute paths to the `.caf` files. The AUSampler has a set of rules it uses to search for audio files along known paths. It splits out any paths under `Sounds`, `Sampler Files`, or `Apple Loops` and then searches for those subpaths in the application bundle and other special directories, such as the `Documents` directory. TN2283 has all the details, but the practical upshot is that if you include a folder (not a group) named `Sounds` in your Xcode project, you can put your sounds there and have the `AUSampler` find them, possibly with a little hand-editing of the `.aupreset` to put Sounds at the front of the path. The book's downloadable code has an iOS version of the `AUSampler` app from earlier in this chapter, so you can check that out to see how we bundled the preset and the `.caf` it references.

The Core Audio Community

When you're working with all this and get lost, where do you go? Online, of course. The immensely helpful and cooperative Core Audio community is generous with its time and knowledge.

If you Google for Core Audio topics, you'll likely find a trivial number of hits, often back to the official Apple documentation you already have. You can find some amount of help on Stack Overflow (www.stackoverflow.com) under the core-audio tag, although many developers (particularly newcomers to iOS) don't even know the names and responsibilities of the various media APIs and, thus, don't tag their questions correctly. Still, a lot of common questions about Core Audio have been answered on Stack Overflow (and if you see the user invalidname, that's the same person writing this chapter).

There's a higher signal-to-noise ratio, if you will, on the Apple Developer Forums, at http://devforums.apple.com. There you'll find Core Audio forums on both the Mac OS X and iOS sections. Note that you need to be a member of Apple's developer programs to log into these.

If you're on IRC, check out the small channel of Core Audio developers hanging out at the #coreaudio channel on irc.freenode.net, port 6667.

The longest-lived and most useful Core Audio community online is the coraudio-api mailing list, hosted at http://lists.apple.com. For years, this has been the online hangout for the most experienced Core Audio developers, the ones whose products depend on CA. Apple's Core Audio engineers have also been extremely generous with their time on the coreaudio-api list and have answered many questions related to the coding and writing of this book. You'll pick up a lot about Core Audio, including what it can do and where it gets tricky, just by subscribing to this list and reading the daily posts.

Summary: Sounds Good

The Mac OS X and iOS platforms make the deepest commitment to media of any operating systems in history. Seriously, go look at the competition. Windows at least takes media seriously with its oft-rearchitected frameworks (DirectShow, Media Foundation, and so on). Linux's dueling frameworks (OSS and ALSA) are no match for Core Audio's breadth and depth, and Android has no low-level media libraries. Android's media support consists of the android.media classes, which, according to their own documentation, "are used to play and, in some cases, record media files." No effects, no real-time processing, no MIDI, no OpenAL. Feel free to be underwhelmed.

If you've read this whole book, you probably came in knowing that Apple platforms take media seriously and do it right. With Core Audio, they've put together a low-level framework that enables application developers to handle sound in real time or offline; to capture, playback, and synthesize; to add effects, filters, splitters, and mixers; to support low-latency audio for games and musical performance; and to deliver world-class quality audio for media professionals.

Now these tools are yours to use as you see fit.

Rock on.

Index

G–H

I

Essential Resources for Mac and iOS Developers

Developer's Library

ESSENTIAL REFERENCES FOR PROGRAMMING PROFESSIONALS

Test-Driven iOS Development

Graham Lee

ISBN-13: 978-0-321-774187

The iOS 5 Developer's Cookbook, Third Edition

Erica Sadun

ISBN-13: 978-0-321-75426-4

Programming in Objective-C, Fourth Edition

Stephen G. Kochan

ISBN-13: 978-0-321-81190-5

Other Developer's Library Titles

TITLE	AUTHOR	ISBN-13
Objective-C Phrasebook, Second Edition	David Chisnall	978-0-321-81375-6
Android™ Wireless Application Development, Second Edition	Lauren Darcey / Shane Conder	978-0-321-74301-5
Cocoa® Programming Developer's Handbook	David Chisnall	978-0-321-63963-9
Cocoa Design Patterns Applications for the iPhone	Erik M. Buck / Donald A. Yacktman	978-0-321-53502-3

Developer's Library books are available at most retail and online bookstores. For more information or to order direct, visit our online bookstore at **informit.com/store**.

Online editions of all Developer's Library titles are available by subscription from Safari Books Online at **safari.informit.com**.

Addison
Wesley

Developer's Library

informit.com/devlibrary

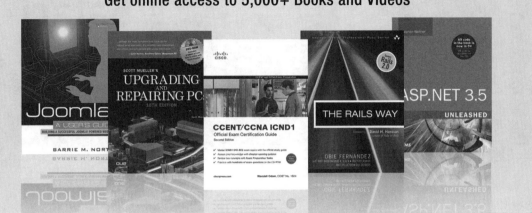

LEARNING Core Audio
A Hands-on Guide to Audio Programming for Mac and iOS

CHRIS ADAMSON
KEVIN AVILA

Safari
Books Online

FREE
Online Edition

Your purchase of *Learning Core Audio* includes access to a free online edition for 45 days through the **Safari Books Online** subscription service. Nearly every Addison-Wesley Professional book is available online through **Safari Books Online**, along with over thousands of books and videos from publishers such as Cisco Press, Exam Cram, IBM Press, O'Reilly Media, Prentice Hall, Que, Sams, and VMware Press.

Safari Books Online is a digital library providing searchable, on-demand access to thousands of technology, digital media, and professional development books and videos from leading publishers. With one monthly or yearly subscription price, you get unlimited access to learning tools and information on topics including mobile app and software development, tips and tricks on using your favorite gadgets, networking, project management, graphic design, and much more.

Activate your FREE Online Edition at
informit.com/safarifree

STEP 1: Enter the coupon code: GGGJGWH.

STEP 2: New Safari users, complete the brief registration form.
Safari subscribers, just log in.

If you have difficulty registering on Safari or accessing the online edition,
please e-mail customer-service@safaribooksonline.com

 Addison Wesley Adobe Press ALPHA Cisco Press Press IBM Press Microsoft Press New Riders O'REILLY

 Peachpit Press PRENTICE HALL que Redbooks SAMS SAS Publishing vmware PRESS WILEY wrox